What Kind of Future
Will Our Children Inherit?

The Glass Half Empty – The Glass Half Full

ISBN 978-1-947112-51-3

Humboldt State University Press
Humboldt State University Library
1 Harpst Street
Arcata, California 95521-8299
hsupress@humboldt.edu
digitalcommons.humboldt.edu/hsu_press

Cover Art by Eva Swartz
Layout and Design by Aaron Laughlin
Editorial by Aaron Laughlin, Maximilian Heirich and Audra
Sim

What Kind of Future
Will Our Children Inherit?

The Glass Half Empty – The Glass Half Full

Samuel P. Oliner, Editor
Ronnie Swartz, Associate Editor
Altruistic Behavior Institute

Humboldt State University Press
Arcata, California

Sam Oliner (Ph.D. University of California at Berkeley) is an Emeritus Professor of Sociology at Humboldt State University and Founder of the Altruistic Behavior Institute. He has authored important publications on the Holocaust, altruism and prosocial behavior, and race and ethnic relations in national and international contexts. Sam has appeared on numerous national television shows and has lectured widely in the US and several other countries on the topic of rescuers of Jews in Nazi-occupied Europe.

Ronnie Swartz has consulted with young people, families, adults, and organizations in education, healthcare, behavioral health, substance abuse, juvenile justice, child welfare, and advocacy systems. His current research, teaching, writing, and practice includes narrative therapy and community work, harm reduction in relation to problematic drug use and drug policy, social/economic policy, values, ethics, and the cultivation of love, kindness, and care skills.

Ronnie received a BA in Philosophy from Brown University, a Master of Social Work from the University of Michigan, and a Ph.D. in Human and Organizational Systems from Fielding Graduate University. He served as Chair of the Department of Social Work at Humboldt State University from 2009-2018 and has been Director of the Altruistic Behavior Institute since 2010.

Contents

Chapter 2 focuses on varieties of war and state violence as well as the causes of war, including acquisition of territories, desire for vengeance, alliances among nations, mobilization for war, acquisition of weaponry, and economic factors.

Chapter 3 addresses contemporary societal trends related to hatred and violence including mass killings by gun violence

Chapter 4 explores differences and similarities between the Holocaust and other genocides: antecedent causes such as racism, antisemitism, economic and political factors, and the dehumanization of the other.

Chapter 5 highlights sexism, discrimination, child marriages, female genital mutilation, gender discrimination, female impoverishment, and other forms of violence perpetrated against women.

1

Introduction

SAMUEL P. OLINER

Nor can that endure which has not based its foundation upon love. For love alone diminishes not, but shines with its own light; makes an end of discord, softens the fires of hate, restores peace in the world, brings together the sundered, redresses wrong, aids all, and injures none. And those who invoke its aid will find peace and safety and have no fear of the future ill.
—Jadwiga, first queen of Poland (r. 1384–1399)

One word frees us from all the weight and pain of life; that word is love.
—Sophocles

All that I'm saying is that the energy of hate will take you nowhere, but the energy of pardon, which manifests itself through love, will manage to change your life in a positive sense.
—Paulo Coelho

Over the years, my students, research associates, and I have reviewed the literature of psychology, ethics, ecology, climatology, and other areas of study to consider the direction in which our world is going and what kind of future our children will inherit. Our previous work focused on the nature of good and evil—with concern especially for goodness—through which we have considered good in the world and the application of good to achieve a better world. (Oliner & Oliner, 1988, 1995; Oliner, 2003, 2011). Our books concerned altruism, kindness, empathy, and moral responsibility for diverse others. In this book we will concentrate on the areas of greatest concern regarding our future as a species.

The Glass Half Empty

Increasingly, scholars are warning us about the direction we are taking in this interconnected world. Many of these experts view our global situation as a "glass half empty"; their studies reveal a future that is bleak and on the verge of catastrophe. Ethicists tell us that corporate greed, tax evasion (especially through tax havens), the outsourcing of jobs, the externalization of corporate costs (such as air and water pollution, which are left for government and taxpayer remediation), and a number of other destructive events have already had huge negative impacts, and that humanity is not doing enough to remedy it. Some even say that in the near future there may be wars over potable water and arable land.

Some point out that our world is becoming increasingly divided between the rich and the poor. Oxfam reports that, as of 2017, just eight of the world's richest men own the same amount of wealth as the poorest half of all humanity. However, this great divide manifests with distinct qualities. in some poorer countries and some democratic countries. For example, in many poorer countries there has recently been a large shift out of poverty, while in some democratic countries, such as the United States, there has been a steady widening of the gap in income and wealth. At the same time, millions of people continue to grow hungry and women are still marginalized in many societies. Women continue to face violence, oppression, genital mutilation, and child marriages and, especially in developing societies, continue to possess few legal rights. Regarding conflicts between nations, there is much strife between different ethnic minority groups within countries that can often spill over into contiguous regions. There are also movements by ethnic groups to establish independent nations in their eagerness to assert their autonomous rights, such as the Kurds in Iraq and Iran, the South Sudanese in 2011, the Palestinians, as well as separatist movements within the United States. Another example is Catalonia, whose parliament declared independence from Spain in October 2017. Global, political, and economic integration efforts like the European Union, NAFTA, and other regional, economic, and political alliances have recently been threatened, as seen in Great Britain's exit from the European Union (Brexit). Additionally, President Trump's threats to dismantle NAFTA, withdrawal from the Paris Climate Agreement, and disparagement of the Iran nuclear deal (also known as the Joint Comprehensive Plan of Action) represent further economic and political destabilization.

Scientists around the world increasingly warn us about climate change. Human activity continues to negatively impact the earth's fragile ecosystems in unprecedented ways, and the continued availability of natural resources is now in question. In particular, the UN reports that the current world population of 7.3 billion is expected to reach 9.7 billion by the year 2050 (United Nations, 2015).There is concern that snowballing national populations could deplete available water supplies in the near future, and that many countries are abusing their resources to the point where we may soon experience catastrophes such as those predicted in Malthus's 1798 *Essay on the Principle of Population*. In addition to water shortages due to population growth, climate change also threatens civilization as melting ice caps may cause the coastlines of many countries to become submerged in the not-too-distant future.

The Glass Half Full

There are, however, other scholars who view the world and humanity's future in more optimistic terms—those who see the "glass half full." When researching more optimistic schools of thought about the kind of future we may inherit, we see that there are millions of people who volunteer in this country and around the world. If they were paid for it, they would be earning billions of dollars. In 2014 alone, Doctors Without Borders worked in 63 countries to provide 8.3 million outpatient consultations, 511,800 inpatient admissions, and assistance with the delivery of 194,000 babies. Similarly, Habitat for Humanity has helped more than 13.2 million people obtain affordable housing since 1976.

In *The Better Angels of Our Nature*, Steven Pinker (2011) argues that violence has substantially subsided in relation to the past, with the exception of World War II when 60 million civilians and soldiers were killed. He shows us that we have become more concerned with each other and with the survival of our humanity. He also shows that there has been improvement in the treatment of children and an increase in literacy, and that nations, having become stronger, now try to avoid war. In addition, there is an increase in world trade, and there appears to be a civilizing process as well as a feminizing process (e.g., women taking part in politics, economics, science, education, etc.) in various parts of the world. Lastly, Goldstein (2011) maintains that the decline of violent behavior has been paralleled by a decline in attitudes that tolerate or glorify violence. In *Modern Ethics in 77 Arguments*, edited by Peter Catapano and Simon Critchley

(2017), philosopher Leif Wenar maintains that humanity is improving and that altruism is not only possible but on the rise.

In *The Empathic Civilization*, author Jeremy Rifkin (2009) argues that the world is evolving into a more altruistic, caring, empathetic, and compassionate place. He sees the 21st century as a time when people throughout the world are becoming increasingly conscious of the forthcoming entropy, the destruction of the biosphere, and the need for sustainability. Rifkin views the shift as an emergence of a global brain, a revolution of communication and information about what is occurring around the world. This rapid awareness is accompanied by disillusionment, which affects people's views of good and evil. It arouses an empathic response among our fellow human beings, which we have witnessed in the global response to the tragic earthquake in Haiti and other natural disasters. People's consciousness can also be influenced by a dual inheritance from genetic and cultural evolutionary processes simultaneously. Neuroscience and other social science fields see dual inheritance theory as articulating an important convergence between the human brain and social situations. According to this theory, the human brain contains mirror neurons that cross the barrier between the self and others, allowing people to empathize with other human beings.

Another author who supports the notion of a burgeoning global consciousness is Edmund J. Bourne. In his book entitled *Global Shift: How a New Worldview Is Transforming Humanity* (2008), Bourne focuses on global crises and makes specific suggestions for how changes could take place on a global scale for the better. He sees, as expressions of global consciousness, processes like volunteerism and the development of respectful and cooperative relationships, along with an increasing sense of union between all peoples and compassion for all beings, the decline of consumerism, and the growth of intuitive feminine knowledge and natural ethics in many parts of the world.

Other "glass half full" scholars point to the fact that people around the world are becoming cognizant of the process of genuine forgiveness and reconciliation. My own recent books, *The Nature of Good and Evil* (2011) and *Altruism, Intergroup Apology, Forgiveness, and Reconciliation* (2008), indicate that goodness, defined as concern for others and for making the world a better place, is on the rise. There are many nations and ethnic groups that have apologized to each other for inflicting harm. In other words, these nations and ethnic groups have apologized to their victims, who, in turn, have accepted and appreciated the apologies offered. Relationships between harm-doers and the harmed can improve; for example, one might consider the current relationship between Germans and Jews, or Israel and Germany. Recently in 2008 and again in 2017, Canadian authorities have also acknowledged and apologized for their country's role in committing acts of cultural genocide against First Nations Peoples.

The Duality of Progress and Globalization

Making the world a better place is not simply about the glass being half full or half empty; it is both at the same time. With the complexity of global trends comes major challenges, and one cannot say that one perception is correct and the other incorrect. It is much more complicated than that. For example, on the one hand we have better availability of technology, medicine, and food; on the other hand, this also means that world populations are increasing at unsustainable rates that the planet cannot support.

Thus, we have an emergence of those who see the future as promising and perhaps even more harmonious than we have ever imagined, as well as those who believe that we are declining and ruining ourselves through rapid and rampant consumerism and what we are doing to the environment. One can readily observe the waste that human beings are responsible for. Every day one sees millions of tons of waste from wrapping paper to plastic boxes infiltrating the planet's ecosystems. The ocean is full of garbage, especially plastic containers, bottles, toothbrushes, and much more. Some of this garbage washes up on the shores of Hawaii and other coasts.

Peter Diamandis and Steve Kotler and other futurologists argue that the everyday human experience has improved massively for populations around the world. They note that the past few centuries have seen the gap between wealthy and poor nations close over time: people are living longer, healthier, and wealthier lives. They argue that there is better access to goods and services, health, information, transportation, education, lifesaving medicines and procedures, and means of communication; also that there has been greater recognition of the value of human rights and the importance of democratic institutions, available shelters, available calories, available employment, and affordable energy. They believe that technologies (specifically communication technologies), robotics, and nanotechnology will replace much manual labor and improve the lives of many human beings. Nonetheless, as previously stated, bleaker futures are convincing for some because of the evidence that scholars have offered. A reminder for us is clearly found in the ongoing oppression of women, the state of war and violence throughout the world, in homicidal massacres, and the overwhelming fear of nuclear weapons. A large part of the world is still in poverty, lacking education and suffering from environmental degradation. A number of nations still do not have access to democratic institutions; thus, oppressive governance prevails over those citizens.

Dani Rodrik (2011), in writing of the globalization paradox, advocates a sane globalization approach from which all nations can benefit. Current research on altruism, morality, social solidarity, and gratitude suggests that these elements are crucial to building a "real utopia." Robert A. Emmons (2007) points out the importance of gratitude in human relations and how it may improve kindness. Scientists should undertake research that helps bring about a more caring society. The John Templeton Foundation recently devoted five million dollars to the study of gratitude, which could contribute to a more just society. Where education is concerned, there are recent studies about "altruists" who help reduce the number of bystanders and, importantly, increase the number of upstanders—people who get actively involved in improving others' lives.

A number of institutions, groups, governments, and individuals have taken these challenges to humanity seriously—have "seen the light"—and are trying to do something about the future state of the world. Among the progressive solutions they propose are making alternative energy sources such as hydroelectric, solar, and wind power more accessible and affordable. In the political arena, people are beginning to speak about nuclear terror and how we might prevent it; they are beginning to spread awareness of nations that threaten the world with nuclear weapons in hopes that they might be stopped in time.

The latest medical research and developments bode well for health issues. Ranging from disease prevention to AIDS research, the World Health Organization is attempting to alleviate many of the ailments that afflict much of the world's population, especially in developing countries. There are attempts being made to eradicate diseases, such as malaria, that poor people around the world suffer from. They include taking steps to prevent disastrous climate change by reducing the use of fossil fuels and the emittance of greenhouses gases and other such pollutants that contribute to the toxicity of the world (especially through water pollution). Plus, other attempts are being made to preserve the living species that are currently threatened. In the economic sphere, unions and various governments are also trying to improve the rights of workers and advocate for more fair-trade conditions in their countries.

In this book, we focus on individuals, corporations, and governments and the roles these groups may play in conflict resolution as well as group apology, forgiveness, and reconciliation. Recent research indicates that apology and forgiveness between groups and nations have a positive effect on both the recipients and the harm-doers. We will also emphasize what people are doing to combat poverty, especially efforts put forth by nongovernmental organizations (NGOs) such as Habitat for Humanity, Catholic Relief Services, Global Action International, the Bill & Melinda Gates Foundation, and MAZON, a group that focuses on elimination of world hunger. Other institutes foster and conduct research. The Fetzer Institute and John Templeton Foundation, for instance, funded our past research. We will also address research that has been done on disease control. Johns Hopkins University has conducted malaria research, for example, and we will examine similar efforts by other health organizations, including Doctors Without Borders and the World Health Organization. Other organizations have been committed to the rainforest movement and other environmental preservation efforts.

The chapters of this book deal with the following topics:

Chapter 2, "Causes of War and Violence," focuses on a variety of wars and violence as well as the causes of war, which include acquisition of territories, the desire for vengeance, alliances among nations, mobilization for war, acquisition of weaponry, and a variety of economic factors.

Chapter 3, "The Nature of Contemporary Hatred," deals with contemporary societal trends related to hatred and violence.

Chapter 4, "The Holocaust: How It Differs From Other Genocides," addresses what all genocides have in common and what differentiates the Holocaust from other genocides.

Chapter 5, "The Status of Women," deals with sexism, discrimination, child marriages, female genital mutilation, gender discrimination, female impoverishment, and various forms of violence perpetrated upon women.

Chapter 6, "Families of the Future," addresses the impact of the future on the family, including topics such as new emerging family forms, the gender revolution, the values revolution, economies of the future, new technologies, and artificial intelligence.

Chapter 7, "Climate Change," deals with the degradation of the environment, including factors such as pollution caused by the overuse of fossil fuels and pollution of the oceans, and consequences such as droughts and natural disasters like storms and earthquakes.

Chapter 8, "Heroic Acts of Extraordinary People," discusses Christian rescuers of Jews in Nazi-occupied Europe, hospice volunteers, and volunteers in other settings.

Chapter 9, "Sorokin's Vision of Love and Altruism," explores the prominent sociologist Pitirim Sorokin's (1889–1968) descriptions of the association between love and altruism, which could suggest an antidote to a divided world.

Chapter 10, "Altruism in Different Religions," considers the following religious traditions: Judaism, Christianity, Islam, Buddhism, Hinduism, Taoism, Confucianism, and Native American traditions. All of these religions teach similar concepts, which include love, justice, compassion, and "clothing the naked and feeding the hungry."

Chapter 11, "Ecumenism of the Deep Well," describes how some of the world's religious traditions are coming together in new ways, forming partnerships based on mutual respect and understanding and the sharing of important values.

Chapter 12, "Apology and Forgiveness," describes the importance of intergroup apology and forgiveness among institutions of different kinds, including religious, governmental, and corporate.

Chapter 13, "Elimination of Suffering," deals with a variety of different types of suffering and with individuals who help reduce suffering.

Chapter 14 is the summary and conclusion.

References

Bourne, E. J. (2008). *Global shift: How a new worldview is transforming humanity.* New Harbinger Publications; Noetic Books.

Catapano, P., & Critchley, S. (Eds.). (2017). *Modern ethics in 77 arguments: A Stone reader.* Liveright Publishing Corporation.

Diamandis, P. H., & Kotler, S. (2012). *Abundance: The future is better than you think.* Free Press.

Emmons, R. A. (2007). *Thanks! How the new science of gratitude can make you happier.* Houghton Mifflin Company.

Goldstein, J. S. (2011, September/October). Think again: War. *Foreign Policy,* (188), 53–56.

Oliner, S. P. (2003). *Do unto others: Extraordinary acts of ordinary people.* Westview Press.

Oliner, S. P. (2008). *Altruism, intergroup apology, forgiveness, and reconciliation.* Paragon House.

Oliner, S. P. (2011). *The nature of good and evil: Understanding the acts of moral and immoral behavior.* Paragon House.

Oliner, S. P., & Oliner, P. M. (1988). *The altruistic personality: Rescuers of Jews in Nazi Europe.* The Free Press.

Oliner, S. P., & Oliner, P. M. (1995). *Toward a caring society: Ideas into action.* Praeger.

Pinker, S. (2011). *The better angels of our nature: Why violence has declined.* Viking Press.

Rifkin, J. (2009). *The empathic civilization: The race to global consciousness in a world in crisis.* Jeremy P. Tarcher; Penguin.

Rodrik, D. (2011). *The globalization paradox: Democracy and globalization in the world economy.* W. W. Norton & Company.

Wright, E. O. (2010). *Envisioning real utopias.* Verso.

2

Causes of War and Violence

SAMUEL P. OLINER

There are a variety of human behaviors. Some of them are altruistic, caring and compassionate to fellow humans. Stephen Post (2002) in a chapter entitled *Traditions of Agape* maintains that *Agape* is used to describe the love that is of and from God, whose very nature is love itself. "God is love." (1 John 4:8). There are other forms of love that represent human behavior.

The most destructive human behavior is war and violence. According to Paul Goodman (2019), war is a state of armed conflict between states, governments, societies and informal paramilitary groups, such as mercenaries, insurgents and militias. It is generally characterized by extreme violence, aggression, destruction and mortality, using regular or irregular military forces. Goodman lists causes and kinds of war as follows:

1. Economic Gain. This is when one state or country wishes to take control of another's wealth. Hence, there are economic reasons for war. In preindustrial times, the reasons for war may have been to gain precious materials such as gold, silver or even livestock such as cattle and horses. In more modern times, the resources sought were more likely to be oil or material used for manufacturing.

2. Territorial Gain. Over 65 civil, national, and world wars were fought between 1700 and 1939 that included the loss/ gain of territories.

3. Religious Reasons. Some wars purport to seek revenge for an historical slight from the past. An example of this would be Protestant and Catholics or Shia and Sunni.

4. Nationalism. These wars attempt to prove that one country is superior to another through violent subjugation that often manifests as an invasion of another country. Nationalism is related to imperialism as well as racism. This is what happened in Hitler's Germany. Another example of this is Germany invading Russia because the thinking was that the Slavs were an inferior race.

5. Revenge. Revenge means to punish, redress a grievance or simply just strike back for a perceived grievance. Unfortunately, says Paul Goodman, this can lead to an endless chain of retaliatory wars being set in motion.

6. Civil War. Among the wars mentioned above, a great number of them are civil wars. Civil wars can also be sparked by separatist groups wanting to establish an independent country without striving to overthrow the government of the nation as a whole. An example in the United States is the southern states wanting to secede from the Union.

7. Revolutionary Wars. This occurs when a large section of a country revolts against the authorities because they are dissatisfied with their leadership. Revolution can also begin for a variety of reasons including economic hardships against a certain section of the population, or perceived injustices committed by the authorities. Revolutionary wars can easily

descend into civil wars depending on the success of unifying people against the perceived oppressive leadership.

8. Defensive/Preventative War. In the modern world, where military aggression is more widely questioned, countries will often argue that they are fighting in a purely defensive capacity against a potential aggressor and, therefore, their war is "just."

Besides the above factors, other authors suggest additional factors for war such as, overpopulation, climate change which will result in shortage of water and food, putting cars ahead of people, and wasting of food. Still other authors maintain that cause of war is associated with racism, extreme poverty and wealth, unbridled nationalism and religious strife. Geoffrey Blainey in his book *The Causes of War*, informs us that, in deciding for war or peace, national leaders seem to be influenced by at least seven factors:

1. Military strength to apply in war.

2. Predictions how outside nations will behave if war should occur.

3. Perceptions of whether there is internal unity or discord in their land and in the land of the enemy.

4. Knowledge or forgetfulness of the realities or suffering of war.

5. Nationalism and ideology.

6. The state of the economy and also its ability to sustain the kind of war envisaged.

7. The personality and experience of those who share in the decision.

Violence

Violence is a behavior that involves physical force intended to harm, damage, or kill someone. Violence comes in a variety of forms.

1. Physical Violence. This type of violence includes physical force which causes pain, discomfort or injury. Examples are hitting, punching and a number of other acts of violence.

2. Medical Abuse. In the medical area, examples of abuse include the withholding of medication.

3. Restraints Abuse. Another form of abuse is restraints abuse, which is forceable confinement.

4. Sexual abuse. This is non-consensual and/or unwanted sexual activity, with perpetrators using force, making threats or taking advantage of victims not able to give consent.

5. Emotional Violence. This type of abuse includes name calling, humiliating or making fun of a person.

6. Psychological Violence. This type of violence includes threatening to harm a person or his or her family.

7. Spiritual Violence or Religious Violence This type of violence includes when someone uses a person's spiritual belief to manipulate or dominate a person.

8. Cultural Violence. This type of violence includes hurting a person because of his cultural practices or religious tradition.

9. Verbal Abuse. This type of abuse involves the use of language that is spoken or written to cause harm to a person.

10. Financial Abuse. This type of abuse occurs when some one controls another's financial resources without the person's consent or misuses the resources.

11. Neglect. This type of abuse occurs when someone has the responsibility to provide care or assistance but does not.

We have discussed above the causes of war and violence. Conversely, Stephen Pinker in his book, *The Better Angels of Our Nature,* informs us that violence and war have declined. Pinker, in his thorough research, was surprised to find that violence has decreased in the past century. Contrary to public perception, he claims that in fact we are living now in the most peaceful era in the existence of our species since WWII. Evidence of bloody history during the time of the Old Testament, the British monarchy as well as other countries that beheaded a lot of victims, tribal wars and violence that were pervasive, and murder and rape in medieval Europe was thirty times what it is today. Slavery, sadistic punishment and frivolous executions were frequent. He points out that during WW II over 70 million people died, while since then, we have had the Korean War, the Vietnamese War and other smaller conflicts. In all of these wars combined, a fraction of the 70 million were killed. Pinker asks how is it possible that violence has declined? He poses the question: should we offer a Nobel Peace Prize for preventing WW III? Pinker argues that the key to explaining the decline of violence is to understand the inner demons that inclined us towards violence such as revenge, sadism, tribalism, and the better angels of our nature that steer us away. He continues to say thanks to the spread of agriculture, democracy, feminism, homosexual rights, children's rights and animal rights, literacy, trade, and cosmopolitanism where we increasingly control our impulses, empathize with others, bargain rather than plunder, debunk toxic ideologies and deploy our power of reason to reduce the temptation to violence.

References

Blainey, G. (1973). *The causes of war*. Macmillan.
Goodman, P. (2019, February 5 [updated]). The 8 main reasons for war. *Owlcation*. Retrieved May 2018, from https://owlcation.com/social-sciences/The-Main-Reasons-For-War
Post, S. G., Underwood, L. G., Schloss, J. P., & Hurlbut, W. B. (Eds.). (2002). *Altruism and altruistic love: Science, philosophy, and religion in dialogue*. Oxford University Press.
Pinker, S. (2011). *The better angels of our nature: Why violence has declined*. Viking Press.

3

The Nature of Contemporary Hatred

EVAN S. OLINER

There is ample evidence that we live in a time of what one might call moral progress. This evidence includes survey data on racial attitudes[1], an increasing institutional focus on gender equality[2], and upward trends in charitable giving[3] among much else. There is an ongoing sea of change in our civilization, whose implications are widely disagreed upon but which points toward a more integrated world and a more cosmopolitan culture. Fukuyama's "End of History" theory[4] did not quite hold, but at the very least, represents a still-prevalent sentiment of cautious optimism that liberal peace and stability lie on some kind of unprecedented bedrock. That the incendiary presidency of Donald Trump has not seen violent interstate conflict on a large scale is perhaps evidence of this bedrock.

---

1. See Krysan & Moberg, 8/25/2016, "Trends in racial attitudes". University of Illinois Institute of Government and Public Affairs. Retrieved from http://igpa.uillinois.edu/programs/racial-attitudes.
2. See McKinsey & Company, October 2018, "Women in the Workplace 2018". Retrieved from https://www.mckinsey.com/featured-insights/gender-equality/women-in-the-workplace-2018.
3. See Charity Navigator, "Giving Statistics". Retrieved from https://www.charitynavigator.org/index.cfm?bay=content.view&cpid=42.
4. Fukuyama famously theorized in The End of History and the Last Man that, with the collapse of the Soviet Union, liberal democracy had defeated alternative systems and would be "the final form of human government". See Francis Fukuyama, 1992, The End of History and the Last Man.

All of this belies a deeply troubling reality, which has reared its ugliest head in just the last five years: acts of violence based on hate, and the political power of xenophobic and radical right groups, are both on the rise. Further, this trend is occurring globally and in an unprecedentedly networked manner. Racism, xenophobia, and nationalism are the basis for a growing set of behaviors and political phenomena to which we thought ourselves immune. And the root causes are as numerous as they are confounding.

Per data from the FBI, incidents of hate crime in the United States have risen 31% between 2014 and 2017, a period marked by political polarization and increased race-related rhetoric, reversing a downward trend in reported hate crime during the preceding period. What's worse is that this breaks down into increases in crime, targeting nearly every victim group the FBI tracked during that time period. To name a few, incidents of anti-Hispanic hate crime have increased 42.8%, anti-Jewish hate crime incidents have increased 54%, and anti-Muslim incidents have increased a staggering 77.3%. Crimes against Jews constitute the largest religious category. Crimes against blacks constitute the largest race category. Crimes against Muslims constitute the fastest-growing religious category. The statistics go on and the picture remains bleak[5].

---

5. FBI UCR crime database. Retrieved from https://ucr.fbi.gov/hate-crime; It is important to note that these data represent reported offenses, and thus an increase in hate crime may partially be a function of law enforcement agencies' raised awareness of religious or ethnic bias in motivating criminals. The staggering nature of the increases would seem to show that higher reporting is only partially explanatory, and a real increase has occurred as well. Many large jurisdictions still do not report hate crimes.

The Nature of Contemporary Hatred

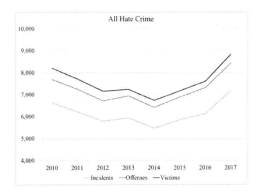

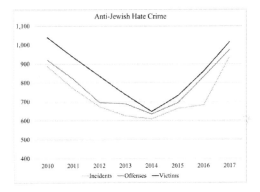

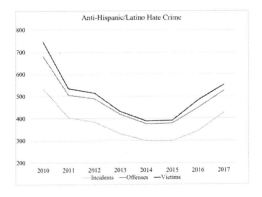

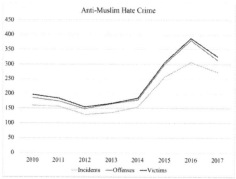

Source: FBI UCR Data

The above charts underscore the recency of the trend, and is contrasted with what seemed to be progress in prior years. The trend reversal occurred in the vicinity of 2014 or shortly thereafter, coincident with the rise of radical right parties in Europe and North America.

These regions of the world have both seen troubling incidents of Islamic extremist violence in the 21st century, but a growing and equally nefarious set of right-wing ideologies associated with white nationalism are now comparable drivers of global terrorism. Anti-Defamation League (ADL) data shows that there have been 129 incidents of extremist murder by white supremacists in the US since 2010, making white supremacy the leading motivator of extremist murder nationally[6].

The Mass Murder Network

At their worst, these ideologies are manifested in the form of massacres in cities throughout the democratic world. Christchurch, Pittsburg, Oslo/Utøya, Munich, London, and

---

6. Anti-Defamation League H.E.A.T. Map. Retrieved from https://www.adl.org/education-and-resources/resource-knowledgebase/adl-heat-map.

Quebec City, among countless others, have been host to deadly rampages by far-right extremists. Though widespread, these incidents are far from isolated. The man who carried out the Christchurch murders, for instance, drew inspiration from the killers in Norway and Quebec City according to the manifesto posted online before his attack[7]. A school shooter in New Mexico corresponded directly with the teenage boy who perpetrated the Munich attacks, who was also inspired by the Norway killer and carried out his attack on the anniversary of the Norway atrocity[8]. All of these individuals held white nationalist views of some flavor[9]. Heidi Beirich, director of the Southern Poverty Law Center, underscored this common ideological footing in saying "the Christchurch killer didn't see himself as an Australian; he saw himself as part of a white collective"[10].

The phenomenon of "media contagion," whereby media coverage brings salience to shootings increasing the likelihood that they will inspire others, has been studied extensively in academic literature. One highly-cited paper by scholars from Arizona State University and Northeastern Illinois University showed that mass killings involving firearms temporarily increase the probability of similar incidents. The

7. See Ravndal, Jacob Aasland, Foreign Policy, 3/16/2019, "The Dark Web Enabled the Christchurch Killer". Retrieved from https://foreignpolicy.com/2019/03/16/the-dark-web-enabled-the-christchurch-killer-extreme-right-terrorism-whitenationalism-anders-breivik/.
8. See Wikipedia, "2016 Munich Shooting". Retrieved from https://en.wikipedia.org/wiki/2016_Munich_shooting#cite_noteinquirySchulze-53.
9. The Munich shooter's association with white nationalism is less certain. A commissioned panel of three political scientists determined that he was influenced by xenophobia and far-right ideology, but a later report by the Bavarian State Office of Criminal Investigation concluded that his motivations were not political.
10. Cai, Weiyi & Landon, Simone, New York Times, 4/3/2019, "Attacks by White Extremists Are Growing. So Are Their Connections." Retrieved from https://www.nytimes.com/interactive/2019/04/03/world/white-extremist-terrorismchristchurch.html.

study found that, on average, the heightened risk level lasts 13 days and a given incident leads to .3 new ones[11]. Other literature widely confirms the statistical significance of media contagion[12].

These studies pertain primarily to the United States and to the news media, but the advent of social media gives scope for the contagion to globalize. Perhaps the most prominent unintended consequence of the internet has been its unique ability to connect violent racists from around the world. Websites such as Gab and 8chan have been called breeding grounds for mass murderers. The shooters at both Christchurch and Pittsburg frequented these sites and felt a sense of solidarity with the communities using them[13]. Studies have shown that these sites exhibit more racist and anti-Semitic behavior in the wake of major political events, like the election of Donald Trump or the fatal rally in Charlottesville[14]. Further, there is quantitative evidence that expressions of such sentiment on social media propagate hate crime[15].

---

11. Towers S, Gomez-Lievano A, Khan M, Mubayi A & Castillo-Chavez C, 7/2/2015, "Contagion in Mass Killings and School Shootings". Arizona State University, Northeastern Illinois University. Retrieved from https://www.ncbi.nlm.nih.gov/pubmed/26135941.
12. See also Pew A, Goldbeck L & Halsted C, "Does Media Coverage Inspire Copy Cat Mass Shootings?". National Center for Health Research. Retrieved from http://www.center4research.org/copy-cats-kill/. Jetter M & Walker J, October 2016, "The Effect of Media Coverage on Mass Shootings". IZA Institute of Labor Economics Discussion Paper Series. Retrieved from http://ftp.iza.org/dp11900.pdf.
13. See "Gab and 8chan: Home to Terrorist Plots Hiding in Plain Sight". Anti Defamation League. Retrieved from https://www.adl.org/resources/reports/gab-and-8chan-home-to-terrorist-plots-hiding-in-plain-sight.
14. See Finkelstein J, Zannettou S, Bradlyn B, Blackburn J, 9/5/2018, "A Quantitative Approach to Understanding Online Antisemitism". Retrieved from https://arxiv.org/abs/1809.01644.
15. See Müller K & Schwarz C, 11/30/2018, "Fanning the Flames of Hate: Social Media and Hate Crime". Retrieved from https://papers.ssrn.com/sol3/papers.cfm?abstract_id=3082972.

Concurrently, we have seen the rise of organized far-right groups. These groups run a spectrum from criminal gangs to legitimate political parties. The former include groups like the Aryan Brotherhood, a racist gang found in most American prisons[16]. Some groups are faith-based organizations like the Westboro Baptist Church. Some are nongovernment organizations, like the Alliance Defending Freedom, whose attorneys work to build case law limiting gay rights[17]. Finally, some are political parties on the floors of legislatures throughout the democratic world.

Cultural Insecurity and the Far-right

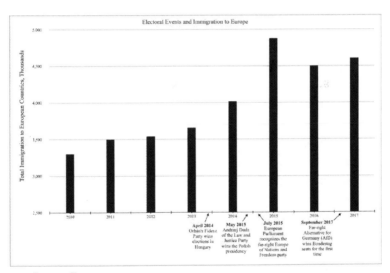

Source: Eurostat

---

16. See Southern Poverty Law Center, "Aryan Brotherhood". Retrieved from https://www.splcenter.org/fightinghate/extremist-files/group/aryan-brotherhood.
17. See Southern Poverty Law Center, "Alliance Defending Freedom". Retrieved from https://www.splcenter.org/fightinghate/extremist-files/group/alliance-defending-freedom.

Ostensibly, far-right political parties can proliferate when phenomena like immigration waves appear to threaten some concept of tradition or identity. This is most salient in the case of far-right European politicians, whose messages gained traction as the European migrant crisis took place. Take for example the below quotes by Marine Le Pen, President of the National Rally party in France, Viktor Orbán, Prime Minister of Hungary and leader of the Fidesz party, and Matteo Salvini, Deputy Prime Minister of Italy and leader of La Lega Nord, a far-right party:

Le Pen[18]
"It is right for us not to want our country transformed into a mere corridor, a giant railway station"
"I am opposed to a multicultural France. I think that those who have a different culture and who arrive in France have to submit themselves to French culture"

Orbán[19]
"Is it not worrying in itself that European Christianity is now barely able to keep Europe Christian? If we lose sight of this, the idea of Europe could become a minority interest in its own continent"
"Take seriously the traditions, the Christian roots, and all the values that are the basis of the civilization of Europe"

---

18. BrainyQuote, "Marine Le Pen Quotes". Retrieved from https://www.brainyquote.com/authors/marine_le_pen.
19. Ker, S, 9/13/2015, "Is Europe Losing Control Over Its Destiny?". Retrieved from https://www.gatestoneinstitute.org/6490/europe-control-destiny; BrainyQuote, "Viktor Orbán Quotes". Retrieved from https://www.brainyquote.com/authors/viktor_orban_4. 22

Salvini[20]
"We are under attack. Our culture, society, traditions, and way of life are at risk"
"Centuries of history risk disappearing if Islamization, which up until now has been underestimated, gains the upper hand"

Some Europeans who identify with the far-right exhibit an adoration of art, history and culture that is classically "European", "Western" or associated with their home nations. In the private café in Lille, France, which is the effective headquarters of Génération Identitaire, the youth wing of the French Identitarian movement (a movement which lies even to the right of Marine Le Pen), a statue of Joan of Arc sits in the corner, along with various medieval décor. One BBC reporter called it "a medieval hunting lodge"[21]. This adoration can border on the absurd: fringe far-right parties in Italy and Greece reject Catholicism for polytheistic religions of antiquity—that is to say the pantheons of Greek and Roman gods[22]. Whatever the fetish, the premise that "European culture is under attack" assumes some demarcation of which artifacts and ideas are European, and which are not. Far-right parties have leaned on different identities to make this demarcation.

In Eastern Europe, religion has tended to serve this

---

20. Balmer C, Reuters, 1/15/2008, "Northern League leader says Italian society threatened by Islam". Retrieved from https://www.reuters.com/article/us-italy-election-league/northern-league-leader-says-italian-society-threatened-by-islamidUSKBN1F4249.
21. See Channel 4 News, 3/24/2017, "Far-right documentary: Could Génération Identitaire help Le Pen to French election victory?". Retrieved from https://www.youtube.com/watch?v=_kJNc2iIbzg.
22. See Nugent, A, OZY, 6/26/2017, "Inside the European Far-right's Weird Obsession with Paganism". Retrieved from https://www.ozy.com/fast-forward/inside-the-european-far-rights-weird-obsession-with-paganism/79101.

purpose. The Law and Justice party (PiS) of Poland and the Fidesz party of Hungary are both grounded in a Christian nationalism. In these instances, Christianity has served the dual purpose of defining national identity and providing the basis for a morality that has guided policy. The PiS party has advocated socially conservative policies targeting gay marriage and abortion, attempted to restrict demonstrations like the Equality March in Warsaw, and appointed ministers whose track records include homophobia and anti-Semitism[23]. In a similar Christian moralist vein, Orbán added an article to the Hungarian constitution giving formal preference to traditional marriage between a man and a woman[24].

There is no discounting the importance of political opportunism here. In a nation that is 87.2% Catholic[25], a faith-focused message was most certainly the path of least resistance for the Polish far-right. In a more religiously pluralistic country like France, which has significant minorities of nonbelievers and Muslims[26], and whose secularism is highly codified in law (an 1872 law, reaffirmed in 1978, prevents census-taking for religious affiliation[27]), the message is less about religion, and the far-right is more overtly, more "secularly", xenophobic. This partially explains why the far-right has not been as electorally successful in France. The current president, Emmanuel

---

23. See Human Rights Watch, 6/4/2006, "Poland: Official Homophobia Threatens Basic Freedoms". Retrieved from https://www.hrw.org/news/2006/06/04/poland-official-homophobia-threatens-basic-freedoms-0.
24. Library of Congress, 3/19/2013, "Hungary: Constitutional Amendments Adopted". Retrieved from https://www.loc.gov/law/foreign-news/article/hungary-constitutional-amendments-adopted/.
25. CIA World Factbook, "Poland". Retrieved from https://www.cia.gov/library/publications/the-world-factbook/geos/pl.html.
26. CIA World Factbook, "France". Retrieved from https://www.cia.gov/library/publications/the-world-factbook/geos/fr.html.
27. Cosgrove M, Le Figaro.fr, 4/7/2011, "How does France Count its Muslim Population?". Retrieved from http://plus.lefigaro.fr/note/how-does-france-count-its-muslim-population-20110407-435643.

Macron, can be described as the antithesis of the European far-right: a liberal internationalist, pro-EU former banker.

Italy, roughly 80% Christian[28], lies somewhere between the two on the spectrum of religious cohesiveness, and although the leaders of Italy's far-right have not used religion as any direct basis for policy, churchgoing Christians form their base, and tend to align with their vision for the country.

In all three cases, the policy prescription of the far-right is to dramatically restrict immigration, not just for reasons relating to the capacity of the economy, but based on concepts of cultural invasion and the preservation of heritage.

Across the Atlantic, the story is fundamentally similar, but takes place in a different political context. To be certain, the U.S. balance of power has shifted to the right due to the presidential election of 2016, and white nationalist elements have gained a louder voice. But in an effectively two-party system, individual parties are much more pluralistic and the simple composition of congress cannot be used as a barometer for the success of the radical right. Still, the alt-right, nationalistic coalition within the Republican party associated with Donald Trump is ideologically similar to European analogues.

On the campaign trail and beyond, Trump made appeals to national cultural identity reminiscent of the European radical right. At one rally in Arizona, he said "They're trying to take away our culture. They're trying to take away our history".[29] As if to confirm this Transatlantic solidarity, Trump has offered condolences to his European brethren. In an interview in Brussels he said that immigration "changed the fabric of

---

28. CIA World Factbook, "Italy". https://www.cia.gov/library/publications/the-world-factbook/geos/it.html.
29. This sentence, in context, was aimed at the media and at liberal politicians, not immigrants.
See Bradner E, Tatum S & Liptak K, CNN, 8/24/2017, "After angry rally, Trump calls for healing in Nevada". Retrieved from https://www.cnn.com/2017/08/23/politics/donald-trump-nevada-speech/index.html.

Europe" and counselled "I think you are losing your culture. Look around."[30]

To answer the question of whether Trump is emboldening perpetrators of hate crime, one need to look no further than the words of the perpetrators themselves. The shooter at Christchurch called Trump "a symbol of renewed white identity and common purpose"[31]. A depressing foray into the annals of YouTube comments or websites of 8chan's ilk will further confirm that radical rightists feel "liberated", normalized, by Trump. There is no reason we shouldn't take them at their word.

The data seem to be there too: a statistical study by the Washington Post looked at the counties that hosted Donald Trump's 275 presidential campaign rallies and analyzed their hate crime prevalence, controlling for various factors, as compared to the rest of the country. To quote the Post directly: "We found that counties that had hosted a 2016 Trump campaign rally saw a 226 percent increase in reported hate crimes over comparable counties that did not host such a rally"34. From this we cannot conclude whether the rhetoric causes the hate, merely fuels it, or is simply a manifestation of it. But the correlation is glaring.

---

30. Allen, C, The Conversation, 7/13/2018, Trump's claim that Europe is 'losing its culture' is racism – and it must be challenged". Retrieved from http://theconversation.com/trumps-claim-that-europe-is-losing-its-culture-is-racism-and-it-mustbe-challenged-99962.
31.Al Jazeera, 3/16/2019, "New Zealand mosque attacks suspect praised Trump in manifesto". Retrieved from https://www.aljazeera.com/news/2019/03/zealand-mosques-attack-suspect-praised-trump-manifesto-190315100143150.html. 34 Feinberg A, Branton R & Martinez-Ebers V, Washington Post, 3/22/2019, "Counties that hosted a 2016 Trump Rally saw a 226 percent increase in hate crimes". Retrieved from https://www.washingtonpost.com/politics/2019/03/22/trumps-rhetoricdoes-inspire-more-hate-crimes/?noredirect=on&utm_term=.dcd6aa1ee824#click=https://t.co/bYXsN60xzH

The Rhetorical Bridge[32]

White nationalism is a well-documented phenomenon in the United States, as are racialist science and xenophobia. In the early 20th century, elements of the political mainstream flirted with racialist ideas, namely that a "white genocide" was nigh if whites and nonwhites were allowed to intermix culturally. President Warren Harding gave a speech to that effect in 1921, and his vice president Calvin Coolidge wrote an article echoing the idea. In the wake of World War II and the Civil Rights Movement, these ideologies became muffled, if not reduced.[33] The modern alt-right, some say, has enabled their resurgence.

A quick etymological background is in order. The term "alt-right" is more commonplace in the United States than in Europe. The term was coined, originally as the unabbreviated "Alternative Right", by Philosopher Paul Gottfried in a 2008 address. Gottfried is a mainstay of paleoconservatism, a political philosophy which stresses tradition, social order, and nationalism but, contemporarily, is usually defined by its opposition to neoconservatism. Gottfried and other paleos are opposed to interventionist neoconservatives who he claims hijacked the right, were in fact "those from the Left who had occupied the Right"37. Ten years after this original formulation, the alt-right has maintained this militant independence from modern mainstream conservatism, perhaps best illustrated by the "drain the swamp" imperative levelled by the Trumpian wing against the whole traditional spectrum—Democrats and Republicans alike.

---

32. This term is attributable to Stephanie L. Hartzell, California State University, Long Beach.
33. See Serwer A, The Atlantic, April 2019, "White Nationalism's Deep American Roots". Retrieved from https://www.theatlantic.com/magazine/archive/2019/04/adam-serwer-madison-grant-white-nationalism/583258/ 37 Gottfried P, November 2008 address, "The Decline and Rise of the Alternative Right". Retrieved from http://www.unz.com/article/the-decline-and-rise-of-the-alternative-right/.

The alt-right as we know it is arguably an instantiation of paleoconservatism.

It would be hyperbolic to synonymize the alt-right with white nationalism, but it has been theorized that the alt-right has built a "rhetorical bridge" connecting white nationalism with the political mainstream. Dr. Stephanie Hartzell argued, in the Journal of Contemporary Rhetoric, that this was done with "appeals to intellectualism and political correctness", that is to say a rejection of them[34]. Essentially, by crying foul of a national discourse that long had a tendency to moralize and censor, the alt-right has carved space for radicals to smuggle white nationalism into a more politically legitimate arena.

Trump, thankfully, has had limited success implementing the most nationalistic and identitarian policies he advocated, like the travel ban imposed on seven Muslim-majority countries, and the border wall. But perhaps more concerning than the policy effects of the rhetorical bridge, is the bridge's tendency to normalize hateful ideology and embolden white nationalists. The latter, after all, is what has led to terror and bloodshed that no modern civilization should be prepared to accept.

An Uncertain Future

Civilizational trends toward economic globalization, ethnic diversity and open-mindedness are both seen and felt: seen in various data, felt by anyone who has lived in a major economic hub like London, or attended an internationally renowned university. Yet a chorus of voices opposing the logical end of these trends in the United States and Europe has reached a new tenor in recent election cycles. Due in part to political opportunism, and in part to genuine ideological

---

34. Hartzell S, 2018, "Alt-White: Conceptualizing the "Alt-Right" as a Rhetorical Bridge between White Nationalism and Mainstream Public Discourse". Retrieved from http://contemporaryrhetoric.com/wpcontent/uploads/2018/02/Hartzell8_1_2_2.pdf

anchoring, actors espousing ideas long considered danger-ously radical have gained a seat at the table.

One hopes that the emergence of racism and xenopho-bia as increasingly legitimate political positions may prove a transitory phenomenon, a "swinging back of the pendulum" to use the popular metaphor. But for its duration and likely beyond it, previously-suppressed prejudice and hatred, giv-en voice by the internet and a global cadre of radical-right politicians, threaten to manifest themselves in the form of violence. Our edifices of law enforcement are increasingly aware of this threat, and that is important. These edifices face an open question, strategically but also ethically, of how to deal with hateful speech online in a way that minimizes the body count but satisfies the principle of free speech.

The upcoming European parliamentary elections and the 2020 United States presidential election will be telling tests for the strength of radical rightism. In a potential future where Europe's far-right can establish a consequential coali-tion in European Parliament, and an incumbent Trump wins the presidency again, there will certainly be more incendiary rhetoric to come from a very high podium. If this does not come to pass, we will truly see whether hate subsides along-side its political enablers. In either case, a deep interconnec-tivity within our society is here to stay. May we use it well.

References

Al Jazeera, 3/16/2019, "New Zealand mosque attacks suspect praised Trump in manifesto". Retrieved from https://www.aljazeera.com/news/2019/03/zea-land-mosques-attack-suspect-praised-trump-manifes-to-190315100143150.html.

Allen, C, The Conversation, 7/13/2018, Trump's claim that Europe is 'losing its culture' is racism – and it must be challenged". Retrieved from http://theconversation.

com/trumps-claim-that-europe-is-losing-its-culture-is-racism-and-it-mustbe-challenged-99962

Anti Defamation League, "H.E.A.T. Map". Retrieved from https://www.adl.org/education-and-resources/resourceknowledge-base/adl-heat-map.

Balmer C, Reuters, 1/15/2008, "Northern League leader says Italian society threatened by Islam". Retrieved from https://www.reuters.com/article/us-italy-election-league/northern-league-leader-says-italian-society-threatened-by-islamidUSKBN1F4249.

Bradner E, Tatum S & Liptak K, CNN, 8/24/2017, "After angry rally, Trump calls for healing in Nevada". Retrieved from https://www.cnn.com/2017/08/23/politics/donald-trump-nevada-speech/index.html.

BrainyQuote, "Marine Le Pen Quotes". Retrieved from https://www.brainyquote.com/authors/marine_le_pen.

BrainyQuote, "Viktor Orbán Quotes". Retrieved from https://www.brainyquote.com/authors/viktor_orban_4.

Cai, Weiyi & Landon, Simone, New York Times, 4/3/2019, "Attacks by White Extremists Are Growing. So Are Their Connections." Retrieved from https://www.nytimes.com/interactive/2019/04/03/world/white-extremist-terrorismchristchurch.html.

Channel 4 News, 3/24/2017, "Far-right documentary: Could Génération Identitaire help Le Pen to French election victory?". Retrieved from https://www.youtube.com/watch?v=_kJNc2iIbzg.

Charity Navigator, "Giving Statistics". Retrieved from https://www.charitynavigator.org/index.cfm?bay=content.view&cpid=42.

CIA World Factbook, "France". Retrieved from https://www.cia.gov/library/publications/the-world-factbook/geos/fr.html.

CIA World Factbook, "Italy". https://www.cia.gov/library/publications/the-world-factbook/geos/it.html.

CIA World Factbook, "Poland". Retrieved from https://www.cia.gov/library/publications/the-world-factbook/geos/pl.html.

Cosgrove M, Le Figaro.fr, 4/7/2011, "How does France Count its Muslim Population?". Retrieved from http://plus.lefigaro.fr/note/how-does-france-count-its-muslim-population-20110407-435643.

Eurostat data. Retrieved from https://ec.europa.eu/eurostat/en/web/products-datasets/-/MIGR_IMM3CTB.

FBI UCR crime database. Retrieved from https://ucr.fbi.gov/hate-crime.

Feinberg A, Branton R & Martinez-Ebers V, Washington Post, 3/22/2019, "Counties that hosted a 2016 Trump Rally saw a 226 percent increase in hate crimes". Retrieved from https://www.washingtonpost.com/politics/2019/03/22/trumps-rhetoricdoes-inspire-more-hate-crimes/?noredirect=on&utm_term=.dc-d6aa1ee824#click=https://t.co/bYXsN60xzH

Finkelstein J, Zannettou S, Bradlyn B, Blackburn J, 9/5/2018, "A Quantitative Approach to Understanding Online Antisemitism". Retrieved from https://arxiv.org/abs/1809.01644.

Francis Fukuyama, 1992, The End of History and the Last Man.

Gottfried P, November 2008 address, "The Decline and Rise of the Alternative Right". Retrieved from http://www.unz.com/article/the-decline-and-rise-of-the-alternative-right/.

Hartzell S, 2018, "Alt-White: Conceptualizing the "Alt-Right" as a Rhetorical Bridge between White Nationalism and Mainstream Public Discourse". Retrieved from http://contemporaryrhetoric.com/wpcontent/uploads/2018/02/Hartzell8_1_2_2.pdf

Human Rights Watch, 6/4/2006, "Poland: Official Homophobia Threatens Basic Freedoms". Retrieved from https://www.hrw.org/news/2006/06/04/poland-offi-cial-homophobia-threatens-basic-freedoms-0.

Jetter M & Walker J, October 2016, "The Effect of Media Coverage on Mass Shootings". IZA Institute of Labor Economics Discussion Paper Series. Retrieved from http://ftp.iza.org/dp11900.pdf.

Ker, S, 9/13/2015, "Is Europe Losing Control Over Its Destiny?". Retrieved from https://www.gatestoneinstitute.org/6490/europe-control-destiny.

Krysan & Moberg, 8/25/2016, "Trends in racial attitudes". University of Illinois Institute of Government and Public Affairs. Retrieved from http://igpa.uillinois.edu/programs/racial-attitudes.

Library of Congress, 3/19/2013, "Hungary: Constitutional Amendments Adopted". Retrieved from https://www.loc.gov/law/foreign-news/article/hungary-constitutional-amendments-adopted/.

McKinsey & Company, October 2018, "Women in the Workplace 2018". Retrieved from https://www.mckinsey.com/featured-insights/gender-equality/women-in-the-workplace-2018.

Müller K & Schwarz C, 11/30/2018, "Fanning the Flames of Hate: Social Media and Hate Crime". Retrieved from https://papers.ssrn.com/sol3/papers.cfm?abstract_id=3082972.

Nugent, A, OZY, 6/26/2017, "Inside the European Far-right's Weird Obsession with Paganism". Retrieved from https://www.ozy.com/fast-forward/inside-the-european-far-rights-weird-obsession-with-paganism/79101.

Pew A, Goldbeck L & Halsted C, "Does Media Coverage Inspire Copy Cat Mass Shootings?". National Center for Health Research. Retrieved from http://www.center4research.org/copy-cats-kill/.

Ravndal, Jacob Aasland, Foreign Policy, 3/16/2019, "The Dark Web Enabled the Christchurch Killer". Re-

trieved from https://foreignpolicy.com/2019/03/16/
the-dark-web-enabled-the-christchurch-killer-ex-
treme-right-terrorism-whitenationalism-anders-breivik/.
Serwer A, The Atlantic, April 2019, "White Nationalism's Deep American Roots". Retrieved from https://
www.theatlantic.com/magazine/archive/2019/04/ad-
am-serwer-madison-grant-white-nationalism/583258/
Southern Poverty Law Center, "Alliance Defending Freedom". Retrieved from https://www.splcenter.org/fight-
inghate/extremist-files/group/alliance-defending-free-
dom.
Southern Poverty Law Center, "Aryan Brotherhood". Retrieved from https://www.splcenter.org/fighting-hate/
extremistfiles/group/aryan-brotherhood.
Towers S, Gomez-Lievano A, Khan M, Mubayi A & Castillo-Chavez C, 7/2/2015, "Contagion in Mass Killings
and School Shootings". Arizona State University, Northeastern Illinois University. Retrieved from https://www.
ncbi.nlm.nih.gov/pubmed/26135941.
Wikipedia, "2016 Munich Shooting". Retrieved from
https://en.wikipedia.org/wiki/2016_Munich_shoot-
ing#cite_noteinquirySchulze-53.
"Gab and 8chan: Home to Terrorist Plots Hiding in Plain
Sight". Anti Defamation League. Retrieved from https://
www.adl.org/resources/reports/gab-and-8chan-home-
to-terrorist-plots-hiding-in-plain-sight.

4

The Holocaust:
How It Differs From Other Genocides

PAT DEVINE

The words *holocaust* and *genocide* sound very different from each other, but they both conjure images of death and destruction of a people and their culture. Both words convey a victory, at least temporarily, of darkness over light, evil over good, the worst of humanity over the best of humanity, the shadow of civilization over enlightened consciousness. Both terms connote systemic death and destruction of an out-group and its culture. There have been genocides throughout history and they continue up to the present day in various parts of the world. The 20th century alone was witness to the Armenian genocide, the Jewish Holocaust, the Cambodian genocide, and the Rwandan genocide, to name a few. All holocausts are genocides, but not all genocides are holocausts. The Jewish Holocaust is unique in that it is the only time in human history where there was what is commonly referred to as an "industrialization of death" using the most advanced, scientific methods of the day to obliterate an out-group. It was the first time in human history that the element of fire in combination with a modern gas was used on such a devastating scale to reduce a people to ash.

Before examining the Jewish Holocaust and how it differed from other types of genocide, it is helpful to understand the words "holocaust" and "genocide" themselves, their roots, and their evolution into the 20th century. The former has its roots in sacred offerings, while the latter has its roots in describing a group of people and the desire to destroy.

Webster's New World College Dictionary defines the word *holocaust* as coming from the Greek word *holo*, meaning "whole," and *kaustos* meaning "burning" or *kaiein* meaning "to burn." More specifically, the word *holocaust* describes "an offering the whole of which is burned; burnt offering." Secondarily, "great or total destruction of life, especially by fire" (Webster's New World 2007). The Greek god Prometheus, who is credited with the act of stealing divine fire to benefit mankind, gave way to a darker, primal deity in the 20th century.

It has been a long journey from the meaning of the word *holocaust*, which represents a burnt offering, to the word Holocaust used to describe the death and destruction of over six million European Jews. Fire, not only one of the most ancient elements used to illume the night but also an object of special worship by ancient priests and priestesses in various cultures, lost its sacred way in the 20th century.

Whereas *holocaust* began from the idea of a burnt offering, only later coming to connote the darker idea of destruction by fire, *genocide* appears to have been a part of the world of darkness and shadow from its inception.

The word *genocide* has its roots in the Greek prefix *geno*, meaning "race," which was combined with the Latin word *caedere*, meaning "to strike, to kill" (Webster's New World 2007). Massacres and mass killings have taken place since the beginning of human history, but over the centuries such phenomena were never given a precise name. Until very recent times, vague terms such as crimes against humanity were used. It has been a problem that has been crying out to us to be named from mass graves over the centuries. It was not until December 11, 1946 that the General Assembly of the United Nations, in its resolution 96 (I), declared genocide a crime under international law. Article II of the resolution defined the crime of genocide as follows:

(a) Killing members of the group;
(b) Causing serious bodily or mental harm to members of the group;
(c) Deliberately inflicting on the group conditions of life calculated to bring about its physical destruction in whole or in part;
(d) Imposing measures intended to prevent births within the group;
(e) Forcibly transferring children of the group to another group.

(United Nations Convention 1946)

We have just examined the definitions of the terms *holocaust* and *genocide*. As stated at the beginning of this essay, all holocausts are genocides, but not all genocides are holocausts. In the remainder of this chapter, we will explore how this statement is true. We will first look at the qualities that all genocides have in common. We will then look at what differentiates the Holocaust from other genocides. In the following breakdown, Gregory Stanton, a human rights scholar, delineates for us the ten stages of genocide:

1. CLASSIFICATION: In the first stage of genocide, groups of people are singled out as the "other." In this stage, ethnicity, race, religion or nationality all play a part in classifying human beings and distinguishing them as "us" and "them." This type of classification is common to all cultures.
2. SYMBOLIZATION: In the second stage of genocide, names or symbols are assigned to the out-groups. In this stage, examples of such symbols would be the yellow

star worn by the Jewish people under Nazi rule or the blue scarf required to be worn by people from the Eastern Zone in Cambodia during the reign of the Khmer Rouge.

3. DISCRIMINATION: In the third stage of genocide, genocide is formalized in a society. In this stage, the dominant group uses law, custom, and political power to deny the rights of the out-groups.

4. DEHUMANIZATION: In the fourth stage of genocide, denial of the humanity of those considered the other in society takes place. At this point, members of the out-groups are looked upon as animals or some form of insect or disease.

5. ORGANIZATION: In the fifth stage of genocide, opposition to the out-groups is organized in the following ways: (1) the state hides behind the use of militias to accomplish its goals; (2) informal groups such as local mobs led by militants are used; (3) decentralized terrorist groups are employed; (4) special army units or militias are trained and armed; (5) plans for genocide are drawn up.

6. POLARIZATION: In the sixth stage of genocide, a wedge is inserted between the society's in-group and its out-groups to drive them apart. In this stage, this is accomplished through the use of divisive propaganda or through laws that impede social interaction or intermarriage. At this point, attempts are made to silence the moderate elements of the society.

7. PREPARATION: In the seventh stage of genocide, leaders of national or perpetrator groups begin the planning stage for eliminating the out-groups. At this stage, it justifies its plans by using such terms as ethnic cleansing, purification or counter-terrorism.

8. PERSECUTION: In the eighth stage of genocide, segregation of the out-groups takes place. Victims are

identified and segregated on the basis of ethnicity or religion. This is the point at which death lists are created, property confiscated, ghettos formed to name a few examples.

9. EXTERMINATION: In the ninth stage of genocide, elimination of the out-groups takes place. This is the point where the act of genocide is carried out. The perpetrators of genocide at this point do not view their victims as human beings.

10. DENIAL: In the final stage of genocide, denial sets in among the perpetrators and persists long after the horrendous crime of genocide is over. At this point, those responsible try to hide evidence of their deeds (Stanton n.d.).

The ten stages of genocide that Stanton has defined can be used as a tool to understand the nature of genocide, as well as to identify its early warning signs when manifest in some part of the world. By understanding the genocidal stages, early interventions can be designed and employed to thwart the crime of genocide before it progresses (Stanton n.d.).

The Bystander

In any given culture, how could good citizens stand by and allow genocide to take place? What academics and others have known for a long time is that genocide never exists in a vacuum. The genocidal elimination of an out-group requires the complicity of *bystanders*. Bystanders are those citizens who stand by passively while atrocities are being committed around them. Author Elie Wiesel, a Holocaust survivor, said in his Nobel Peace Prize acceptance speech: "Neutrality helps the oppressor, never the victim. Silence encourages the tormentor, never the tormented. Sometimes we must interfere" (as quoted in Eisner 2018, p. 17).

Sociologist and Holocaust scholar, Samuel P. Oliner, offers the following framework for identifying the role of bystander which he sees as present in all genocides.

- First are the "Innocent Bystanders" who claim, for one reason or another, that they had no knowledge of a situation. Scholars and others have cast doubt on this claim of innocence. According to Oliner, innocence cannot be claimed when there are opportunities for individuals to stand against what is happening around them.
- Second are the "Individual Bystanders," who, when not influenced by group behavior, are more likely to assist and stand up for people in distress.
- Third are the "Institutional Bystanders," who may be members of governmental institutions, churches, schools, the military, and so forth. These individuals, who are part of larger institutions, are prone to giving up their individual identities and adhering to institutional cultures.
- Last are the "International Bystanders," a category that includes governments of nation–states, international organizations, and other institutions that stand by as genocide takes place (Oliner 2011).

Understanding the role of the bystander is critical to understanding the crime of genocide in all societies. More specifically, it is critical to understanding the role of the bystander at the time of the Holocaust, when large segments of German society took on the role of bystander or became complicit with the Nazis. What follows is a description of two segments of society—women and the business elite—and the bystander roles that they played during the time of the Holocaust.

Female Bystanders

Historian Wendy Lower examined the female bystander, looking at the roles women played in the administration of the Nazi regime. According to Lower, women's roles were not limited to the few women who worked in the extermination and concentration camps; rather, women from all levels of German society, including secretaries, office workers, nurses, and social workers, participated in the planning and implementation of the Holocaust. It was not uncommon for young women from the provinces to seek to make their mark on the world by working their way up the career ladders offered by the new government of the Reich. Many left home as innocents but soon became bystanders, while others became complicit in the Holocaust (Lower 2013). While Lower gives us a perspective on how women participated in the plans of the Reich, it is important to emphasize at this point that the role of bystander was filled by both men and women in German society.

We shall now look at the business elites in Germany who also took on the role of bystander and, in many cases, were complicit in the Holocaust. Many German companies chose to aid and abet the Nazis in their efforts to exterminate the Jewish population:

> Leaders of banks, insurance companies, and other commercial and industrial businesses participated in the persecution of Jews. Many of them played a role in the "Aryanization" of the German economy, the expropriation of Jewish assets, and the use of forced labor during the war (United States Holocaust Memorial Museum [U.S. Holocaust Museum], 2019a).

It is important to note that not all German businesses were complicit in the Holocaust. We now know, however, that many were.

One of the better-known companies to participate in the Final Solution to exterminate the Jews was the Volkswagen company. Volkswagen started out in the Third Reich building a "people's car" for the German populace. By the beginning of the war, however, it was focused on military needs and even used forced labor from Nazi concentration camps. "One VW plant engineer traveled to Auschwitz and selected 300 skilled metalworkers from the massive transports of Hungarian Jews in 1944. In addition, 650 Jewish women were transferred to assemble military munitions" (U.S. Holocaust Museum, n.d.-c). The Volkswagen company ran four concentration camps and eight forced-labor camps over the course of the war (U.S. Holocaust Museum, n.d.-c).

Another company, Bayer, a pharmaceutical firm known for its anti-inflammatory pain reliever "Aspirin," also became complicit in the crimes of the Third Reich. In the absence of legal and ethical restraints, it tested its drugs on unwilling human subjects at Dachau, Auschwitz, and Gusen concentration camps (U.S. Holocaust Museum, 2019b).

Volkswagen and Bayer are just two among many companies we know about today that were complicit with the Third Reich. The involvement of some companies we may never know about because their histories are shrouded in silence or lost in time. Bayer has never owned up to its past. Despite this fact, it remains a global pharmaceutical company (U.S. Holocaust Museum, 2019b). On the other hand, Volkswagen has acknowledged its corporate complicity with the Nazis and has made efforts at reparations. For example, it has given money to support former forced laborers from various countries, and it has committed to financially supporting Israeli institutions in aiding elderly survivors of the Holocaust and non-Jewish victims of forced labor (U.S. Holocaust Museum, n.d.-c).

As stated earlier, not all businesses were complicit in the Holocaust. Some businessmen, for instance, were rescuers. The one businessman who is most familiar to us is Oskar Schindler. He was an ethnic German, born in Moravia but later a citizen of Czechoslovakia, who became a rescuer.

Schindler and his wife saved more than a thousand lives by employing Jewish workers in their factories. In 1993 Yad Vashem, the primary memorial and educational organization in Israel honoring "Righteous Gentiles" as well as the victims of the Holocaust, awarded Schindler and his wife Emilie the title "Righteous Among the Nations"—in recognition of everything they had done to save Jews from being sent to Auschwitz (U.S. Holocaust Museum, n.a.).

It is important to emphasize at this point that in any given genocidal situation there are people who do not remain passive or indifferent bystanders. These are the rescuers who stand up against oppression and atrocities. The Jewish organization Yad Vashem has counted 6,706 Polish men and women as "Righteous Among the Nations," making Poland the country with the highest number of rescuers in the world (Eisner 2018, p. 18). At the same time, there were other European countries where many citizens became rescuers. For example, both Denmark and Bulgaria rescued a significant number of their Jewish citizens from the hands of the Nazis. In Bulgaria, 48,000 Jewish lives were saved. The rescue effort was carried out with the help of the Minister of Justice, officials of the Bulgarian church, and ordinary members of the citizenry. Also, in Germany there were those who took a stand against the killing of the physically and mentally handicapped (Oliner 2011, p. 51).

In summary, it is best not to paint with too broad a brush on the subject of bystanders and to keep in mind that there are always individuals who chose not to remain passive and uninvolved and who stand up for others when genocide appears.

One cannot close this discussion on bystanders without remarking on the anti-Semitism that existed in Germany at the time of the Nazi regime and in Poland where, despite the fact many Poles were rescuers, a deep-seated form of anti-Semitism existed in Polish society. Anti-Semitism has existed across Europe for hundreds of years. In Germany, the early 20th century, bogus anti-Semitic document entitled "The Protocols of the Elders of Zion", which spoke about a Jewish plan for world domination, was used for propaganda purposes by the Nazis. It was also used by some teachers in the German school system (Segel, Levy 1995, p. 30). In Poland, the words of a Polish resistance fighter, uttered during the occupation, speak to how deeply embedded anti-Semitism was in Polish society. "The Germans will throw stones at Hitler's death, because he brought about the downfall of the German people, but the Poles will bring flowers to his grave as a token of gratitude for his freeing Poland from the Jews" (Eisner 2018 p. 18). Today, remnants of this attitude still exist in Poland but in a more subtle form. For example, in legislation that is crafted to make it difficult for Jewish people to reclaim property (Eisner 2018, p 19). Also, the document "The Protocols of the Elders of Zion" is now being circulated on the Internet. At the same time, today, we frequently hear accounts depicted in the media of how the embers of anti-Semitism are being stoked once again in Europe.

In the first part of this essay we looked at the characteristics that are common to all genocides. First, we looked at the definition of genocide as defined by International Law. Second, we looked to a classification system which delineated the ten stages of genocide. Third, we explored the role of bystander and the various types of bystanders that enable the perpetrators of genocide. As examples, we explored the role of corporate bystanders in German society as well as the role of female bystanders. We also looked at the role of rescuer and how there are always citizens who choose to stand up and not remain passive or indifferent to what is going on around them when genocide threatens a people. Conversely, from this point on, we will look at what differentiates the Holocaust from other genocides. We will begin with the Nazi plan for the elimination of the Jewish population from Europe. While other genocides have included governmental plans to eliminate an out-group, what came to be known as The Final Solution, developed by the Nazi regime, reached a level of centralized planning, organization and efficiency that surpasses what we know about other genocides.

The Final Solution

In January of 1942, Hitler's top aides met to discuss a plan to eliminate Jews from Europe. What followed was the development of an official policy of extermination known as the Final Solution. There were two programs that served as models for the Final Solution: Operation T-4 and the mobile killing units called Einsatzgruppen (Roleff 2002).

The earlier Nazi elimination program known as Operation T-4 focused on eliminating physically and mentally handicapped children, the elderly, the incurably ill, the mentally ill, and the emotionally disturbed. The killings were carried out by gas in a room disguised as a shower, by lethal injection, or by starvation, and the remains were cremated. "It is estimated that between seventy and eighty thousand people were killed between 1939 and 1945 in the T-4 Program" (Roleff, 2002, p. 13).

Author Elie Wiesel describes the mobile killing squads used in Russia, the Ukraine and Lithuania in the following passage:

The Einsatzgruppen carried out the final solution by turning their machine guns on more than a million Jews, men, women, and children, and throwing them into huge mass graves, dug just moments before by the victims themselves. Special units would then disinter the corpses and burn them. Thus, for the first time in history, Jews were not only killed twice but denied burial in a cemetery (Wiesel, 2006, p. viii).

The Einsatzgruppen entered other counties as well. In Latvia, Estonia and Poland, for example, the Jewish populations were also decimated (Einsatzgruppen, U.S. Holocaust Museum n.d. b).

As the Final Solution progressed, the methods used for mass extermination proved inefficient for the Nazis. These earlier elimination programs would later be replaced by death camps, specifically designated extermination centers where mass killings could be handled on an efficient, assembly-line basis. In addition, a new poison made of hydrogen cyanide that was experimented with at the Auschwitz camp proved much more efficient at killing than previous methods used. The new chemical, Zyklon B, in combination with the modern-day furnace called a crematorium, made the extermination process complete. The Einsatzgruppen were relieved of their killing duties, and the Nazis began to focus on sending Jews directly to death camps to be exterminated (Roleff 2002).

The following death camps were established in Poland, where millions of people (including Jews, Poles, Roma, and Soviet prisoners of war) lost their lives: Chelmno, Belzec, Sobibor, Treblinka, Majdanek , and Auschwitz (Roleff 2002, p.15). Among these, it was Auschwitz, the largest of the camps, that became known as the headquarters of mass extermination.

The following quote describes the role that Auschwitz played in the extermination of over a million Jewish people:

The gruesome history and enduring horror of Auschwitz can be attributed primarily to the machinery for mass extermination of human beings created by the Nazis at the nearby Birkenau Camp, a unit of Auschwitz. The location was designated by Himmler as the centerpiece for "the final solution" of the Jewish question in Europe. From 1942 until fall 1944, the operation designed to annihilate European Jews functioned almost without let-up as transport trains delivered Jews from Nazi-occupied countries and European Satellites of the Third Reich (Gutman, 1994, p. 6).

We will now examine closely this "centerpiece" of mass extermination, the Auschwitz–Birkenau death camp, in order to understand what scientific genocide looks like. Through the lens of the chemical Zyklon B and the modern-day crematoria in Auschwitz, one will hopefully be able to fully understand what differentiates the Holocaust from all other genocides.

What began as a harmless pesticide used in Germany later became a potent killing agent. The actual chemical ingredient in the pesticide was hydrocyanic acid, also known as prussic acid. It was generally considered benign because it was known to only vaporize at a temperature of 27 °C. It had initially been used at Auschwitz as a fumigation agent (Pressac, 1994).

The gas Zyklon B was first used in Auschwitz to kill large numbers of Soviet prisoners. Any doubts Commandant Hoss of Auschwitz had about Zyklon B's efficiency as a killing agent were put to rest when he heard about its success with the Soviet prisoners (Gutman 1994).

But the adoption of Zyklon B was not without its problems. There was a learning curve involved for the executioners. Its first use was experimental, which caused problems not only for the administrators of the gas but for the victims as well. Many prisoners suffered horribly because they were still alive two days after the gas was administered. The executioners were not aware that prussic acid was not deadly until it vaporized at 27 °C. Other issues had to be worked out as well. For example, how much Zyklon B was lethal for how many people? Ventilation posed a problem. These were some of the issues facing the engineers and other professionals that needed to be resolved before gassing operations using Zyklon B could be effective (Pressac 1994).

The next phase of the operation using Zyklon B took place in two temporary cottages near Birkenau. The victims were Jews who had been transported from Upper Silesia and Slovakia. After this success at mass killing, the use of Zyklon B reached a whole new level: "from March 1943 on, four gas chambers and crematoria, designed and built specifically for mass murder by German engineers and companies, were in operation at the Birkenau camp. At their top capacity, these installations could "process" 4,416 victims in 24 hours" (Gutman 1994, p. 30).

From 1941 to 1943, Jews destined for extermination arrived in Auschwitz on trains from the following places: Upper Silesia, Slovakia, Germany, the Netherlands, Belgium, France, Italy, Greece, Yugoslavia and parts of occupied Poland, Theresienstadt in Czechoslovakia, Greece, the Majdanek camp and ghettos of Zaglebie in Poland, the Bergen-Belsen camps, and Italy (Gutman, 1994). According to Gutman "With the establishment of the death factory, Jews arrived in mass transports from Nazi-occupied countries or satellites of the Third Reich. Most transports carried entire families uprooted from their residences as part of the process of total eradication of Jewish communities, their only offense being their "racial" and national origins" (Gutman, 1994, pp. 30-31).

Just as prussic acid began as a harmless pesticide for general use, the crematorium began in England in the late 1800s as a public health solution for the handling of human remains in heavily populated areas. The idea to use crematoria spread quickly to the European continent, and firms in Germany were involved in their construction.

Through an engineer by the name of Kurt Prüfer, of the reputable German firm of Topf and Sons in Erfurt, Germany secured the first contract issued by the SS to build a single muffle furnace for the Reich (the muffle holds the human remains). By the end of 1939, the first furnace was in full operation at the Dachau camp. The following year Prüfer secured a second contract to produce two furnaces for the price of 9,000 Reichsmarks—one at Auschwitz and another at the Flossenburg concentration camp in Germany: "The new contract must have pleased Prüfer, and not only because of the 2 percent commission he received on the profit of each order. With Topf furnaces in Dachau, Buchenwald, Flossenburg, and Auschwitz, he was on his way to acquiring a monopoly in what could only be an expanding market" (Pressac, 1994, p. 187).

Just as there were problems that needed to be worked out with the use of prussic acid, there were many problems with the furnaces to be worked out by Topf engineers and other professionals. Furnaces broke down and there were frequent alterations, modifications, and redesigns that needed to be made. Ventilation was a problem with the furnaces as well. Also, smokestacks needed to be constructed or repaired. At one point, fuel shortages forced Topf to redesign a model furnace to use coke burners instead of oil burners. Plans for an electric forced-air draft fan fitted with an electric blower needed to be perfected. On August 15, 1940, crematorium I at Auschwitz became fully operational, and the first crema-tion took place. Prüfer estimated that the furnace would pro-cess 30 to 36 bodies in a 10-hour cycle or about 70 bodies if it were run for a 20-hour cycle (Pressac 1994). For Prüfer, the Topf furnace ensured an efficient, cost-effective operation.

Crematorium I was the first of the crematoriums to be built at Auschwitz, but plans for more crematoria soon fol-lowed. Crematorium II was to be built in Birkenau, and plans were on the drawing board for crematoria III, IV, and V. As plans for the additional crematoria progressed, so did the evo-lution of the single-muffle furnace. It was not long until two-, three-, and four-muffle furnaces were required (Pressac 1994).

In late 1942 the Nazis began to formulate plans to build crematorium VI because they were becoming insecure about the increased demand for cremation created by the influx of new arrivals at the camp. Commandant Hoss of Auschwitz described one of the new furnaces under consideration as "in the shape of a huge brickworks with a ring furnace" conjuring an image of a continuous ring holding hundreds of human corpora encircling a huge brick building (Piper 1994, p. 176). Fortunately, the war was winding down and crematorium VI was never built. More than a million Jews lost their lives in the gas chambers of Auschwitz–Birkenau, and it was the gas chambers and crematoria that enabled killing on such a massive scale (Piper 1994).

For Topf and Sons, as well as for many other German businesses, professionals, and SS staff, supplying labor and materials for the Holocaust was filling a need. The Holocaust stands out as an example of 20th-century industrial organizing, planning, time management, cost-benefit and assembly-line mentalities:

> As thousands of women, children, and old people disappeared into the flames, the Zentralbauleitung and Topf were settling their accounts. The Zentralbauleitung had paid practically all of its outstanding bills during the last trimester of 1943 and at the beginning of February 1944. But it wanted Topf to pay for the jobs it had commissioned the metalwork shop at the DAW to do and for various little things that Topf needed on the work sites and that the Zentralbauleitung had procured (Pressac 1994, p. 239).

By January of 1945 all of the crematoria in the Auschwitz death camps had been destroyed (Pressac 1994). Although the camps with their gas chambers and ovens no longer exist, the memory of the horrors of Auschwitz will go down in

history as the place where the first industrial, scientific genocide in human history took place.

Other Genocides

The crime of genocide has plagued humanity for thousands of years, and the 20th century was one of the worst for
this crime against humanity. A total of nineteen genocides
were perpetrated worldwide during this century, with the
Holocaust and the genocides of Armenia, Cambodia and
Rwanda being just a few that marked this horrific period in
history. In the Armenian genocide of 1915, 1.5 million Armenian lives were lost in a systematic government attempt to
eliminate the Armenian population. Denial of the genocide
by the Turkish government persists to the present day. The
Jewish Holocaust followed from 1941 to 1945, where, again,
there was a systematic government attempt to eliminate an
out-group, and six million Jews lost their lives (in addition
to several million more people deemed undesirable). On the
other side of the world, from 1975 to 1979, the Khmer Rouge
regime in Cambodia carried out a systematic extermination
of the Cambodian people, killing 1.7 million Cambodians.
Rwanda, where the last genocide of the 20th century took
place, saw a systematic attempt by the Hutu elite majority
to eliminate the minority Tutsi, Twa, and moderate Hutu. A
total of 800,000 Rwandans lost their lives during this brutal
time in the country's history (Genocide Watch, n.d.).

Genocide reared its ugly head again early in the 21st century in Darfur, erupting in 2003 and lingering for many years.
According to humanitarian affairs scholar Mukesh Kapila
in his paper entitled "Darfur: The World's Longest Running
Genocide," this was again "a systematic and organized attempt by supremacist–racist perpetrators (the Janjaweed aided by their government allies and led by the dominating military–political elite) to 'do away' with another group of people
because of their black African identity" (Kapila 2014).

Unfortunately, Darfur is not the only genocide of the 21st century. According to a *New York Times* report, the three-member panel of the United Nations Fact-Finding Mission on Myanmar has judged the actions of Myanmar's Buddhist-majority security forces against Rohingya Muslims a genocide (Cumming-Bruce 2018). Forces in Myanmar had begun a campaign of ethnic cleansing in August 2017 that included slaughter, gang rape, and the burning of hundreds of villages. Since then, more than 10,000 Rohingya have died in what have been described as "clearance operations." Another 74,000 Rohingya have fled to Bangladesh, while about 120,000 remain internally displaced (Zakaria 2019). The government of Myanmar has launched a repatriation campaign to encourage Rohingya in refugee camps in Bangladesh to return, but few care to comply (Beech 2019).

The Rohingya genocide is linked to the Jewish genocide in a very unique way. Just as Hitler used the new medium of film to transmit Nazi propaganda, the modern-day social communication medium Facebook has been used by government officials and others in Myanmar to circulate propaganda against the Rohingya. According to a *New York Times* article, Facebook had to bar certain individuals and organizations linked to the Myanmar military's human rights abuses from using its platform (Beech 2018). These are two examples of how the perpetrators of genocide employ the latest technologies of their day for propaganda.

We have just reviewed genocides that occurred prior to as well as after the Holocaust. Many thought the Holocaust was the genocide to end all genocides. Yet, the crime of genocide has continued to rear its ugly head. It is a crime that seldom manifests in black and white. Rather, as we have seen, it is a multilayered offense that is carried out on many levels. Factors such as racism, anti-Semitism, economic and political factors, and the dehumanization of the other precede this horrific crime against humanity. Fortunately, today, there are rays of hope worldwide committed to combating the crime of genocide.

One ray of hope is the International Association of Genocide Studies (IAGS). Founded in 1994, it has worked hard over the years to bring about the first academic interdisciplinary study of genocide that is global in its reach. Its main goal is the prevention of the crime of genocide wherever it occurs. Through its conferences, workshops, research centers, publications, public policy efforts, scholarship and many other endeavors, we know more about the crime of genocide than ever before. Goals and objectives based on solid interdisciplinary research are a major step forward in combating the crime of genocide (IAGS n.d.).

Another ray of hope is a new voluntary organization called the Alliance Against Genocide, which operates under the umbrella organization Genocide Watch. The Alliance's approach is decentralized but its mission is proactive. Its many constituent international partner organizations converge with the express goal of preventing genocide. In addition to advocating for institutional reform of the United Nations, the Alliance has implemented its own NGO early warning system, alerting the community to forms of ethnic conflict taking place, as well as its own powerful and rapid response forces at regional and international levels. One of its goals is to have an international police force that can act swiftly whenever genocide threatens (Genocide Watch, n.d.). These are just two out of many outstanding organizations presently working to prevent the crime of genocide wherever it occurs in the world.

Conclusion

The beginning of this essay stated that all holocausts are genocides but not all genocides are holocausts. It also stated that the Jewish Holocaust of the 20th century differed from all other genocides in the history of the world because it was the only genocide where an industrialization of death occurred, utilizing the most modern, scientific, and technological advances of the day to obliterate an out-group. The ensuing discussion of the Holocaust attempted to demonstrate how these two statements are true. We started by looking at the stages of genocide followed by an exploration of the concept of the bystander, which is applicable to all genocides. We explored the role of women bystanders as well as the role of corporate bystanders in German society. We also looked at the role of rescuer. We then turned to the qualities that differentiated the Holocaust from other genocides, beginning with the Nazis' plan called the Final Solution, which was designed to eliminate Europe's Jewish population. We examined closely how Auschwitz, the Nazi "centerpiece" of death, came to represent the first industrial, scientific genocide in human history, by looking through the lens of the chemical called Zyklon B and the modern-day furnace called the crematorium. The new chemical enabled the efficient killing of thousands of people at a time, while the ancient element of fire used in a new way as part of a modern-day furnace, enabled the disposal of thousands of human remains at one time. It was a triumph of industrialized, scientific, genocide, and it was done on a scale never before seen in the history of the world. Hopefully, this line of inquiry has convinced the reader that the Jewish Holocaust of the 20th century differed significantly from all other genocides. The Holocaust was no "sacred offering;" it was an industrialized, scientific attempt to obliterate the Jewish people and their culture from Europe.

The introduction to this essay described fire as an element used in the sacred rituals of the ancients. To conclude, let us look to the fire that illumes the imagination of humankind. Theologian Matthew Fox describes how our greatest gift— the one that sets us apart from other species—is the human imagination, which gives us our unlimited capacity for creativity (Fox 2004). We have minds that can contemplate the furthest galaxies and explore the depths of the oceans; we can build spaceships that go to the moon and probe the complexities of the psyche; we can create super structures and develop nanotechnologies. But there is a dark side to all of this wonderful human creativity. Like many things in life, the human imagination is a double-edged sword. It can be used for good or for evil.

Fox warns us that we can create a world that is "life-giving" or "death-making." Mankind's capacity for the demonic did not emerge in the modern day. Thomas Aquinas, seven centuries ago, warned of this weakness in our species. "One human being can do more evil than all the other species put together" (Fox 2004, p. 35).

The Jewish Holocaust of the 20th century will go down in history as a time when some members of humanity chose to create a world that was "death-making" instead of "life-giving." Brilliant chemists chose to create a lethal poison that would kill millions of people; brilliant engineers and architects chose to design gas chambers and crematoria for the mass killing and disposal of the remains of millions of people. The human imagination, in this instance, was a lethal weapon that needed to be tethered to a higher moral value. Our powers for creativity have to be steered in a positive, healthy direction, as stated by Fox. If we do not do this, "then we are surrendering our ethical decision making to others. And these others, be they individuals or corporations, have their own agendas which may prove to be very distant from our own values and ethics" (Fox, 2004, p.36).

If there is a lesson to be learned from the Holocaust, it is what the consequences might be if we no longer care about our neighbors and if, as Fox stated, we let our responsibility for our creativity be subsumed under others' agendas.

References

Beech, H. (2018, September 1). "Facebook ban, not genocide incites outrage in Myanmar," *The New York Times, A4, September 1, 2018.*

Beech, H. (2019), August 23). "Promises Made: The Rohingya – 730,000 fled Myanmar: Only a few dozen returned, "*The New York Times*, A1, August 23, 2019.

Cumming-Bruce, N. (2018), August 28). "U.N. says Rohingya purge warrants genocide charges for generals," *The New York Times*, August 28, 2018, A4.

Eisner, J. (2018, April). "Collaborators, righteous gentiles or something in between?" *Forward*, April 2018, pp. 16-19.

Fox, M. (2004). *Creativity: Where the divine and the human meet.* Jeremy P. Tarcher; Putnam.

Genocide Watch. (n.d.). *Alliance Against Genocide*. Retrieved September 14, 2019, from http://genocidewatch.net/partners-and-projects/international-allianc

Gutman, Y. (1994). Auschwitz -- An overview. In Y. Gutman & M. Berenbaum (Eds.), *Anatomy of the Auschwitz death camp* (pp. 5-32), Indiana University Press, United States Holocaust Memorial Museum.

International Association of Genocide Studies (IAGS) https://genocidescholars.org/about-us/

Kapila, M. (2014, March 31-April 1). "*Darfur: The world's longest running genocide*," International Conference on Genocide Prevention, Brussels. https://www.genocideprevention.be/sites/default/files/content/mukesh_kapila.pdf

Lower, W. (2013). *Hitler's Furies: German women in the Nazi killing fields.* Houghton Mifflin Harcourt.

Oliner, S.P. (2011). *The nature of good and evil: Understanding the acts of moral and immoral behavior*. Paragon House.

Piper, F. (1994). Gas chambers and crematoria. In Y. Gutman & M. Berenbaum (Eds.), *Anatomy of the Auschwitz death camp* (pp. 157–176). Indiana University Press; United States Holocaust Memorial Museum.

Pressac, J.-C. (with Van Pelt, R.-J.). (1994). The machinery of mass murder at Auschwitz. In Y. Gutman & M. Berenbaum (Eds.), *Anatomy of the Auschwitz death camp* (pp. 183–240). Indiana University Press; United States Holocaust Memorial Museum.

Roleff, T.L. (ed.). (2002). *The Holocaust: death camps.* Greenhaven Press.

Segel, B.W., Levy, R.S. (1995) A lie and a libel: The history of the Protocols of the Elders of Zion, University of Nebraska Press.

Stanton, G. H. (n.d.). *The ten stages of genocide.* Genocide Watch. https://www.genocidewatch.com/ten-stages-of-genocide

United Nations Convention on the Prevention and Punishment of the Crime of Genocide, December 11, 1946, http://www.preventgenocide.org/law/convention/text.htm#II

United States Holocaust Memorial Museum. (n.d.-a). *Oskar Schindler.* The Holocaust Encyclopedia. Retrieved September 19, 2019, from https://encyclopedia.ushmm.org/content/en/article/oskar-schindler

United States Holocaust Memorial Museum. (n.d.-b). Einsatzgruppen, The Holocaust Encyclopedia. Retrieved January 28, 2020, from https://encyclopedia.ushmm.org/content/en/animated-map/einsatzgruppen

United States Holocaust Memorial Museum. (n.d.-c). *Volkswagen.* The Holocaust Encyclopedia. Retrieved September 19, 2019, from https://encyclopedia.ushmm.org/content/en/article/volkswagen-1?parent=en/54588

United States Holocaust Memorial Museum. (2019a, June 4). *The role of business elites*. The Holocaust Encyclopedia. Retrieved September 19, 2019, from https://encyclopedia.ushmm.org/content/en/article/the-role-of-business-elites

United States Holocaust Memorial Museum. (2019b, June 13). *Bayer*. The Holocaust Encyclopedia. Retrieved September 19, 2019, from https://encyclopedia.ushmm.org/content/en/article/bayer

Webster's New World. (2007). *Webster's New World college dictionary* (4th ed.).

Wiese E. (2006) *Night*. Hill and Wang.

Zakaria, R. (2019, May 15). The quandary of Myanmar: Will starving the country of visitors make things better? *The New York Times Style Magazine*. https://www.nytimes.com/2019/05/15/t-magazine/myanmar-travel-quandary-essay.html

5

The Status of Women

NICHOLE WAGNER

Promoting a healthy future for the children of the world requires us to examine the role that all people play in providing social support to one another. Social injustice embedded in relations of power and privilege creates unequal opportunities for people with marginalized identities. In many cultures and societies there is a persistent inequality between people considered male and those identified as female.

Consider for a moment what could be possible in a society where women and girls are unconditionally protected and respected. Imagine a little girl who dreams of being a scientist. Her mother is an engineer, her father is a teacher. The girl is able to eat healthy foods. She feels safe in her neighborhood. She can focus in the classroom and form meaningful relationships. Her parents embolden her to reach for her dreams, work hard, and know that she is intrinsically valued. While in high school she is encouraged to obtain scholarships to help her pay for college, where she has the opportunity to study science. The girl completes her education and eventually makes valuable scientific contributions that improve people's lives. The positive impact this one girl has on the world is made possible because she is supported—socially, physically, and economically—by her family and community. This is the kind of future our children can inherit.

What stands in the way of little girls of the world? Ideas that demean and diminish the value of femininity. Social systems that exclude females. Male favoritism and privilege. Violence in families and communities. Unequal access to education, health care, employment opportunities, and pay. These are clear barriers to unfettered development. Another factor in gender discrimination is the tendency to *essentialize* people's identities—that is, the claim that a category of people have certain characteristics that are inherent in every member of that group. When applied to constructs of gender and femininity, this means that women are frequently perceived as fragile, illogical, and inferior, thereby ignoring social–emotional variation in individuals that is unrelated to their sex or their gender (Wood, 2015). Disproportionate violence towards women is one of the most widespread and difficult impediments to gender equality (Carter, 2014; Wood, 2015). In many places around the world, women cannot vote, drive, own property, or travel abroad without permission from a husband or male relative. Even in industrialized nations, implicit prejudice and discrimination can hold women back from obtaining power and influence comparable to that of their male counterparts. All of these conditions impair the ability of women and girls to participate in their societies, depriving communities and countries of valuable leaders and innovators. Since the focus of this book is on the future and what can be made possible, we felt it was crucial to briefly examine the social status of women in various parts of the world in an effort to understand what can be done to promote justice and equality for all.

Gender inequality refers to the various ways in which women and girls are systemically and systematically disadvantaged in areas of social life. Some of these disadvantages include unequal access to education, health care, job opportunities, and civic leadership. Impediments to the progress of women are too numerous to recount in a single chapter. Instead, we will briefly examine some obstacles to gender equality, and then suggest how ordinary citizens can help promote the advancement of women in their communities.

In his book *A Call to Action: Women, Religion, Violence, and Power* (2014), former United States President Jimmy Carter relates his experience working to combat gender inequality around the world. Jimmy and Rosalynn Carter's nonprofit, nongovernmental organization, the Carter Center, was founded in 1982 with the goals of alleviating human suffering and promoting human rights. The Carter Center has supported efforts to strengthen equality for women and girls in over 80 countries since its founding. Comparing gender discrimination to racism, President Carter describes the former as "extending far beyond a small geographical region to the entire globe . . . based on the presumption that men and boys are superior to women and girls," and as a "system of discrimination . . . supported by some male religious leaders who distort . . . sacred texts to perpetuate their claim that females are, in some basic ways, inferior to them, unqualified to serve God on equal terms" (2014, pp. 1–2). President Carter's criticism of the distortion of religious ideas to justify discrimination against women and girls shows that it provides men with a false moral high ground from which to gain undeserved power and privilege. At times, the perceived inferiority of women is used to justify practices such as female genital mutilation, which is often carried out to preserve a girl's "purity" before marriage and to discourage sexual relations outside of marriage by reducing or eliminating sexual pleasure (Wood, 2015, pp. 264–66).

Another major driving force in gender inequality is the epidemic of gender-based violence. Tolerance for systems of discrimination promotes an underlying acceptance of violence against, and the suffering of, vulnerable social groups (Carter, 2014). According to the World Health Organization (WHO, n.d.), approximately 30% of women globally have experienced violence at the hands of an intimate partner. Data from the *Global Gender Gap Report* shows that as many as 38% of women who were murdered around the world were killed by an intimate partner (World Economic Forum [WEF], 2017). Gender-based violence contributes to other forms of inequality, such as classism and economic injustice. President Carter writes that, in addition to violence and suffering caused by inequality, "there is a devastating effect on economic prosperity caused by the loss of contributions of at least half of the human beings on earth. This is not just a women's issue. It is not confined to the poorest countries. It affects us all" (2014, p. 3). This insight highlights a rallying point in the fight for gender equality. All people are affected by the injustice of gender inequality, and all people have a responsibility to use their voice and social influence to speak out and push back against it. A first step can be calling out injustice in any form. This brings attention to systems of privilege and discrimination.

The status of women and girls can be improved through deliberate, collective efforts. International forums provide space for bringing to light these issues and forming plans of action. The World Health Organization is one such forum. Partnering with the United Nations to create an agenda of humanitarian priorities they call Sustainable Development Goals, the WHO's 2030 Agenda for Sustainable Development includes several goals that relate to the status of women, including a specific goal called Gender Equality. One strategy called for is the creation and utilization of data-sharing systems between humanitarian agencies. Programs that deliver results are developed as a result of implementing policies. Policies require data for measurements of effectiveness. An efficient method of gathering and sharing data between nations is therefore critical (WHO, n.d.).

Due to major barriers to women's health in many regions of the world, women are a primary focus of the WHO and

UN's sustainable development goals, particularly in developing nations. While there is substantial variation across African nations, the average African woman's lifespan is 22 years less than the global average of 80 years. African women are also far more likely to die from pregnancy complications, communicable diseases and nutritional deficiency (Women for Women International, n.d.; WHO, 2017). Female genital cutting tragically remains an accepted practice in too many parts of the world, particularly in regions of Africa and East Asia. Genital cutting is often presented as a rite of passage for young women despite links to premature death and complications during pregnancy, among other health concerns (Wood, 2015; WHO, 2017). In 2017 two U.S. doctors were charged with cutting the genitals of up to 100 young girls in Michigan. This was the first recorded case in the United States of a doctor being criminally charged for genital cutting. As a result, scores of previously silent women spoke out about their own experiences of being subjected to the procedure (Belluck, 2017). This illustrates how social, cultural, and religious norms can greatly affect women's physical and emotional health. It also demonstrates that positive change can occur when women have the opportunity to give input and shape norms under the protection of law.

Another tool for evaluating the status of women is the Global Gender Gap Index, which is a collection of data gathered by the World Economic Forum. The index measures over 70 indicators of the socioeconomic status of women in countries around the world. These include participation in the labor force and professional careers, access to health care, access to wealth and technology, and levels of participation in education and political leadership. The Index's latest report summarizes the importance of closing the gender gap: "To build future economies that are both dynamic and inclusive, we must ensure that everyone has equal opportunity. When women and girls are not integrated—as both beneficiary and shaper—the global community loses out on skills, ideas and perspectives that are critical for addressing global challenges and harnessing new opportunities" (WEF, 2017, p. v).

The United States ranks 49th out of 144 countries on the Global Gender Gap Index. This compares to a ranking of 23rd in the 2006 index. The U.S. has *declined* in its advancement of women in all subindex areas aside from educational attainment, and remains far below average in terms of women's participation in government (96th out of 144). It has comparatively few women in local and national offices, and there have been no female heads of state in the nation's history (WEF, 2017). At 82nd place on the "Health and Survival" subindex, the United States shows that much remains to be done to achieve gender parity within its borders, both socially and politically.

The United States has recently seen the rise of a widespread feminist movement. Unlike in social movements of times past, cultural narratives today can shift dramatically through the strategic use of digital media. Aided by social media and popular personalities, this recent feminist uprising has manifested as what is now popularly referred to as the Me Too movement. Coined in 2007 by social activist Tarana Burke, the phrase "Me Too" has been used as a way to connect the shared experiences of women who have suffered sexual violence and harassment, calling out the need for resources and support (García Giribet, 2018). Burke, a Black woman from the Bronx, noted that women of color have often been sidelined in popular feminist movements. She hoped to make intersectionality—an awareness of the many social identities that all people have and how those identities affect their lives—a main focus of the movement. After a popular actress shared Burke's message in a social media post, an overwhelming public response resulted in the #metoo hashtag on Twitter. More importantly, the

Me Too movement brought issues that had long been suppressed by dominant social narratives to the forefront of national conversations (Garcia, 2017). The subsequent deluge of women publicly sharing their experiences of harassment and violence resulted in accusations against more than 250 high-profile men whose behavior had gone unchallenged for years (North et al., 2019). The global sharing of information and culture, made possible by online media platforms, has brought awareness of the Me Too movement to women in many parts of the world, and it may yet yield major social changes outside of the United States.

Social change takes place at both local and global levels. Nonprofit organizations such as the World Health Organization, Carter Center, World Economic Forum, Women for Women's Rights, and many others represent a collective concern for and interest in the well-being of women and girls in all local communities and in the global community of nations. These organizations exist because of committed individuals who recognize the harm caused by gender bias and violence and who are motivated to organize their efforts in meaningful ways. When individuals are taught respect and compassion for others from an early age, a cultural shift takes place—one that does not allow for passive acceptance of violence and discrimination. Vulnerable groups are offered protection and support, and suffering does not go unaddressed, because in a compassionate society the suffering of one group affects everyone.

The end of gender inequality will not come quickly, but one can draw hope from efforts to educate and encourage people to address systems that diminish the status of women. Nurturing a sense of morality, justice, and other altruistic principles can lead individuals to become involved in the struggle to increase equality (Oliner, 2003). When women suffer, so do their communities. When women prosper, the world prospers. Social, economic, and political systems that

69

permit gender-based violence are the same systems that undergird other forms of discrimination and inequality for people with nondominant social identities. Moral leaders and compassionate individuals can cultivate caring relationships and promote female equality in schools and communities, and thereby realize a hopeful future that our children can inherit.

References

Belluck, P. (2017, June 11). Michigan case adds U.S. dimension to the debate over genital cutting. *The New York Times*, A21.

Carter, J. (2014). *A call to action: Women, religion, violence, and power.* Simon & Schuster.

Garcia, S. E. (2017). The woman who created #MeToo long before hashtags. *The New York Times.* https://www.nytimes.com/2017/10/20/us/me-too-movement-tarana-burke.html

García Giribet, A. (2018, August 21). *Tarana Burke: The woman behind Me Too.* Amnesty International. https://www.amnesty.org/en/latest/education/2018/08/tarana-burke-me-too/

North, A., Grady, C., McGann, L., & Romano, A. (n.d.). *A list of people accused of sexual harassment, misconduct, or assault.* Vox. Retrieved 2019, from https://www.vox.com/a/sexual-harassment-assault-allegations-list

Oliner, S. P. (2003). *Do unto others: Extraordinary acts of ordinary people.* Westview Press.

Women for Women International. (n.d.). *Where we work.* https://www.womenforwomen.org/where-we-work

Wood, J. T. (2015). *Gendered lives: Communication, gender, and culture* (11th ed.). Cengage Learning.

World Economic Forum. (2017). *The global gender gap report 2017.* http://www3.weforum.org/docs/WEF_GGGR_2017.pdf

World Health Organization. (n.d.). *MDG 3: Promote gender equality and empower women.* https://www.who.int/topics/millennium_development_goals/gender/en/

World Health Organization. (2017, May 26). *Leaving no one behind: Equity, gender and human rights policy to practice* [News release]. https://www.who.int/gender-equity-rights/events/policy-to-practice/en/

6

Families of the Future

PAT DEVINE

The human family has been the bedrock social unit of human societies for thousands of years. It has taken on a variety of forms throughout the centuries and has uniquely suited itself for each evolutionary stage and undergone adaptations when required. According to the latest research by social historians, families have always been diverse and we need to modify the understanding that there is one dominant Western type (Zinn, Eitzen, Wells 2011). Speaking in broad terms, however, particular family structures developed historically to meet the economic demands of the times. For thousands of years humans lived in hunter-gather societies where a broad range of social relationships based on kinship and/or the tribe prevailed. With the dawn of agriculture, the large extended family system consisting of parents, multiple children, grandparents, and a network of relatives united by kinship, emerged to meet the necessities of the time period. Thousands of years later, agrarian society gave way to the industrial age. At this point in time, the extended family system prevalent in Western-European culture was trimmed down to a smaller social unit (mother, father and fewer children) to become the nuclear family of the modern era. Some social forecasters predicted that the nuclear family would be a mere blip on the historical timeline. Based on an idealized model of women who were defined by rigid gender roles as stay-at-home wives and mothers, satisfied to live through their husbands and children, it has been a flawed system vulnerable to change. Today we are facing another major evolutionary transition from an industrial society to a post-modern society that is based on information and technology. Where the agrarian age and the industrial age required physical strength and the making of commodities, the new information-technological age requires a high level of cognitive skills for the modern-day work environments. What is required of the nuclear family in this new information-technological age? Will it survive? How will gender roles change? How will new technologies affect the nuclear family? How will the expanding global economy affect the nuclear family? It is the challenge for present-day futurists to assess the impact of future change on the family system. Futurists and other social scientists do not have a crystal ball; they cannot tell us definitively just what form the family of the future will take. Researchers can only identify present-day trends that may give some indication where the family is heading. The following pages seek to explore what some of the present-day trends are related to the nuclear family as well as to look at the impact of future change on the family system.

We will begin with a brief overview of the nuclear family paradigm that was prevalent in the modern era. Secondly, we will proceed to an overview of how the future has already impacted marriage and the nuclear family. Thirdly, we will look at the gender revolution created by the impact of women in the workforce. Fourthly, we will look at the role of technological innovation in creating exponential growth for the economies of the future. Fifthly, we will look at declining and emerging values affecting the family. Sixthly, we will look at the impact of future technologies on the family as well as explore ethical concerns. Lastly, we will hear voices of hope for the families of the future.

In the industrial age, the dominant paradigm of the nuclear family was defined by sociologists and anthropologists "as a group of people who are united by ties of partner-ship and parenthood and consisting of a pair of adults and their socially recognized children." In the recent past, this definition of the nuclear family has been expanded to in-clude same-sex marriage which is based on partnerships of the same gender (Encyclopedia Britannica). It is important to note at this point that while the original definition was initially informed by heterosexual dominance; i.e., one man and one woman, it has recently been expanded to acknowl-edge partnerships with varying sexual identifications.

Today, the definition of family has evolved even further to encompass the following new living arrangements that have emerged in society in recent years. (1) single women having children; (2) people living together without being married; and (3) unmarried couples raising children (Pew Research Center, 2010, Chapter 5). In addition to these changes in liv-ing arrangements, a new term, blended families, has emerged which describes families with mixed parentage whereby one or both parents remarry and bring children from the former marriage into the new marital structure. In the year 2014, it was reported that nearly half (44%) of young people ages 18 to 29 had a step sibling (Krogstad, 2014).

The nuclear family was widely assumed by dominant Western paradigms to be a normative goal since the 1950s. So-ciologist Judith Stacey speaks to a bias in the U.S. social scienc-es that held the belief that the history of the American nuclear family would become a global model. "Westerners presumed that the global diffusion of the modern nuclear family system would come about automatically. Instead industrialization quickly gave way to a globalized information economy and the transition influenced families both in the U.S. and globally to drift toward the "postmodern" stage of diversity, flux and instability" (Stacey, 1996, as cited in Montgomery, 2008).

Futurist Alvin Toffler, in his seminal work about the fu-ture entitled *Future Shock* (1970), warned the American public about the rate of change that was impacting modern-day life and how this accelerated change was affecting American institutions, including the family. Toffler predicted that the family of the future will need to pare down to its most elemental form of man and woman. (It is important to note here that Toffler's book *Future Shock* came out in 1970 and that an updated version would likely characterize this relationship more inclusively, such as two people joined together by a marital bond). The family of the future will need to be mobile and flexible. The primary piece of excess baggage to be cast aside will be children. Some couples may decide to remain childless and navigate through life devoted to their work, professions and other life goals. Toffler also foresaw deferring parenthood to another stage of life. This last prediction has materialized in society. Today, advances in biotechnology have extended a woman's biological time clock and have now presented parenthood as an option to be chosen at a later stage in life.

According to Toffler, anthropologist Margaret Mead is also known to have held the view that the nuclear family was starting to undergo major changes. Mead predicted that the role of parent in the future would be carried out by fewer people who would perform the main task of raising children in society. For the first time in the history of the world, there would be a large segment of the population who would be relieved of childrearing and "free to function-for the first time in history—as individuals" wrote Mead (Toffler 1970, p. 242).

The Impact of the Future on the Family

One need only to look at the status of the present-day family to understand how "future shock" has affected the nuclear family over the past 50 years. The future is here now. Since the publication of the book *Future Shock* in 1970, there has been a quiet revolution taking place in American society

fueled by such factors as demographics, economics and societal changes that have impacted the structure and composition of the American family. Absent from the scene is the
idealized nuclear family unit of mother, father and a couple
of children of the mid-Twentieth Century. Also, absent from
the scene is the idealized media version of the family that
prevailed for some years that depicted the family as white
and European in origin. Marriage and the nuclear family
today are made up of many colors and ethnicities.

According to writer Kristen Bialik, in her Pew Research
Center article *"Key Facts about Race & Marriage 50 Years After
Loving v. Virginia,"* intermarriage has increased steadily since
1967 when the law was passed prohibiting marriage discrimination based on race. Bialik describes how, in 2015, one-
in-six U.S. newlyweds (17%) were married to a person of a
different race or ethnicity. This percentage figure represents
a significant increase from the 1967 rate of three percent. Bialik elaborates further on how overall increases in intermarriage have been driven in part by rising intermarriage rates
among black and white newlyweds. The most dramatic increase, according to Bialik, has occurred among black newlyweds, whose intermarriage rate more than tripled from 5%
in 1980 to 18% in 2015. Among whites, the rates rose from
4% in 1980 to 11% in 2015. Just as the rate of intermarriage
has increased in society, there has been a rise in children who
are multiracial or multiethnic, reports Bialik. Today one in
seven U.S. infants (14%) are multiracial or multiethnic. This
represents a major increase since the year 1980 (Bialik 2017).

According to writers Cilluffo and Cohn in their Pew Research Center article describing demographic trends shaping
the world in the year 2017, in addition to the changing colors of matrimony today is the declining institution of marriage itself. According to the writers, there has been a downward trajectory regarding marriage in this country. They
report that just half of U.S. adults were married in 2015,

representing a significant decline from the year 1950 when 70% of the population was married (Cilluffo, Cohn 2017). At the same time, according to a Pew Research Center article on the decline of marriage, it is pointed out that, contrary to public perception, divorce rates have also declined over the past 20 years. The article describes how divorce rates did rise sharply during the 1960's and 1970's but leveled off and began to trend downward (Pew Research Center, 2010 p. 18). In another Pew Research Center article, the writers describe how there is a new phenomenon occurring regarding the institution of marriage called gray divorce. The authors describe how between 1990 and 2015 the divorce rate among those 50 and older roughly doubled, spawning this new term (Cilluffo, Cohn 2017).

Trends In Cohabitation

At the same time that there has been a decline in marriage rates, there has been a rise in cohabitation rates in this country. According to writers Cilluffo and Cohn, in their Pew Research Center article on the decline of the institution of marriage, there is an increase in unmarried partners living together. Included in this category is a growing number of unmarried parents. At the same time, there has been a growing number of adults in the population who are living without a spouse or partner. In the year 2007, for example, 39% of the adult population were living without a spouse or partner. By 2017, the percentage had reached 42% (Cilluffo, Cohn, 2018).

A report by the Organisation for Economic Co-operation and Development (OECD) entitled "The Future of Families to 2030" addresses this decline in marriage and trend in cohabitation as phenomena that is happening not only in the United States but in Scandinavia and western European countries as well. The report cites Scandinavia and some western European countries where the data indicates that cohabitation appears to be a replacement for marriage. Conversely, in the United States, the research indicates that cohabitation is more of a preliminary stage to marriage (Organisation for Economic Co-operation and Development (OECD), 2011).

Social Scientists do not have a crystal ball about present marriage and cohabitation rates continuing into the future. The present trends could stabilize, increase or reverse. For example, there was a study conducted on U.S. cohorts born in the 1950's and 1960's, where the data points to the conclusion that marriage will remain nearly universal for American women. The researchers conclude that general marriage rates may trend up again in the future should women no longer delay marriage for educational purposes (Jiang et al., op.ci.) (Organisation for Economic Co-operation and Development, 2011). At the same time, according to a Pew Research Center survey, a majority of Americans (53%) say that people will be less likely to get married in the year 2050. When asked about having children, 46% of the respondents answered that people will be less likely to have children than they are now (Cilluffo, Cohn 2019).

The following are some of the projected socioeconomic factors the OECD report forecasts that will affect the family and household structures of the future in the developed world. (1) The present increase in life expectancy rates is projected to grow to levels we have never seen before. The elderly will make up a large portion of the societies of the future. This fact alone will have a major impact on families. (2) A decline in fertility rates will also impact the families and societies of the future. This fact is also related to the projection that there will be a decline of young people by 2030. (3) A growth in broadband technology will transform how families will work and how they will learn in the future. (4) Technology will empower the lives of the elderly, the sick, the frail and disabled in ways that will help them to lead independent, useful lives. Lastly, in the future there will be an expansion of social media to whole new levels across the globe (Organisation for Economic Co-operation and Development, 2011).

The Gender Revolution

In the beginning of the industrial revolution, men left the home and became active in the public sphere and women's lives remained in the realm of the home. As the industrial economy progressed, women also left the home to participate in the public sphere. The major presence of women in the workplace has created transformational changes in the traditional gender roles of the nuclear family system.

According to a Pew Research Center article, women made up only 33% of the U.S. labor force in 1960. There was a significant increase by the year 2009 when participation of women in the work force reached 47%. Over the same time period, women have made major gains in educational achievement. According to the Pew Research Center, in 1960 less than 6% of women had completed college. By 2008, their numbers had escalated to 29%. From 1990 to 2010 women were the majority of new college graduates thereby providing the workforce with more educated women than ever before. These changes regarding women pursuing higher education as well as entering the workforce in large numbers has had far-ranging effects on the nuclear family structure (Pew Research Center 2010).

In an article entitled "The Gender Revolution" published in the Population and Development Review of June 2015, the authors Goldscheider, Bernhardt and Lappegard speak to the idea of a two-part gender revolution. The first stage of the gender revolution began when women left the confines of the home and entered the public realm. In the following quote, the authors describe this first phase of this revolution:

During its early growth, female labor force participation has been linked with trends toward delayed marriage and non-marriage (Espenshade 1985), low and often ul-tra-low fertility (Bernhardt 1993); (Brewster and Rindfuss 2000), and increased union dissolution (Ruggles 1997). However, evidence is accumulating that many of these long-observed linkages are weakening and some are even reversing. As we will argue, these weakening and revers-ing linkages are rooted in changing gender relationships, as female employment has become not only ubiquitous but expected. We refer to these changing gender rela-tionships in the public and private spheres as the gender revolution (Goldscheider, Bernhardt, Lappegard, 2015, p 207).

In the second stage of the gender revolution, men in-creased their participation in the private sphere of home and family. A study by Sullivan, Billari, and Altintas (2014) found that the research data revealed evidence of recent increas-es in 13 European countries in the contribution of younger, more highly educated fathers participating in both childcare and domestic tasks in the home. Also, in another study (Bond, Galinsky and Swanberg 1998) the data revealed that in the United States, among dual-income earners, the amount of parental time fathers spent with their children was above 40% (Goldscheider, Bernhardt, Lappegard, 2015).

In another study regarding fathers' involvement in childcare in the U.S. (Yeung et al. 2001) the data revealed increased involvement of fathers in childcare on weekends. Researchers found that while fathers in employed couples were responsible for 40 percent of childcare during the week, they took on 47 percent on weekends. In another study (Bi-anchi, Robinson, and Milkie, 2006), the data also showed an increase in involvement of fathers with their children. The researchers found that by the end of the twentieth century in the U.S., fathers spent five more hours per week with their children than they had two decades earlier. Researchers Bonke and Esping-Andersen (2008) issue the caveat that it is likely that more progress has been made in terms of men's involvement with children than in their taking responsibility for routine household chores. They stress the importance of studying these two behaviors separately (Goldscheider, Bernhardt, Lappegard, 2015).

The Family and the Global Economy

As society has moved from an industrial age economy to a globalized knowledge-based economy, new opportunities as well as challenges have emerged which have affected all of society's institutions, including the family. Some of the current economic predictions for the global economy of the future are positive for families in general and for women in particular.

In the book *The Long Boom* authors Peter Schwartz, Peter Leyden and Joel Hyatt predict an optimistic view of a globalized future and speak to the technological revolution that has fueled this new economy of the 21st Century. According to the authors, it has created:

> ...a vast economic expansion that could go for decades, spreading prosperity around the world and lifting billions into middle class lifestyles. These same forces that have transformed the economy – technological change, rapid innovation, and global integration – are now moving beyond the economy and beginning to change our society, our politics, our culture, and ultimately, over the course of the coming century, even our civilization (Schwartz, Leyden, Hyatt, 1999, p.v.).

The writers see the long boom as being beneficial to women because it brings them into the new global economy

and utilizes their talents. They also believe it will be beneficial to many other groups who heretofore have not been able
to participate in the economic life on the planet (Schwartz,
Leyden, Hyatt 1999). A similar view is voiced by Futurists
Alvin and Heidi Toffler in their book entitled *Revolutionary
Wealth*, which talks about a wealth revolution that will include new opportunities across the board in a wide-range of
endeavors, including a myriad of new business opportunities
and entrepreneurships, the net effect of which will be the potential of reducing poverty on a grand scale across the globe
(Toffler, Toffler, 2006).

The predictions for the new economy of the future, made
by both Peter Schwartz et. al. and Alvin and Heidi Toffler,
bode well for the completion of the gender revolution. In this
new knowledge-based economy of the future, gender roles in
the family have the potential of being equal for the first time
in human history.

The National Organization for Women (NOW), back in
the 1960's, pointed out how the economy of the new technological world no longer needed masculine muscle strength
but rather it needed higher level cognitive skills and that
women have a right to take part in this new economy of the
future (Toffler,1970). Writers Pamela McCorduck and Nancy Ramsey in their book *The Futures of Women – Scenarios for
the 21ˢᵗ Century* agree and point out the potential for women
in a new technological age and that the research shows that
young girls are better learners than young boys and have
superior symbolic skills as well. "As hunters and gatherers
in the symbolic realm, nobody does it better" (McCorduck,
Ramsey,1996, p.8).

New Emerging Family Values

In their book *Revolutionary Wealth*, the Tofflers address
the idea of an implosion of modern-day institutions that
served a prior era and the emergence of new values that will

accompany the institutions of today. We cannot expect the values of the nuclear family, which were formed in an industrial society, to be applied to the diverse family forms of a postmodern era state. At the same time, we cannot apply the values common to large multigenerational families prevalent in pre-industrial agrarian societies to today (Toffler & Toffler, 2006).

Regarding the implosion of values, in the past fifty years we have seen a cultural war emerge over family values in the political and social arenas of American society. Central to this values war is the nuclear family, where traditional gender roles have changed. Traditional values, moral values, family values, religious values—it is a war that continues to take place on many fronts.

Technology and the Family of the Future

What will be the effect of new technologies on the families of the future? The English writer, Aldous Huxley, attempted to give us a vision of what the future would look like in his book *Brave New World*, which was published in 1932. In it Huxley described a dystopian future where genetic engineering and brainwashing would be used as tools of control in a totalitarian world (Miller 2016). Since Huxley's day, new words have entered the human lexicon such as artificial intelligence, robotics, nanotechnology, bioengineering, and virtual reality to name a few. Such words transport us into a brave new world that most likely would have surprised even Huxley. It is a world that is totally uncharted. Like many innovations in the past, the technologies of the future can be looked at as double-edge swords. They can help to increase satisfaction in life and decrease or eliminate human suffering, or they can propel us into a dystopian future, to use Huxley's term. What follows is an exploration of some of the technologies that will be impacting our families and societies of the future.

To find out about the future, we consult one of the world's foremost Futurists, Ray Kurzweil. Kurzweil is an author and inventor. He has also served as Director of Engineering at Google. Kurzweil, in his book *The Singularity Is Near*, addresses this idea of "Singularity" which, according to Kurzweil, is the moment when technology will become smarter than humans. He predicts this moment to be by 2045 (Caughill 2017).

The Singularity is "…a future period during which the pace of technological change will be so rapid, its impact so deep, that human life will be irreversibly transformed. Although neither utopian nor dystopian, this epoch will transform the concepts that we rely on to give meaning to our lives from our business models to the cycle of human life, including death itself" (Baer 2015). Such a prediction is hopeful and eerie at the same time. On the one hand, according to Kurzweil, nanobot technology will enable the human immune system to defeat disease which will lead to radical life extension. On the other hand, this same technology will have the possibility of curing death itself. A sampling of other extreme predictions by Kurzweil include such things as being able to upload the human mind into computers, connecting the human brain directly into the cloud, being able to 3-D print basically everything that humans will need, and a new world based on virtual reality (Baer 2015).

Kurzweil gives us some words of assurance that this brave new world of computers and artificial intelligence is a world that "is not going to displace us, compete with us, it's not an invasion coming from Mars – these are tools we're creating to basically expand ourselves, who we are. And that's what we've done with tools since we've had tools" (Kurzweil 2010, p. 65).

In his book *The Age of Spiritual Machines*, Kurzweil depicts a future where life as we have known it for thousands of years is replaced by a world based on technologies that will change forever the way we live on the planet. The following delineates what forms Kurzweil feels some of these changes will take: Firstly, in the field of education, virtual teachers will transform the way we learn and neural implants will augment the brain's capacity to process and master information. The progenitor of new knowledge will be machines and not humans. Secondly, in the field of disabilities, there will be an elimination of the disabilities humans have lived with for thousands of years. For example, there will be highly intelligent visual navigation devices for the blind, speech-to-print devices for the deaf, and nerve stimulation intelligence in orthotic prosthetics for the physically disabled. Thirdly, in the field of communications, three dimensional virtual environments, to three-dimensional holographic technology, will be the communication modes of the day. Fourthly, in the fields of production, agriculture and transportation, humans will no longer be required to perform the tasks involved. Fifthly, in the fields of health and medicine, human life will be extended through the use of bionic organs and artificial enhancements for parts of the brain. Life expectancy is predicted to be around 120 years. Lastly, we will fully understand how to read and revise the product of our genetic code (Kurzweil 1999).

In a report by the World Economic Forum regarding healthcare, Melanie Walker, a medical doctor and World Bank advisor, predicts that by 2030 technology will have cured the diseases that currently affect us. She predicts that the hospital, as it has been defined in our lifetimes, will soon become an institution of the past. Our lives will become much safer, she predicts, with the advent of self-driving cars and healthier with an increase in preventive and personalized medicine. In the place of surgery and organ donors, she predicts, will be robotic tubes and bio-printed organs (Parker 2016).

Ethical Concerns Regarding Future Technology

In his book *Intelligent Machines and Human Values*, writer Thomas M. Georges explores the relationship between science and society and voices his concern that artificial intelligence is likely to create changes faster than human societies can absorb them. To avoid risky technological endeavors, in the following quote he proposes using artificial intelligence to produce simulated societies to predict the societal impact of a particular technology.

> Experimenting with simulated societies could help us preview technologies, but also the effects of changing moral values on those impacts. In other words, which ground rules for exploiting technology would produce the most beneficial outcomes for the simulated society? In this way, alternative moral and ethical codes that might offset our self-destructive tendencies could be devised and tested (Georges 2003, p. 245).

Also posing important questions about future technologies is the author Noreen L. Herzfeld, who speaks from a religious perspective regarding artificial intelligence that is predicted to supersede humans. She asks the question: If humankind is made in the image of God, what does that say about an artificial intelligence that surpasses humankind?

Herzfeld looks to her own Christian tradition and to theologian Karl Barth to find an answer to this question. According to Barth, "man is not without but with God" (Herzfeld 2002, p. 86). This human-God relationship, therefore, is a template for our human-to-human interactions. Unfortunately, Barth had little to say about human-to-non-human interactions. After further search through the tradition, Herzfeld suggests looking to the Rule of St. Benedict for guidance on how humans might relate to the world of computers and artificial intelligence. St. Benedict instructs his monks to treat everyone with respect and humility and to treat the material goods of the monastery as sacred vessels. Herzfeld interprets the term sacred vessels in a contemporary sense and applies it to the areas of computers and artificial intelligence. She gives modern-day technologies their due but also issues the caveat that we need to be vigilant in their applications. For Herzfeld, if it should ever come down to a choice between protecting human life and its communities, and artificial intelligence, we need to choose the former (Herzfeld 2002).

In reply to concerns regarding future technologies, Futurist Kurzweil responds with a warning that relinquishment of pursuing technological advances is not desirable because it would deprive humanity of some of technology's greatest benefits. Also, relinquishment would drive technological development underground, where it would take a more virulent form such as bioterrorism, where a bioweapon could be developed by an unscrupulous individual or group. Furthermore, according to Kurzweil, by suppressing scientific inquiry, humanity would be deprived of technologies that would eliminate many forms of suffering in the world. Also, Kurzweil warns that by scientific inquiry going underground, responsible scientists would be hindered in developing the necessary defenses against abuse. He advocates for a world committed to open scientific inquiry (Kurzweil 2010).

We have seen how the technologies discussed by Kurzweil and others in this writing bode well for the relief of human suffering on a grand scale and how our societies and our families will stand to benefit from such technological advancement. We have also been given a glimpse of how some future technologies are questionable as to their value for future families and societies. Although, as stated earlier, technological advancement remains a double-edged sword. Notwithstanding Kurzweil's warnings about limiting science, the scientific community would do well to consider the ethical concerns expressed in this essay. It will be the role of futurists, scientists of all disciplines and ethicists of the future to advocate for and support approaches such as the one voiced by Thomas M. George. His intelligent simulator model would be able to demonstrate possible outcomes in a community as a result of a given technology. Such an approach will be needed in order to safeguard the dignity of our families and our societies of the future.

In addition to ethical concerns about the impact of future technologies on families and societies, is also the concern about which families will benefit from the new technologies and which ones will be left out. Will many be excluded technological access because of race, class, sex, gender, or nationality, just to name a few social identities that can be marginalized? How will racism, classism, sexism, patriarchy, and xenophobia affect the distribution of technological resources for the families of the future? This is a question futurists and other social scientists concerned about the family will need to address.

Voices of Hope for the Future

Authors Pamela McCorduck and Nancy Ramsey in their book *The Futures of Women: Scenarios for the 21st Century*, write of hope from a feminist perspective about a day in the future when societies will reach true equality between the sexes. They look forward to a time when women's rights means the same as human rights. According to the authors, when this day finally arrives, all the old divisions that have separated the sexes throughout the centuries will no longer apply (McCorduck, Ramsey 1996).

Feminist writers Jennifer Baumgardener and Amy Richards in their book *Manifesta: Young Women, Feminism and the Future*, also address continuing a feminist agenda until true gender equality is achieved. Their hope for the future includes a world where there are such things as equal pay for equal work, where co-parenting is the norm for all families, regardless of race or ethnicity, and where the sexes are freed from emotional restrictions and expectations. Their hope is for a world where, ultimately, there will be no need for a feminist movement or agenda (Baumgardner, Richards 2000).

Writer Alexandra Montgomery in her article "U.S. Families 2025: In Search of Future Families," summed up the role of feminists and futurists in the years ahead to assure equality for families. "For future gender roles to reflect equality – equality being both a feminist and a futurist ideal -- futurists should seek personal, professional, and activist opportunities to ensure that more families are empowered to make conscious choices that reinforce the human value of equality" (Montgomery 2008, p. 387).

Summary

In this essay we have explored the future of the family. We reviewed at a sampling of how the future has already impacted the nuclear family to date and various markers of change. We looked at a gender revolution created by women entering the workforce. We surveyed predictions of a long boom and revolutionary wealth that have the ability to transform the economies of the future, eradicating major pockets of poverty across the planet and providing opportunity for gender parity. We explored how family values change as our family structures change. We listened to a prominent futurist who outlined for us a future that will transform life as we have known it on this planet and has the potential for alleviating human suffering on a grand scale. We probed ethical concerns about the effects of future technologies on the family and society. We asked the question, "who are the families that will benefit from the technological innovations of the future?" and, "who are the families that will be left out?" Lastly, we examined visions of hope for the families of the future.

Just as feminists and futurists need to work towards

assuring a future of equality for families, other social scientists, such as sociologists and anthropologists who are concerned about the family, need to work towards the goal of equality as well. They will need to focus on assessing the future's impact on evolving family structures, evolving gender roles and the impact of new economies and technologies on these structures. Also, as previously stated, they will need to advocate for families who have been denied access to technological resources because of race, class or gender as well as advocate for an ethical use of technology as applied to societies, communities and families of the future. Equality is not a linear process and there can be many setbacks to such an ideal. Constant work and vigilance will be required by our social scientists, our professionals, our politicians, our community leaders and our families themselves.

In ending this essay, we look to the future with optimism regarding the survival of the human family. Many in recent years have been willing to sound the death knell for the family, predicting it has outlived its usefulness. Others have refused to give up on the family and predict that the technological future of increasing, accelerated change will be the very factor that will assure its continuation. This latter view depicts the family as a safe harbor, a shelter from the storm, in a future where technology will be transforming the very fabric of human life. It is on this positive note that we look to the future. We know that change will be a constant companion for the families of tomorrow. While some look at the future of the family as being half empty and others look at the future of the family as being half full, what we need to keep in mind is that the glass can always be refilled. As we have seen, history tells us that the family has the unique ability to constantly reinvent itself, thereby refilling the glass. In the societies of the future, it is predicted that there will be several types of family structures coexisting together at one time in a given society. Today, as we have seen, it is not uncommon to find the traditional nuclear family in America sharing space with new family forms. Thus, in the future, it will not be uncommon in societies across the globe for there to be a combination of multiple family forms living side-by-side. One thing we can say for sure is that the family of the future will find its own way. It will adapt and morph into new forms, or old forms, or some combination of old and new. It will survive and possibly, for the first time in human history, the family will become egalitarian.

References

Baer, D. (2015, November 18). *8 shocking predictions for life after 2020 from Google's genius futurist.* Business Insider. https://www.businessinsider.com/ray-kurzweil-most-extreme-predictions-2015-11

Baca Zinn, M., Eitzen, D. S., & Wells, B. (2011). *Diversity in families* (9th ed.). Allyn & Bacon.

Baumgardner, J., & Richards, A. (2000). *Manifesta: Young women, feminism, and the future.* Farrar, Straus and Giroux.

Bialik, K. (2017, June 12). *Key facts about race and marriage, 50 years after* Loving v. Virginia. Pew Research Center, Fact Tank. https://www.pewresearch.org/fact-tank/2017/06/12/key-facts-about-race-and-marriage-50-years-after-loving-v-virginia/

Caughill, P. (2017, October 11). *Ray Kurzweil's most exciting predictions about the future of humanity.* Futurism. https://futurism.com/ray-kurzweils-most-exciting-predictions-about-the-future-of-humanity

Cilluffo, A., & Cohn, D. (2017, April 27). *10 demographic trends shaping the U.S. and the world in 2017.* Pew Research Center, Fact Tank. https://www.pewresearch.org/fact-tank/2017/04/27/10-demographic-trends-shaping-the-u-s-and-the-world-in-2017/

Cilluffo, A., & Cohn, D. (2018, April 25). *7 demographic trends shaping the U.S. and the world in 2018*. Pew Research Center, Fact Tank. https://www.pewresearch.org/fact-tank/2018/04/25/7-demographic-trends-shaping-the-u-s-and-the-world-in-2018/

Cilluffo, A., & Cohn, D. (2019, April 11). *6 demographic trends shaping the U.S. and the world in 2019*. Pew Research Center, Fact Tank. https://www.pewresearch.org/fact-tank/2019/04/11/6-demographic-trends-shaping-the-u-s-and-the-world-in-2019/*Encyclopedia Britannica*. (n.d.). https://www.britannica.com

Georges, T. M. (2003). *Digital soul: Intelligent machines and human values*. Westview Press.

Goldscheider, F., Bernhardt, E., & Lappegård, T. (2015). The gender revolution: A framework for understanding changing family and demographic behavior. *Population and Development Review, 41*(2), 207–239. https://doi.org/10.1111/j.1728-4457.2015.00045.x

Herzfeld, N. L. (2002). *In our image: Artificial intelligence and the human spirit*. Fortress Press.

Krogstad, J. M. (2014, April 30). *5 facts about the modern American family*. Pew Research Center, Fact Tank. https://www.pewresearch.org/fact-tank/2014/04/30/5-facts-about-the-modern-american-family/

Kurzweil, R. (1999). *The age of spiritual machines: When computers exceed human intelligence*. Penguin Books.

Kurzweil, R. (2010). Merging with the machines: Information technology, artificial intelligence, and the law of exponential growth: An interview with Ray Kurzweil. *World Futures Review, 2*(1), 61–66.

McCorduck, P., & Ramsey, N. (1996). *The futures of women: Scenarios for the 21st century*. Warner Books.

Miller, L. (Ed.). (2016). *Literary wonderlands: A journey through the greatest fictional worlds ever created*. Black Dog & Leventhal Publishers.

Montgomery, A. (2008). US families 2025: In search of future families. *Futures*, *40*(4), 377–387. https://doi.org/10.1016/j.futures.2007.08.005

Organisation for Economic Co-operation and Development. (2011). *The future of families to 2030: Projections, policy challenges and policy options: A synthesis report*. https://www.oecd.org/futures/49093502.pdf

Parker, C. (2016, November 12). *8 predictions for the world in 2030*. World Economic Forum. https://www.weforum.org/agenda/2016/11/8-predictions-for-the-world-in-2030/

Pew Research Center. (2010, November 18). *The decline of marriage and rise of new families* (A Social & Demographic Trends Report). https://www.pewsocialtrends.org/2010/11/18/the-decline-of-marriage-and-rise-of-new-families/

Schwartz, P., Leyden, P., & Hyatt, J. (1999). *The long boom: A vision for the coming age of prosperity*. Perseus Books.

Toffler, A. (1970). *Future shock*. Random House.

Toffler, A., & Toffler, H. (2006). *Revolutionary wealth*. Alfred A. Knopf.

7

Climate Change

SITARAM K. SANDIN, RONNIE SWARTZ,
BRYAN KRAUS

"We must do something braver than try to save the world we have known. We must accept the fact that the world we have known is going to change in hideous and damaging ways—and we must nonetheless work as hard as we can to limit that damage, to keep it this side of complete catastrophe, to save as many options for our descendants as are still possible. This, as I say, is hard—it's easier to defend a pristine rainforest than to save a woodlot that's already half cut over. Easier to rally support, easier to keep fired up. Once something's spoiled, it's easier to throw up your hands and walk away, which will be the great temptation for us. Still, we need to try."

-Bill McKibben, founder of 350.org (2011)

The largest and most comprehensive panel on climate change in the history of the world, the Intergovernmental Panel on Climate Change (IPCC), has provided conclusive evidence to support Bill McKibben's call to action with the 2018 publication of "Global warming of 1.5°C". 2018 also saw California experience the worst modern wildfire in the state's history, destroying the entire town of Paradise (Wootson, 2018). Meanwhile, the U.S. President refused to acknowledge the impact of climate change. Although it is difficult to isolate climate change as the singular cause of a specific natural disaster, the science is clear: wildfires are happening more often, they are more severe, and they can be directly attributed to human-caused global warming (U.S. Global Change Research Program, 2018). Storms, floods, hurricanes, wildfires, and other natural disasters are likely to occur more often and be of higher severity as the result of climate change (Schiermeier, 2018). We can expect widespread disease, drought, food shortages, and social and economic instability as a consequence (Watts et al., 2018). This trend will not reverse unless steps are enacted to stop global warming. Planet Earth will be largely uninhabitable by the end of the century if we do not act (IPCC, 2018).

Climate change is solvable if we are willing to take a sober look at its structural and ideological roots as well as the strangling hold of its pervasive vines. This chapter shows that the vines can recede and the roots can be severed, creating space for new and emergent solutions. We are living in a time when seeing the bright side is counter-productive and dangerous without acknowledging the clouds. Our propensity to see the glass as half full can prevent us from taking an actual measurement of volume. The psychological weight of the half emptiness restrains many of us from bearing witness to the resulting despair and thereupon acting for change.

Self-help books that provide do-it-yourself answers to the problem are a growing industry, frequently highlighting actions such as changing your light bulbs and unplugging "vampire" appliances when not in use. These solutions confuse the magnitude of the problem and what is required to remedy it. Meanwhile, there is a well-funded and vocal minority that twists public perception about the science to muddy the waters, creating an illusion of reasonable doubt that amounts to nothing more than a multi-billion dollar set of smoke and mirrors.

There are also growing numbers of activists, scientists,

business leaders, politicians and concerned citizens stepping up to make real and lasting change, as reviewed below. There are viable theories, strategies, and innovations that have been developed to help us save a livable planet for future generations. Most scientists do not advocate pessimism; there is something that can be done. But for our solutions to be real, we need to understand just how large and unruly a beast climate change is, and we need to be honest about our inability to rein it in.

This chapter is going to look at climate change from a systems perspective, placing a heightened focus on environmental racism, classism, and the legacy of global colonialism in this current crisis. Climate change is already having an impact on every single aspect of life and can no longer stay isolated to the realm and expertise of atmospheric scientists. It has weaved itself into our social, spiritual and psychological fabric, and it demands responses and solutions from all of these domains.

This chapter is divided into three sections. First there is a summary of the science of climate change as it is now known, including a discussion on the overwhelming evidence of consensus among climate scientists. Second, there will be an overview of many effects of climate change, including the disproportionate relationship with environmental racism, classism and colonialism. Third, potential solutions will be considered from multiple domains such as technology, politics, the courts, ideology, and the economy. Lesser-heard perspectives will be highlighted including those from Indigenous Communities, anti-capitalist movements, and the Global South.

What We Know

"Let there be light" (Genesis, 1:3)

In the core of the Sun the weight of 2-octillion-tons of mass squeezes four hydrogen nuclei into one helium atom.

Excess mass from this fusion is released as energy, which stays trapped in the Sun's core for around 100,000 years as it fights its way through the shackles of gravity towards the Sun's surface where it bursts forth at the speed of light. The Sun, our cosmic nuclear fusion reactor, emits 38,460 septillion watts of this energy every second. These rays of light dance across the solar system, radiating outward as they pass the concentric elliptical orbits of Mercury and Venus on their 92,000,000 mile journey to reach Earth, a trek that takes just over eight minutes.

Of course the light does not stop at our planet, and it was not made for it. That we may think so is understandable. These rays of light are central to life on Earth. They provide the energy that fuels plants, algae and bacteria, seeding the first link of a food chain that sustains our entire planet. They also provide another form of energy: heat. But, like an open fire under the starry skies of a winter night, this heat would quickly escape back to the depths of space if it wasn't for an added layer of insulation. Add a structure around the fire and it has the opportunity to heat an entire house. In this case, the "walls" of the earth are a layer of atmosphere that contains greenhouse gasses, namely water vapor (H_2O), methane (CH_4), and carbon dioxide (CO_2). These gasses absorb some of the heat before it escapes to space, effectively "bouncing" some of it back to earth. Without this layer the earth would be an estimated 30° C colder and life as we know it would not be possible (Ma, 1998).

Water vapor makes up the largest percentage of this atmospheric stratum and acts as the largest insulator. The amount of water is fairly stable and not something that can be injected into the system from the outside. For this reason, it is not considered to be a climate "forcer," or that which can force global warming (Hansen, 2009). Still, water vapor's relationship to heat means it is part of a positive feedback loop for global temperature. As Earth's temperature rises, there will be more evaporation, which will place more water vapor into the atmosphere and will amplify the effects of climate change (Hansen, 2009). This amplifying effect will change weather patterns across the globe and is likely the reason why we are currently experiencing an increase in storms. More water vapor means more rainfall; as temperatures continue to rise, warm humid air could lead to heightened extreme-weather events such as tropical storms and hurricanes (Riebeek, 2005). This is one example of "climate change," or the changes to our climate due to global warming.

Carbon dioxide, nitrogen dioxide (NO_2), and methane are being added to the atmosphere through human activity, with CO_2 being the biggest contributor to our planet's warming. These chemicals are climate forcers; they can alter global temperatures by being added to or subtracted from the atmosphere (Hansen, 2009). Just as there is a natural water cycle, there is a natural carbon cycle. Carbon is added to the atmosphere through animal and plant respiration, wildfires, volcanic eruptions, and thawing permafrost. Carbon is subtracted from the atmosphere by plants, oceans and soil (NOAA, 2011). Although oversimplified, the inputs and outputs of carbon to/from our atmosphere are the math formula that establishes our "carbon budget." Going over our carbon budget means we add more carbon to our atmosphere than we take away, effectively adding more insulation to the lower atmosphere and increasing global warming. Deforestation has increased CO_2 by roughly 11% through the removal of forest ecosystems that sequester CO_2 from the atmosphere and turn it into biomass. Methane has increased by 15%, largely due to animal agriculture, and NO_2 has increased 7% due to agricultural soils. While these are significant percentages, the largest culprit by far is the increase in CO_2 from digging ancient fossil fuels from beneath the earth's surface and burning them for electricity, heat, transportation, and manufacturing. Fossil fuels account for over 80% of the increase in greenhouse gasses (EPA, 2019).

How We Know

The science for global warming is conclusive. Over the last 50 years, scientists and engineers from multiple fields across the world have collected data to clearly demonstrate warming of the Earth's temperature. Some 150 years ago John Tyndall discovered that carbon dioxide traps heat. In 1957 climatologist Roger Revelle and Hans Seuss discovered that people were releasing CO2 into the atmosphere faster than the ocean could absorb it. They noted, "human beings are now carrying out a large-scale geophysical experiment" (Chew, 2008, 51). In order to test Revelle's and Seuss' hypothesis, monitoring stations were set up to measure atmospheric concentrations around the world. The basic science of climate change was so well understood by 1979 that predictions in that year's National Research Council "Charney Report" continue to be supported to this day: if we double the atmospheric carbon from pre-industrial levels, global temperatures will rise 3° C, higher than any time in the last 3 million years (Lindsey, 2018). We have since fine-tuned our understanding and predictive models, but all of the basic science we know now was understood at the end of the 1970s. In fact, when we have erred, we have tended to err on the side of minimization and understatement (Brown & Caldeira, 2017; Wigley & Santer, 2013). In 1988, a worldwide scientific panel, the Intergovernmental Panel on Climate Change (IPCC) was established. This group has grown in size, their science has improved, and their overwhelming consensus has solidified. There is now 97% agreement among peer-reviewed climatologists for the basic science of human-caused global warming (Cook et al., 2016).

Consensus

Since the late 1980s, skeptics have put forth alternative theories about climate change, including variations on "it's not happening," "it's not caused by humans," "it's not that bad," and "it offers a net-positive impact." Science is not about blindly accepting consensus and some of these "alternative theories" may have been conceivable (although still largely disputed) at the time they were made. However, even the most plausible counter-theories have failed to withstand the test of time while others were never reasonable to begin with. Popular "alternative theories" for global warming include: natural planetary cycles, variations from solar output, heat from the Earth's core, and volcanoes. They can also include alternative predictive models that lessen the impact of global warming or even that rising atmospheric carbon will increase agricultural yields (Cook, 2019a).

Skeptical Science, a non-profit science education organization, responds to the most popular climate change misconceptions with peer-reviewed research (Cook, 2019b). For instance, it is true that the earth goes through natural temperature cycles. Humans did once live in an ice age, of course. However, scientists have heavily researched the causes of past ice ages and come to the firm conclusion that the amount of greenhouse gasses in the atmosphere is the biggest predictor of global temperature. Today, the largest contributors of CO_2 are not natural processes that take place over geologic time. In as little as 150 years, humans have changed the atmospheric composition of CO_2 from 280 ppm (parts per million) to 400 ppm, an unprecedented rate of increase that is "more than 100 times faster than the increase that occurred when the last ice age ended" (NOAA, 2013). By the end of the century, CO_2 levels could reach 1,000 ppm. As Ward (2010) states, "That is the level of the Mesozoic Period [65-250 million years ago] and will cause the ice sheets to rapidly melt—all of them" (p. 57).

Another contributor to past changes in global temperature has to do with the distance of the Earth to the Sun. Over geological time our planetary orbit changes, which affects how sunlight is distributed across the globe. However, the rate of change over the last 50 years is far greater than what can be accounted for by this measurement. Furthermore, for the last 35 years, as the Earth has steadily heated up, we have been moving away from the Sun (Cook, 2019a). And while it is true that there are variations in the amount of sunlight that hits the Earth's surface, this is also precisely measured. Observable variations do not match the rising global temperature. Volcanoes, to be clear, do not produce enough CO_2 to account for the changes we are seeing. In fact, humans produce about a hundred times more CO_2 than volcanoes do, and many recent eruptions have actually had a cooling effect (Cook, 2019a). Any agricultural gains attributable to increases in CO_2 are offset by lower yields due to higher temperatures, less available water, and more arid land (Zhu, Chiariello, Tobeck, Fukami & Field, 2016). There are many more arguments than these; this is what can be so exhausting: the deniers are relentless. Every time a conjecture is disproved, skeptics either produce a new argument, develop a new "theory," or just wait a few years to recycle an old one. This continually confuses public perception and creates a sense of false equivalency in the media.

John Cook (2019b) remarks, "When you peruse the many arguments of global warming skeptics, a pattern emerges. Skeptic arguments tend to focus on narrow pieces of the puzzle while neglecting the broader picture" (para. 2). He continues, "Often, the reasons for disbelieving in man-made global warming seem to be political rather than scientific… However, what is causing global warming is a purely scientific question" (Cook, 2019b, para. 3). Over the last 30 years each of these theories has been proven false while the evidence for the prevailing view, that human-caused climate change will make the planet unlivable for human life if nothing is done to stop it, has only gotten stronger.

This leads us to where we are today: 97% consensus among climate scientists and 70% consensus among the general public (Cook et al., 2013; Leiserowitz et al., 2018). Established in 2013, this consensus has been hotly contested by a small and vocal minority that is made up mostly of non-scientists, but it has failed to yield even after rigorous scrutiny. Cook et al. (2016) produced a meta-analysis of seven different consensus studies and checked their results to self-surveys filled out by lead authors of each study, confirming the 2013 finding of 97% consensus. Their analysis also examined methods used by skeptics to challenge scientific conclusions and found that skeptics' methods are not regarded as acceptable by related scientific disciplines. For example, if skeptics' methods were applied to the field of plate tectonics they would reject "consensus on well-established theories" that are not contested (Cook et al., 2016, p. 1). The 97% consensus among scientists is firm. However, public confusion about this is understandable; it is impossible for us to know everything. We require experts to relay their findings so we can make sense of the world. Basic trust in specialized knowledge is compromised when ideology and complacency blind us at the same time as well-funded fringe groups actively spread disinformation.

Impact

We have heated the planet 1° C since the industrial revolution by adding CO2 to the atmosphere. In 150 years we have heated the planet more than it was warmed in the entire duration of human history (Hansen, 2009). Two-thirds of this has occurred since 1975. If we are unable to curb our CO_2 emissions, we will heat another .5° C as early as the year 2032 (IPCC, 2018), placing us at 1.5° C above pre-industrial levels. We will reach 2° C by 2065, and almost 4° C by the end of the century (IPCC, 2014a).

A single degree—even a few degrees—may not seem like much, but it is. One and a half degrees Celsius above pre-industrial levels will drastically alter life on the planet. A 2° C increase will make many large population areas largely uninhabitable for human life (IPCC, 2018). The Paris Agreement (also known as the Paris Climate Accord), which is the most aggressive worldwide compact for stopping climate change, will only limit us to a 3° C increase (United Nations Environment Programme [UNEP], 2018) and this is only if all signatories meet their emissions goals. Very few countries are presently on target to do this and most have increased CO_2 emissions since signing the agreement (UNEP, 2018). Meanwhile, the current U.S. administration has initiated withdrawal from the agreement and is rolling back environmental regulations (Popovich, Albeck-Ripka, & Pierre-Louis, 2017).

At 1.5° C above pre-industrial levels, droughts will lengthen by an average of two months, and 271 million more people will experience water scarcity, with 132 million exposed to severe drought. We will have an increase in severe weather events and a 48 cm sea-level rise. By 2055 both of these factors will contribute to 28 million more people displaced each year due to ocean surges and flooding, increasing to 60 million by the end of the century. Crop yields will decrease, which will be exacerbated by an increase in both arid land and population, heightening the odds of resource wars and other mass violent conflicts over natural resources. Global GDP will decrease by 8% and the cost of flood damage alone will amount to an estimated

$10.2 trillion (Carbon Brief, 2018). Again, this is all at *1.5° C* above pre-industrial levels, which is currently considered the *best-case* scenario (IPCC, 2018).

Another half degree Celsius, and 10 million *more* people will be subject to sea level rise. Severe ecosystem change will double the number of species that lose half their geographic range (Carbon Brief, 2018; Warren, Price, Graham, Forestenhaeusler & Vanderwal, 2018). This means those organisms stop contributing toward the regulation of those ecosystems (Gramling, 2018). Some of these important inputs include plant pollination and water and air purification, which are necessary for both thriving ecosystems and agriculture. We will lose all of our coral reefs. *All of them.* The chance of having an ice-free arctic summer goes up by 70%, and the chance of any given population experiencing a severe heat-wave rises 20%. Droughts will last an additional four months. Moreover, added sea level rise means it is much less likely we will be able to adapt quickly enough to mitigate damage (Climate Nexus, 2018).

At 3° C, which is the Paris Agreement's current goal, the average drought length will increase by 10 months (Carbon Brief, 2018). The Greenland ice sheet will almost completely melt, and sea levels will rise seven meters, drastically changing the geography of rivers, estuaries, and villages (Climate Nexus, 2018). Almost half the Himalayan glaciers will vanish. Marine ecosystems will be at risk of collapse, and many fish species will go extinct.

A predictable outcome if we continue with business as usual is 4° C of increase. This would be enough to melt all the polar ice caps, releasing latent methane gas and rapidly sending us upwards in a heat spiral that peaks well above 6° C. The IPCC notes, "Continued emission of greenhouse gases will cause further warming and long-lasting changes in all components of the climate system, increasing the likelihood of severe, pervasive and irreversible impacts for people and ecosystems" (2014a, p. 8). Without swift and comprehensive reforms, the future is bleak.

It's Already Happening

Extreme heat and cold events, wildfires, hurricanes, and flooding are just the tip of the melting iceberg. Rice yields are decreasing due to rising nighttime temperatures (Peng et al., 2004). We are experiencing significant decreases in protein, zinc, and iron in our food due to increased CO_2 in the atmosphere (Myers et al., 2014). Climate change is responsible for increasing extreme-weather events such as tropical storms, hurricanes, typhoons, and forest fires (Schiermeier, 2018; Westerling, Hidalgo, Cayan & Swetnam, 2006; USGCRP, 2018). Extreme heat events are raising mortality rates (Medina-Ramón & Schwartz, 2007). Pollen-based allergies are increasing and allergy season is lengthening (Rogers et al., 2006). The oceans are becoming more acidic due to increases of oceanic CO_2, altering their biological systems. In fact, oceanic CO_2 is at its highest level ever measured and rising 100 times faster than it has in the last 65,000 years (Fabry, Seibel, Feely & Orr, 2008).

Damage from climate change may add stress to our already strained healthcare systems. Watts et al. (2018) write in *The Lancet* "A lack of progress in reducing emissions and building adaptive capacity threatens both human lives and the viability of the national health systems they depend on, with the potential to disrupt core public health infrastructure and overwhelm health services." When asked if we were entering a worst-case-scenario for climate change, Stanford scientist and chair of the Global Carbon Project, Rob Jackson, stated, "We're actually a lot closer than we should be; I can say that with confidence" (Meyer, 2019).

Fortunately, concern among Americans is finally pushing back on the restraints generated by ideology, corporate influence, and complacency. From March to December 2018, Americans who said that climate change is "personally important" rose almost 10 points to 72%. The number who said they were "very worried" also rose about 8 points (Leiserowitz et al., 2018). It is good we are waking up. This gives us a chance to act.

More Than Just Climate

These issues are often broader than acknowledged. Climate change is exacerbated by many other environmental concerns and it will add extra stress to a planet already dealing with habitat loss, deforestation, extinction, food and water scarcity, overharvesting, topsoil erosion, overpopulation, and political instability. Three quarters of the world's fish supply are overharvested, and nearly all of the world's aquifers are over-pumped. According to Rothschild (2007), around one third of the planet's natural resource space has been consumed in the past three decades. Forty percent of waterways are undrinkable in the U.S. and less than four percent of the United States' original forests are left. The U.S. has about five percent of the world's population, uses 30% of the world's non-renewable resources, and creates 30% of the world's waste. Imagine this statistic from another angle: we would need three to five additional planets to support Earth's human population if the world's inhabitants consumed at the same rate as the U.S. (Rothschild, 2007). This disproportionate influence often is not felt since we extract our resources from and export our trash to other countries.

We may have prevented ourselves from feeling it, but we have long surpassed the Earth's capacity. A 2002 study by the U.S. National Academy of Sciences showed that we surpassed the planet's capacity to sustain and regenerate itself in the year 1980 (Wackernagel et al., 2002). The Earth Policy Institute states, "As of 2009 global demands on natural systems exceed their sustainable yield capacity by nearly

30 percent. This means we are meeting current demands in part by consuming the earth's natural assets, setting the stage for an eventual Ponzi-type collapse when these assets are depleted" (Brown, 2009, p.14).

The weak links in this chain are water and food. Emmerson (2011) states: "Over one billion people live in water-scarce or water stressed parts of the world, a number expected to triple over the next few decades as groundwater depletion, climate change and accelerating demands on water extraction take their toll" (p. 5). Water demand is expected to grow by two thirds as soon as 2025 and the United Nations fears a "looming water crisis" (Prud'Homme, 2011, p. 3). About 900 million people in the world don't have access to clean water, and 2.5 billion people don't have a way to safely dispose of human waste. Many people dispose of waste in their drinking water source causing approximately 3.3 million deaths each year through water-borne bacteria and viruses. Most of these casualties are children under five. Prud'Homme (2011) notes, "In much of the developing world, lack of water is at the center of a vicious circle of inequality" (p. 2).

Our global food supply will be hit just as hard. Soil erosion has contributed to a reduction in crop yields for 30% of the world's agricultural land (Brown, 2009). Countries that have exhausted their own resources are buying agricultural land from countries facing extreme food scarcity. These land acquisitions often include water rights in countries simultaneously stricken with drought. In many countries with ancient rainforests like Indonesia, Brazil, and the Democratic Republic of Congo, this leads to deforestation, feeding right back into the loop. Food and water insecurity are major contributing factors for political instability that often ripples out from host countries to the rest of the world, leaving war, terrorism, and a wake of refugees that many developed nations have been unwilling to help in a time of crisis.

Political Instability

Climate change leads to increased wars and political instability. Findings from the National Academies of Science "suggest that worldwide and synchronistic war–peace, population, and price cycles in recent centuries have been driven mainly by long-term climate change" (Zhang, Brecke, Lee, He & Zhang, 2007). Another National Academies study found that climate change will raise armed conflict in African nations by 54% by the year 2030 with an additional 400,000 deaths (Burke, Miguel, Satyanath, Dykema & Lobell, 2009).

Global warming has been implicated in the Syrian refugee crisis. Global temperature increases contributed to the worst drought on record in the Fertile Crescent, causing massive crop failure and forcing farmers into already resource-stricken cities. This extra stress on local resources supported political instability and the subsequent civil war (Kelley, Mohtadi, Cane, Seager & Kushnir, 2015). Accelerated climate change will lead to failing states, terrorism, and the spread of infectious disease due to lack of medical resources and infrastructure. These problems are not isolated to their countries of origin. They quickly spread throughout the world. The Syrian refugee crisis exacerbated rising xenophobia, populist nationalism, hate crimes, and political distrust in Europe, and there is strong evidence that it contributed to the positive Brexit vote (Postelnicescu, 2016).

Environmental Racism and Classism

Climate change is already happening and the current best case scenario still means we have to adapt and adjust. So the question arises: who will be the winners and losers? Corporations have been researching ways to profit from the effects of global warming since at least the early 1990s, positioning themselves to "sell more weapons systems to the military, more air conditioners to sweltering civilians, and more medications to people afflicted with tropical diseases"

(Schulman, 2017, para. 2). Plans are underway to profit off the policing of victims and the militarization of crisis zones. Raytheon, one of the world's largest weapons contractors, has said they are planning for "expanded business opportunities" that include "military products and services as security concerns may arise as results of droughts, floods, and storm events occur as a result of climate change" (Klein, 2014, p. 9).

Americans who can afford to are strategically buying real estate based on predictive climate models, displacing working-class neighborhoods and causing "climate gentrification" (Keenan, Hill, & Gumber, 2018). Major publications such as *The Guardian* and *Business Insider* have produced articles with titles like, "Where should you move to save yourself from climate change?" (Milman, 2018) and "The best US cities to live in to escape the worst effects of climate change" (Brodwin, 2017). Major cities in the U.S. and Europe are adjusting their infrastructure accordingly.

Indigenous Peoples, people of color, those experiencing poverty, and those from the Global South—people who have contributed the least to climate change—experience the brunt of climate change's negative effects. History suggests these communities that have the least resources to adapt are often the communities the world is least willing to help and most likely to police in a time of crisis. Racism and classism intersect. Histories of slavery, racism and the global impact of European colonialism mean the world's poor are usually people of color.

Toxic facilities that emit harmful chemicals such as mercury, arsenic and lead are often the same facilities that emit CO_2 and methane into the atmosphere. According to the NAACP (2018), the primary factor for the placement of these toxic facilities is race. They are disproportionately located in communities of color that are more likely to face health concerns than white communities (NAACP & CATF, 2017; Mikati, 2018; Hayward, Miles, Crimmins & Yang, 2000). When detrimental health impacts are observed from these pollutants, we can see racism playing out, such as in the Flint water crisis or "cancer alley" in Louisiana. Whether cleaning up pollutants from a spill, fining companies for bad practices, or providing relief from national emergencies, white communities receive quicker responses, more funding, and more media attention (NAACP, 2018).

Hurricanes Harvey, Maria, Sandy, and Katrina all saw this manifest on a national stage. Hurricane Katrina hit New Orleans in 2005, killing 2,000 people and displacing over a million. According to the Center for American Progress, African-American communities were disproportionately affected by the storm and reported an appalling lack of services, slow response times, and policing of their bodies (Maxwell, 2018). The Army Corps of Engineers had been told for years that local levees were in serious need of repair, but they did not act on the reports and neglected the predominately African-American community that faced the danger (Klein, 2017). Ten years after Katrina, 90% of all affected residents had returned to their homes, while only 37% from the predominantly Black areas returned (Maxwell, 2018). Klein's (2017) investigative reporting showed that corporate interests used the crisis to gentrify many of the African-American neighborhoods for profit. Louisiana State Representative Richard Baker demonstrated the role of race on disaster response in his public statement, "We finally cleaned up public housing in New Orleans. We couldn't do it, but God did" (Saulny, 2006).

In 2012, Hurricane Sandy cost $70 billion and killed 159 people in New York and New Jersey (Maxwell, 2018). Although it hit hardest in African-American and Latino communities, the disaster relief disproportionately helped white, middle-class homeowners. The practices were so egregious that Fair Share Housing Center, NAACP New Jersey, and Latino Action Network won a settlement with the New Jersey government.

Further evidence for discriminatory disaster response was provided in the wake of Hurricane Harvey. Black and Latino residents in Texas and Louisiana were twice as likely to experience financial hardship and lack of federal aid, while white residents were twice as likely to report that they had been approved for relief by FEMA. Hurricane Maria tore through Puerto Rico right after Harvey ended with $100 billion in damage reported and 1,000 lives lost. As of early 2019, Congress has approved $23 billion in aid, less than a quarter of what was requested and far less than any of the other storms mentioned (Maxwell, 2018). Many people believe this is because Puerto Rico is primarily a territory of color.

In the first nine days of Harvey, the federal government allocated over $140 million, deployed 30,000 disaster relief workers, provided 5 million meals and 4.5 million liters of water to the people of Texas. In the first 9 days of Maria, they allocated $6 million dollars, deployed 10,000 workers, and provided 1.5 million meals and 2.8 million liters of water to the people of Puerto Rico (Vinik, 2018).

Working-class people and communities of color are the most likely to be harmed by climate change disasters and are the least likely to be helped. The Global South will continue to suffer the pains of environmental racism through pollution, deforestation, privatization of resources, and lack of global aid. Industry practices that contribute to climate change are disproportionately poisoning these communities through harmful toxins, pollution, and oil spills. Climate change, then, is both the result of structural violence and will soon be one of its primary causes.

Global Indigenous Peoples

Indigenous Peoples are rarely part of climate change discussions, despite their decades' long documentation of its effects. Though they have a generally lower ecological footprint, Indigenous Peoples are at higher risk from the negative effects of climate change. Many Indigenous Peoples have been pushed onto drought-ridden and resource-depleted reservations/reserves with fewer water, land and hunting rights than they enjoyed since time immemorial. The United Nations Permanent Forum on Indigenous Issues (2008) stated, "Indigenous peoples are among the first to face the direct consequences of climate change, due to their dependence upon, and close relationship, with the environment and its resources. Climate change exacerbates the difficulties already faced by indigenous communities including political and economic marginalization, loss of land and resources, human rights violations, discrimination and unemployment" (para. 3).

There are many Indigenous communities worldwide that will be required to relocate as sea levels rise. Small-island countries such as Tuvalu, Vanuatu and Kiribati could be underwater by the end of the century (Chemnick, 2017). Displacement from home is difficult for anyone, even more so for those experiencing poverty. However, many Indigenous Peoples' worldviews, identities, spiritualities, sources of resilience, and ontological frameworks are rooted in place (Coulthard, 2010). Standing Rock Sioux tribal member and professor Vine Deloria, Jr., explained why this is so difficult for Westerners to understand. He said, "Ideology is divided according to American Indian and Western European [traditions]...this fundamental difference is one of great philosophical importance. American Indians hold their lands–places–as having the highest possible meaning, and all their statements are made with this reference point in mind" (Coulthard, 2010, p. 1). According to Patricia McGuire Kishebakabaykwe (2010) of the Anishinaabe people in Ontario, "Indigenous place-based resilience requires understanding the traditions and sustained relationships with the land. Relationships are embedded in the land" (p. 123). She continues, "This becomes tied to the personal identity, spiritual development of people, and their overall relationships with others" (p. 123). For many Indigenous Peoples, place is of central importance. However, displacement is not the only issue they face.

Some of the specific effects of climate change included in the United Nations Permanent Forum on Indigenous Issues (2008) are: loss of water and livelihood for rural dwellers of the high Himalayas as glacial melt depletes seasonal water sources, drought-caused wildfires in the Amazon that destroy large portions of the rainforest, and inability of Indigenous Peoples in Arctic regions to hunt their traditional foods. As with displacement, these effects don't just hinder food security and local economies, they erode the heart of traditional cultures and traditions.

As illustration, Humboldt State University's Altruistic Behavior Institute, founded by Pearl Oliner and this book's editor, Sam Oliner, is located in Northwest California, near the ancestral lands of the Yurok people. The Yurok's traditional homeland included over 50 villages covering 765 square miles—although their federally recognized land is now about one tenth that size—centered along the Klamath River, referred to by the Yurok as the "lifeline of our people" (Yurok Tribe, [n.d.]; O'Rourke, 2017). The Yurok Tribe has a robust environmental program and has conducted their own climate change research, which is unique in its strong focus on the impact climate change will have on their "cultural and spiritual identity" (Sloan & Hostler, 2011, p. 28). They list "Protecting and Preserving Yurok Lifeways, Culture and Traditions" (p. 28) as their top priority.

The Yurok Environmental Report identifies the need to protect the "plants and animals used for ceremonies & medicines" (Sloan & Hostler, 2011, p. 38). The loss of these due to climate change or other environmental factors cannot be overstated. Cultural healing is an important aspect of overall well-being (Bassett, Tsosie, & Nannauck, 2012), and cultural practices are often more effective and more likely to be used by Indigenous Peoples than Western methods for psycho-spiritual healing (American Psychological Association, 2010). These cultural practices are embedded in a relational worldview that sees everything as interconnected. Land and resources are tied to culture, spirituality, ancestors, identity, and how one sees and understands the world (Wilson, 2008).

Solutions

Climate change is solvable. We know what we need to do and we have the capabilities to do it. All that is needed is will. Our lack of will thus far is not a failure in human nature. Rather, it is stifled by special interests and ideologies that fail to recognize how our lives are part of the rhythms of the natural world. These obstacles can be overcome, but victory is not inevitable. It's going to take activism on every level of society. This may sound daunting, but there is much that gives hope. California was burning when this chapter was being written. In the last few months there has been a resurgence in media attention on climate change and it has gained larger attention in the U.S. Congress due to Representative Alexandria Ocasio-Cortez and Senator Ed Markey's introduction of the "Green New Deal."

It seems fitting that as the final touches were being put on this chapter, after months of grueling research into just how bad climate change will be, thousands of students across Europe skipped school to protest their government's inability to deal with it (Specia, 2019). There is a habit of accusing young people of idealism and naivety (*viz.* the counter-response to these protests happened right away). Rep. Ocasio-Cortez, only a few years younger than one of the chapter authors, has received this same criticism since her election. But apathy has gotten us nowhere, and a look at the research shows that we really can be carbon-neutral by 2050, and it really will take a massive effort (Jacobson et al., 2017). Countries from the Global South such as India, Morocco, and Ethiopia are leading the way in their climate change efforts (Climate Action Tracker, 2018). Sweden already provides over half of its energy from renewable sources and is on track to be completely fossil-fuel free by 2045 (UN Climate Change, 2017). Denmark is close behind and will reach that goal by 2050. These countries show us that the technology is here and ready to be utilized.

Ideology

An analysis of the history of neoliberalism's rise creates an opening to tackle our current climate crisis. Milton Friedman knew well the central role of crises in creating change. He wrote, "Only a crisis—actual or perceived—produces real change. When that crisis occurs, the actions that are taken depend on the ideas that are lying around" (Friedman & Friedman, 1982, p. ix). In his case, the crisis was the oil embargo of 1973 and the energy crisis of 1978. These events created skyrocketing gas prices that resulted in "stagflation," or the simultaneous inflation and stagnant growth in the economy. This economic failure rendered visible a blind spot in the economic models of the time and it created an opening for neoliberalism to finally have its day. Friedman had already predicted stagflation and had a solution ready to go: privatization of government, deregulation of economic markets, and cutting taxes on the rich. Friedman, Hayek and the Mont Pelerin Society had taken 25 years to develop the ideas of neoliberalism so they could be used in such a crisis. After assuming the Presidency in 1980, Ronald Reagan took on the mantle of these ideas and the world has not really looked back.

One way to look at our current situation is that, for the last 30 years, climate scientists, activists and politicians have been laying out the groundwork for government intervention in climate change. In the last few years we experienced some of the worst fires, floods, and other natural disasters in modern history. During this same time a majority of the American population has come to agree with the findings of basic climate science. Other ideas have been laid out during this time as well. The growing concern with income inequality, money in politics, tax evasion, and intersectionality are all ideas now "lying around," to borrow Freidman's term. History shows that these ideas can change politics and ideologies in ways that make drastic and sudden change possible. Below are some of the ideological frameworks and activist strategies that are currently lying around.

Sustainable Development

Changing our agriculture, logging, and land-management practices will have substantial positive effects on climate change. Fargione et al. (2018) suggest better management of our forests, grasslands, and farmland could offset up to 21% of greenhouse gas emissions. Many scientists are hopeful about the findings but cautious. Timothy D. Searchinger of Princeton University and World Resources Institute says, "I'm intrigued and hopeful but also a little skeptical. They've provided a very rough map of these lands, and it would be a good idea to go out and examine this land more closely to see if they're right and if so, more closely determine what it would take to reforest it" (Plumer, 2018, para. 6). However, even if high-end predictions are exaggerated practices such as replanting trees, utilizing sustainable logging and agricultural practices, and limiting future deforestation can offset many of our greenhouse gasses. The authors are clear that this should not be a replacement for renewable energy. Lead researcher Faglione states, "We're not saying these strategies are a substitute for getting to zero-carbon energy; we still need to do that too. But we think that natural climate solutions generally get overlooked" (Plumer, 2018, para. 4).

There is an ethical concern with limiting farmland while the world experiences rising demands for food. A report in *The Lancet* offers a solution for this, detailing how changing our agricultural practices can relieve the pressure from population growth, decreasing crop yields, and overharvesting (Willett et al., 2019). Some findings, like the need for countries to reduce annual wasted food—30% of food in the United States is wasted—are gaining traction. Other solutions are less popular, like reducing red meat and sugar intake by 50%. It is mostly the Western, "developed" world that will have to decrease meat intake; countries experiencing malnutrition and food insecurity could have modest increases as a part of their path to health and sustainability. A study in *Nature* came to similar conclusions (Springmann et al., 2018).

As we brace for 10 billion mouths to feed in 2050, we need solutions regardless of climate change (Willett et al., 2019). *The Lancet* report accounts for greenhouse gasses, water use, fossil-fuel fertilizers, biodiversity, worldwide nutrition, and food insecurity in their findings. Today, more than 820 million people experience food insecurity and many more consume unhealthy diets that contribute to morbidity and early death. Moreover, "global food production is the largest pressure caused by humans on Earth, threatening local ecosystems and the stability of the Earth system" (Willett et al., 2019, p. 2). Current trends in diet and global population growth will exacerbate this, furthering Brown's (2009) claim that food is the "weak link" in our climate change crisis. By changing our agricultural and dietary nutrition practices, we can help stop climate change while improving our global health, ending 11 million premature deaths annually and ensuring that we continue to feed our growing population. All this can be accomplished without deforestation or overharvesting. These are important considerations, however the biggest contributor to climate change is CO_2 from fossil fuels.

Renewable Energies

We already have all of the technology we need to be completely independent of fossil fuels. Jacobson et al. (2017) provide energy roadmaps for 139 countries across the globe. They maintain that it is feasible and reasonable to convert all energy to 80% renewables by 2030 and 100% by 2050. The energy roadmaps do not require any technological equivalents of a Hail Mary pass like blocking out the sun or carbon-capture technologies (Holden, 2018; Nace, 2018). They do not require biofuels or nuclear plants and their power comes entirely from wind, water, and solar technologies (WWS). Increased reliance on biofuels would overburden our natural systems and would compete with the needs of agriculture, biodiversity, and other ecosystem functions (IPCC, 2018). Nuclear, though carbon-neutral, is not clean energy, even with recent technological advances. As the IPCC (2014b) states, there is "robust evidence and high agreement" that increased reliance on nuclear reactors would involve "operational risks and the associated safety concerns, uranium mining risks, financial and regulatory risks, unresolved waste management issues, nuclear weapons proliferation concerns, and adverse public opinion" (p. 517). While the Union of Concerned Scientists (2019), say that increased nuclear may need to be a part of the solution, they admit that it "faces substantial economic challenges, and carries significant human health and environmental risks" (para. 5). They suggest "policies and measures to strengthen the safety and security of nuclear power" (para. 5). In Europe, every country on track to be carbon neutral has significant nuclear power as part of their plan. If nuclear will need to play a role, utilizing best practices is a must. The best route to sustainable energy is to switch to 100% WWS, or at least head in that direction.

Since WWS are all zero-emission technologies, they can virtually eliminate 4-7 million premature deaths and hundreds of millions of illnesses caused by pollution from fossil fuels. They are more energy-efficient than carbon technologies and switching to 100% WWS would mean a 42.5% decrease in energy consumption because of increased efficiency (Jacobson et al., 2017). It would also mean a net-gain of 24.3 million permanent, full-time jobs. We will see more stable fuel prices and increased access to energy with less disruption due to decentralized power sources (Jacobson et al., 2017). Jacobson et al.'s (2015) energy roadmaps for the United States found that each person in the country will save $260 in energy costs and $1,500 in healthcare costs annually. The Green New Deal, rather than being a naive pet project of the left, is a scientifically-grounded strategy to reverse climate change, create jobs, and lessen U.S. citizens' financial burdens.

Legislative/Economic Action

Land use, agriculture, and energy solutions that sustain a future for us to inherit require government intervention. The hand of the market, rendered invisible by a cloud of greenhouse gasses, will not correct this on its own. The *Economists' Statement on Carbon Dividends*, signed by prominent economists, including former Chair of the Federal Reserve of the United States (and stated fan of neoliberalist Milton Friedman), Alan Greenspan, admits that carbon emissions are a "well-known market failure" (Climate Leadership Council, 2019, para. 2). Environmental and corporate regulation, carbon taxes, renewable subsidies, and government spending programs will be necessary. This is why Robert Kennedy, Jr. is so fond of saying, "It's more important to change your politician than your light bulb" (Navasky, 2016, para. 39). At every level of government, we need people in office who are willing to stand up to industry pressure and make necessary changes.

Even simple regulations that phase out greenhouse gas

refrigerants from air conditioners could reduce global warming .5°C by 2100 (Zaelke, 2019). Electric car subsidies put in place by the Obama administration have shown to be effective in nudging consumer choices. These can be renewed and expanded by offering price reduction at the time of purchase rather than when tax season arrives (Samaras, 2019). At the local level, planning walkable and bikeable neighborhoods known as "complete streets" can reduce commute times and lower reliance on cars. This simultaneously cuts carbon emissions and promotes public health. The majority of Americans are in favor of this (Atherton, 2019). There are many more legislative changes than this that can be made and each country, state and municipality will need to pass laws that make sense within their own communities.

Taxing carbon is almost universally supported among economists across the political spectrum. Two former Treasury secretaries, four Federal Reserve chairs, more than two dozen Nobel laureates, and almost every U.S. Council of Economic Advisers chair since the 1970s have endorsed a bipartisan carbon tax. They state, "A carbon tax offers the most cost-effective lever to reduce carbon emissions at the scale and speed that is necessary" (Climate Leadership Council, 2019, para. 2). The budget neutral plan avoids debates over the size of government by returning revenue to taxpayers in the form of lump-sum rebates. This keeps the government from growing while offsetting potential increased consumer costs. The statement notes, "The majority of American families, including the most vulnerable, will benefit financially by receiving more in 'carbon dividends' than they pay in increased energy prices" (para. 6). While the plan currently may not have Congressional bipartisan support, it certainly has ideological bipartisan support among economics experts. As the public's concern for climate change continues to grow, the carbon taxation plan could be one of the first truly effective and bipartisan pieces of legislation to combat climate change in the United States.

The Green New Deal (GND) is steadily gaining support. It is well summarized by David Roberts (2019) of Vox: "It refers, in the loosest sense, to a massive program of investments in clean-energy jobs and infrastructure, meant to transform not just the energy sector, but the entire economy. It is meant both to decarbonize the economy and to make it fairer and more just" (para. 11). U.S. Representative Alexandria Ocasio-Cortez and Senator Ed Markey's document is more of a list of goals than specific policy. As policy wonks hash out the details there are bound to be debates and disagreements, but the basics of the GND have been around for a while. In fact, then Senator Barack Obama ran on the concept in 2008, and many see his economic stimulus package as a precursor to the GND. Not only was the $90 billion allocation by far the biggest clean energy package in history, it was also wildly successful. According to award-winning journalist Michael Grunwald, it revived a dead industry and kickstarted the continuing renewable renaissance (Roberts, 2012). In President Obama's first term, the United States doubled clean energy production, birthed entire industries, and created new jobs.

Industry Accountability and Responsibility

Although the fossil fuel industry and other special-interest groups have deliberately slowed or halted progress, there are many more industries that have a vested interest in stopping climate change. The media, for instance, can be more forceful and direct in stating the harms of climate change and linking it with human activity. Yale University's Program on Climate Change Communication (2019) outlines effective strategies to connect with audiences about the issue.

Overlooked industries can be allies, such as the medical industry. The United States' medical system accounts for 10% of all emissions in the country. If U.S. healthcare was considered its own country, it would have a GDP of $3.3 trillion and rank seventh in the world for emissions. There is a sad irony that the industry working to save lives, relieve suffering, and keep us healthy, is also a serious contributor to the climate change that causes us harm (Solomon & LaRocque, 2019). There is reason to believe change here is possible and the sizable influence of the medical industry presents an opportunity. Many hospitals are transitioning towards 100% clean energy. Doctors and other health professionals are more clearly connecting climate change to public health in their education and outreach. Healthcare companies are divesting from fossil fuel industries (Solomon & LaRocque, 2019). While many companies have a vested interest in ethics and sustainability, there are more that can be nudged or persuaded through public pressure.

The fossil fuel divestment movement has been going strong for a few decades now. When large institutions and local governments divert investments from fossil fuels they make a powerful statement of values. They also free up funds to be redirected into clean energy technologies. While acknowledging that divestment campaigns have been effective at raising consciousness and building public pressure campaigns, Pollin and Hansen (2019) question how effective divestment strategies have been and suggest they have limited potential to hit corporate pocketbooks because someone else is always willing to purchase available stocks. Activists' time, they suggest, would be better spent directly reducing fossil fuel consumption and CO2 emissions.

Another strategy that shows promise follows in the footsteps of resistance to the tobacco industry. Lawsuits against fossil fuel corporations and governments for damage caused by their direct contributions to or failure to protect us from global warming have started to proliferate. Fossil fuel companies and the U.S. government knew climate change was real, knew the catastrophic costs, and continued to damage the earth while actively misleading the public. This is the basis for several recent lawsuits. The Pacific Coast Federation of Fishermen's Associations currently has a lawsuit against 30 oil companies for causing ocean acidification that has made Dungeness crab and other shellfish unsafe for human consumption. Several governments such as the Maryland city of Baltimore, the California county of Marin, and the state of Rhode Island are suing oil companies for their role in blocking effective climate change action (Bland, 2018). Over 30,000 teens and eight members of Congress are suing the federal government for violating their right to live in a "climate system capable of sustaining human life" (Parker, 2019, para. 7). Once viewed as a longshot, the lawsuit has defied the odds and was recently allowed to go forward by the U.S. Supreme Court. Similar lawsuits by young people can be found across the globe including in India, Colombia, and Belgium. A 2015 citizen lawsuit forced the Dutch government to reduce carbon emissions by 25% over a five year period (Livni, 2018). Continuous quality improvement related to research technologies will strengthen the association between natural disasters and climate change, enhancing outcomes for future lawsuits (Schiermeier, 2018).

Traditional Ecological Knowledge

Indigenous Peoples and Indigenous researchers need to be included in climate change strategy discussions and they need resources to develop and implement their own solutions. Dennis Martinez, a Tohono O'odham/Chicano ecologist, says "traditional ecological knowledge (TEK) and [W] estern science cannot be integrated and cannot be bridged," but mutual dialogue between these worldviews is critical to addressing the negative effects of climate change (Wall, 2009, p. 1). The Indigenous Peoples' Biocultural Climate Change Assessment Initiative aims to "empower local communities to do their own assessments" (Wall, 2009, p. 2). Indigenous

TEK has identified specific effects of climate change before western science and it has added granularity to new discoveries. For instance, Alaskan Natives knew that Arctic ice was thinning in the 1960s and they possess knowledge about the relationships between different animals, kinds of ice, and Tribal communities that represent quantitative data (Wall, 2009).

Climate Justice

Wealthy people have disproportionately occupied global atmospheric space and have appropriated local, national, and global commons for profit. They have overused their share of public resources and have caused massive environmental destruction in their wake. A debt is owed. Climate justice is a restorative process that aims to decolonize the atmosphere by restoring and returning it to the people's commons (Warlenius, 2018). Since some forms of restoration are not possible right now (i.e., the planet will continue to heat up), compensation for damage done is a viable solution.

Repayment can take several forms, but the debt needs to be paid *in full* for true climate justice. Warlenius (2018) states, "losses that cannot be restored physically should be compensated economically or otherwise" (p. 140). The debt includes paying for mitigation efforts as well as helping Indigenous Peoples and the Global South catch up developmentally through return of patents and intellectual property rights to their peoples of origin. Returning land that was taken forcibly or through manipulation would go a long way toward repayment as well.

There are differing opinions in the climate justice movement as to what development looks like. The People's Agreement, a collective document from a broad coalition of climate activists and Indigenous Peoples throughout the world, maintains that true sustainable development must move past a patriarchal and capitalist model of growth "based on the submission and destruction of human beings and nature" and, instead, work towards "a new system that restores harmony with nature and among human beings" based on the "ancestral practices of Indigenous Peoples" (Warlenius, 2018 p. 42). For them, capitalism and sustainability cannot abide:

Under capitalism, Mother Earth is converted into a source of raw materials, and human beings into consumers and a means of production, into people that are seen as valuable only for what they own, and not for what they are. Capitalism requires a powerful military industry for its processes of accumulation and imposition of control over territories and natural resources, suppressing the resistance of the peoples. It is an imperialist system of colonization of the planet. Humanity confronts a great dilemma: to continue on the path of capitalism, depredation, and death, or to choose the path of harmony with nature and respect for life (World People's Conference on Climate Change and the Rights of Mother Earth, 2010, para. 4-7).

Personal Accountability and Responsibility

Several strategies and solutions have been discussed thus far. Each step we make increases the likelihood that we will preserve a viable planet for our children to inherit. The above actions can bring us into a fossil fuel-free future at the same as they create a healthier, sustainable, and harmonious society. One might then ask, "What can I do?" We all have a role to play.

We should be circumspect of quick fixes and easy answers. Individualism is a central thread running through the discourse responsible for human-caused climate change. Individualistic solutions can seem like a simple way to feel better. But this is temporary. Joanna Macy (1995) reminds us that feeling pain for the world is a natural human response and, if nurtured and cared for, this feeling of pain contains the seeds of justice and healing. She writes, "What is it that allows us to feel pain for our world? And what do we discover as we move through that pain? To both these questions there is one answer: interconnectedness with life and all other beings" (p. 14).

It's true we can change our light bulbs and unplug the appliances that consume energy even while they are off. A quick internet search will provide a whole host of do-it-yourself answers. Make those changes for sure. But also remember Robert Kennedy, Jr.'s guidance, "It's more important to change your politician than your light bulb" (Navasky, 2016, para. 39). He recommends that more citizens get involved in politics: vote, join local environmental groups, and run for office.

As individuals we can, in the words of Mari J. Matsuda (1991), "ask the other question." She describes an intersectional lens when she says,

> The way I try to understand the interconnection of all forms of subordination is through a method I call "ask the other question." When I see something that looks racist, I ask, "Where is the patriarchy in this?" When I see something that looks sexist, I ask, "Where is the heterosexism in this?" When I see something that looks homophobic, I ask, "Where are the class interests in this?" (p. 1189).

As we move forward with climate change activism, let us continue to ask the other question. When we consider where to put wind and solar farms, let's ask, "Whose lands are going to be displaced?" When we consider building sea walls to protect our cities, let's ask, "What do we owe to those who cannot afford to do this?" When we latch on to the promise of future technologies that allow us to continue with business as usual, let's ask, "Who profits from this?" When we see environmental destruction, let's ask, "Where is the racism, patriarchy, heterosexism, ableism, classism and colonialism in all this?"

The consequences for not acting are grave. Though we have largely failed in our efforts thus far, the work done in the last 30 years has not been in vain. We really can live a life where each of us thrives; where our physical, mental and spiritual health progresses with the health of the planet; where *my* success is not dependent on *your* suffering; where we acknowledge that our interdependence is beneficial for us all. There is considerable reason for hope. The solutions described in this chapter show that this hope is rooted in the best science, technology, and research.

References

American Psychological Association. (2010). Indigenous Peoples: Promoting Psychological Healing and Well-Being. *Office of Ethnic Minority Affairs.*

Atherton, E. (2019, January 2). Make it easier to live without cars. In Post Opinions Staff (eds) Here are 11 climate change policies to fight for in 2019. *The Washington Post.* Retrieved from https://www.washingtonpost.com/news/opinions/wp/2019/01/02/feature/opinion-here-are-11-climate-change-policies-to-fight-for-in-2019/?noredirect=on&utm_term=.a39fd0487101#2

Bassett, D., Tsosie, U., & Nannauck, S. (2012). "Our Culture Is Medicine": Perspectives of Native Healers on Posttrauma Recovery Among American Indian and Alaska Native Patients. *The Permanente Journal, 16*(1), 19-27.

Bland, A. (2018, December 4). Fishermen Sue Big Oil For Its Role In Climate Change. Retrieved April 1, 2019, from NPR website: https://www.npr.org/sections/the-salt/2018/12/04/671996313/fishermen-sue-big-oil-for-its-role-in-climate-change

Brodwin, E. (2017, September 24). The best US cities to live in to escape the worst effects of climate change. *The Business Insider.* Retrieved February 9, 2019, from https://www.businessinsider.com/best-us-cities-escape-climate-change-2017-9

Brown, L. (2009). *Plan B.* Earth Policy Institute. New York: W. W. Norton & Company. Retrieved from http://www.earth-policy.org/images/uploads/book_files/pb-4book.pdf

Brown, P. T., & Caldeira, K. (2017). Greater future global warming inferred from Earth's recent energy budget. *Nature, 552,* 45-50. doi:10.1038/nature24672

Burke, M. B., Miguel, E., Satyanath, S., Dykema, J. A., & Lobell, D. B. (2009). Warming increases the risk of civil war in Africa. *Proceedings of the National Academy of Sciences,* 106(49), 20670–20674. https://doi.org/10.1073/pnas.0907998106

Carbon Brief. (2018). The impacts of climate change at 1.5C, 2C and beyond. Carbon Brief. Retrieved January 19, 2019 from https://interactive.carbonbrief.org/impacts-climate-change-one-point-five-degrees-two-degrees/?utm_source=web&utm_campaign=Redirect

Chemnick, J. (2017). Island nations urge aggressive action at U.N. climate meeting. *Scientific American.* Retrieved from https://www.scientificamerican.com/article/island-nations-urge-aggressive-action-at-u-n-climate-meeting/

Chew, S. (2008). *Ecological futures: What history can teach us.* Lanham: Altamira Press.

Climate Action Tracker. (December 2018). Some progress since Paris, but not enough, as governments amble towards 3°C of warming. Retrieved from https://climateactiontracker.org/publications/warming-projections-global-update-dec-2018

Climate Leadership Council. (2019). *Economists' Statement on Carbon Dividends.* Retrieved from https://www.clcouncil.org/economists-statement/

Climate Nexus. (2018). Comparing climate impacts at 1.5°C, 2°C, 3°C and 4°C. Climate Nexus. Retrieved on January 19, 2019 from https://climatenexus.org/international/ipcc/comparing-climate-impacts-at-1-5c-2c-3c-and-4c/

Cook, J. (2019a). Global Warming & Climate Change Myths. Skeptical Science. Retrieved from https://www.skepticalscience.com/argument.php

Cook, J. (2019b). About. Skeptical Science. Retrieved from https://www.skepticalscience.com/about.shtml

Cook, J., Nuccitelli, D., Green, S. A., Richardson, M., Winkler, B., Painting, R., . . . Skuce, A. (2013). Quantifying the consensus on anthropogenic global warming in the scientific literature. *Environmental Research Letters,* 8(2), 024024. doi: 10.1088/1748-9326/8/2/024024

Cook, J., Oreskes, N., Doran, P. T., Anderegg, W. R., Verheggen, B., Maibach, E. W., . . . Rice, K. (2016). Consensus on consensus: A synthesis of consensus estimates on human-caused global warming. *Environmental Research Letters,* 11(4), 048002. doi: 10.1088/1748-9326/11/4/048002

Coulthard, G. (2010). Place against empire: Understanding Indigenous anti-colonialism. *Affinities: A Journal of Radical Theory, Culture, and Action,* 4(2), 79-83. Retrieved from http://pages.ucsd.edu/~rfrank/class_web/ES-114A/Week%203/Coulthard-Affinities%204-2.pdf

Emmerson, C. (2011). Environment: Worlds Of Water. *The World Today,* 67(4).

Environmental Protection Agency (2019). Inventory of U.S. Greenhouse Gas Emissions and Sinks: 1990–2017. Retrieved from https://www.epa.gov/sites/production/files/2019-02/documents/us-ghg-inventory-2019-main-text.pdf

Fabry, V. J., Seibel, B. A., Feely, R. A. & Orr, J. C. (2008). Impacts of ocean acidification on marine fauna and ecosystem processes. *ICES Journal of Marine Science*, 65(3), 414–432. Retrieved from https://doi.org/10.1093/icesjms/fsn048

Fargione, J. E ., Bassett, S., Boucher, T., Bridgham, S. D., Conant, R. T., Cook-Patton, S. C., Ellis, P. W., Falcucci, A., Fourqurean, J. W., Gopalakrishna, T., Gu, H., Henderson, B., Hurteau, M. D., Kroeger, K. D., Kroeger, T., Lark, T. J., Leavitt, S. M., Lomax, G., McDonald, R. I., Megonigal, J. P., Miteva, D. A., Richardson, C. J., Sanderman, J., Shoch, D., Spawn, S. A., Veldman, J. W., Williams, C. A., Woodbury, P. B., Zganjar, C., Baranski, M., Elias, P., Houghton, R. A., Landis, E., McGlynn, E., Schlesinger, W. H., Siikamaki, J. V., Sutton-Grier, A. E., & Griscom, B. W. (2018). Natural climate solutions for the United States. *Science Advances*, 4(11).

Friedman, M., & Friedman, R. (1982). Capitalism and freedom. Chicago: University of Chicago Press.

Gramling, C. (2018, May 30). Keeping global warming to 1.5 degrees C helps most species hold their ground. Retrieved February 3, 2019, from https://www.sciencenews.org/article/keeping-global-warming-15-degrees-c-helps-most-species-hold-their-ground

Hansen, J. (2009). Tipping point: a perspective of a climatologist. *State of the Wild*. 2008-2009, 6-15. Retrieved from https://pubs.giss.nasa.gov/docs/2008/2008_Hansen_ha04310w.pdf

Hayward, M., Miles, T., Crimmins, E., & Yang, Y. (2000). The Significance of socioeconomic status in explaining the racial gap in chronic health conditions. *American Sociological Review*, 65(6), 910-930. doi: 10.2307/2657519

Holden, E. (2018, October 17). Could carbon-capture technology be a silver bullet to stop climate change? Re-

trieved March 24, 2019, from https://www.theguardian.
com/environment/2018/oct/17/carbon-capture-tech-
nology-climate-change-solutions

IPCC. (2014a). Climate Change 2014: Synthesis Report.
Contribution of Working Groups I, II and III to the Fifth
Assessment Report of the Intergovernmental Panel on
Climate Change [Core Writing Team, R.K. Pachauri
and L.A. Meyer (eds.)]. IPCC, Geneva, Switzerland.

IPCC. (2014b). Energy Systems. In [Edenhofer, O., R.
Pichs-Madruga, Y. Sokona, E. Farahani, S. Kadner, K.
Seyboth, A. Adler, I. Baum, S. Brunner, P. Eickemeier, B.
Kriemann, J. Savolainen, S. Schlömer, C. von Stechow,
T. Zwickel and J.C.Minx (eds.)], Climate Change 2014:
Mitigation of Climate Change. Contribution of Work-
ing Group III to the Fifth Assessment Report of the In-
tergovernmental Panel on Climate Change. Cambridge
University Press, Cambridge, United Kingdom and New
York, NY, USA, 2014.

IPCC. (2018). Summary for Policymakers. In V. Masson-Del-
motte, P. Zhai, H. O. Pörtner, D. Roberts, J. Skea, P. R.
Shukla, A. Pirani, W. Moufouma-Okia, C. Péan, R. Pid-
cock, S. Connors, J. B. R. Matthews, Y. Chen, X. Zhou,
M. I. Gomis, E. Lonnoy, T. Maycock, M. Tignor, T. Wa-
terfield (eds.), Global warming of 1.5°C. An IPCC Special Report on the impacts of global warming of 1.5°C
above pre-industrial levels and related global greenhouse
gas emission pathways, in the context of strengthening
the global response to the threat of climate change, sustainable development, and efforts to eradicate poverty.
World Meteorological Organization, Geneva, Switzerland, 32 pp. Retrieved from https://www.ipcc.ch/pdf/
special-reports/sr15/sr15_spm_final.pdf

Jacobson, M. Z., Delucchi, M. A., Bazouin, G., Bauer, Z.
A. F., Heavey, C. C., Fisher, E., … Yeskoo, T. W. (2015).
100% clean and renewable wind, water, and sunlight

(WWS) all-sector energy roadmaps for the 50 United States. *Energy & Environmental Science*, 8(7), 2093–2117. https://doi.org/10.1039/c5ee01283j

Jacobson, M. Z., Delucchi, M. A., Bauer, Z. A. F., Goodman, S. C., Chapman, W. E., Cameron, M. A., ... Yachanin, A. S. (2017). 100% clean and renewable wind, water, and sunlight (WWS) all-sector energy roadmaps for 139 countries of the world. *Joule*, 1(1), 108–121. https://doi.org/10.1016/j.joule.2017.07.005

Keenan, J. M., Hill, T., & Gumber, A. (2018). Climate gentrification: from theory to empiricism in Miami-Dade County, Florida. Environmental Research Letters, 13(5), 054001. https://doi.org/10.1088/1748-9326/aabb32

Kelley, C. P., Mohtadi, S., Cane, M. A., Seager, R. & Kushnir, Y. (2015). Climate change in the Fertile Crescent and implications of the recent Syrian drought. *Proceedings of the National Academy of Sciences*, 112(11), 3241-3246. doi:10.1073/pnas.1421533112

Klein, N. (2014). *This changes everything: Capitalism vs. the climate*. New York :Simon & Schuster.

Klein, N. (2017). How power profits from disaster. *The Guardian, July 6*.

Leiserowitz, A., Maibach, E., Roser-Renouf, C., Rosenthal, S., Cutler, M., & Kotcher, J. (2018). *Climate change in the American mind: March 2018*. Yale University and George Mason University. New Haven, CT: Yale Program on Climate Change Communication. Retrieved from http://climatecommunication.yale.edu/wp-content/uploads/2019/01/Climate-Change-American-Mind-December-2018.pdf

Lindsey, R. (2018). *Climate Change: Atmospheric Carbon Dioxide.* National Oceanic and Atmospheric Administration. Retrieved from https://www.climate.gov/news-features/understanding-climate/climate-change-atmospheric-carbon-dioxide

Livni, E. (2018, July 24). Kids suing governments over climate change keep winning. *Quartz.* Retrieved April 1, 2019, from https://qz.com/1334102/kids-around-the-world-are-suing-governments-over-climate-change-and-its-working

Ma, Q. (March 1998). Science briefs: Greenhouse gases: Refining the role of carbon dioxide. NASA GISS. Retrieved February 9, 2019, from https://www.giss.nasa.gov/research/briefs/ma_01/

Macy, J. (1996) Working through environmental despair. In T. Roszak, M. Gomes & Kanner (Eds.), *Ecopsychology: restoring the Earth, Healing the Mind.* A. San Francisco: Sierra Club Books. Retrieved from http://www.morning-earth.org/CE6109/EARTHJOURNAL/JOURNALING%20PDFs/PDFs%20copy%201/EARTH%20&%20SURVIVAL/MACY%20WORKING%20THRU%20DESPAIR.pdf

Matsuda, M. J. (1991). Beside My Sister, Facing the Enemy: Legal Theory out of Coalition. Stanford Law Review, 43(6), 1183–1192. https://doi.org/10.2307/1229035

Maxwell, C. (2018, April 05). America's sordid legacy on race and disaster recovery. Retrieved February 3, 2019, from https://www.americanprogress.org/issues/race/news/2018/04/05/448999/americas-sordid-legacy-race-disaster-recovery/

McGuire, P. D. -Kishebakabaykwe. (2010). Exploring Resilience and Indigenous Ways of Knowing 1. Pimadiswin, 8(2). 117-131. Retrieved from https://www.researchgate.net/publication/266473001_Exploring_Resilience_and_Indigenous_Ways_of_Knowing_1

McKibben, B. (2011). Something braver than trying to save the world. In K. Moore & M. P. Nelson, (Eds.), *Moral ground: Ethical action for a planet in peril* (pp. 174-177). San Antonio: Trinity University Press.

Medina-Ramón, M. & Schwartz, J. (2007). Temperature, temperature extremes, and mortality: a study of acclimatisation and effect modification in 50 US cities. *Occupational and Environmental Medicine*, 64(12), 827-833. Retrieved from https://oem.bmj.com/content/64/12/827

Meyer, R. (2019, January 15). The climate-change disaster scenario. *The Atlantic*. Retrieved February 4, 2019, from https://www.theatlantic.com/amp/article/579700/

Mikati, I., Benson, A. F., Luben, T. J., Sacks, J. D. & Richmond-Bryant, J. (April 1, 2018). Disparities in distribution of particulate matter emission sources by race and poverty status. *American Journal of Public Health* 108 (4),p. 480-485. DOI: 10.2105/AJPH.2017.304297

Milman, O. (2018, September 24). Where should you move to save yourself from climate change? *The Guardian*. Retrieved February 9, 2019, from https://www.theguardian.com/environment/2018/sep/24/climate-change-where-to-move-us-avoid-floods-hurricanes

Myers, S. S., Zanobetti, A., Kloog, I., Huybers, P., Leakey, A. D., Bloom, A. J., Carlisle, E., Dieterich, L. H., Fitzgerald, G., Hasegawa, T., Holbrook, N. M., Nelson, R. L., Ottman, M. J., Raboy, V., Sakai, H., Sartor, K. A., Schwartz, J., Seneweera, S., Tausz, M., … Usui, Y. (2014). Increasing CO2 threatens human nutrition. *Nature*, *510*(7503), 139-42. doi: 10.1038/nature13179

Nace, T. (2018, December 5). Harvard Scientists Begin Experiment To Block Out The Sun. Forbes. Retrieved from https://www.forbes.com/sites/trevornace/2018/12/05/harvard-scientists-begin-experiment-to-block-out-the-sun/?fbclid=IwAR1xh_TzwVut5MWzZ12EvY4Eys8fkZaYqguTRNuF34tlnz-JR1nbswH_4044#529b31140c24

National Association for the Advancement of Colored People (2018). Environmental & climate justice. Retrieved

February 3, 2019, from https://www.naacp.org/issues/
environmental-justice/

National Association for the Advancement of Colored People & Clean Air Task Force (November 2017). *Fumes across the fence-line: The health impacts of air pollution from oil & gas facilities on African American communities.* Retrieved from http://www.catf.us/wp-content/uploads/2017/11/CATF_Pub_FumesAcrossTheFenceLine.pdf

National Oceanic and Atmospheric Administration. (2011). Carbon cycle. Retrieved February 8, 2019, from https://www.noaa.gov/education/resource-collections/climate-education-resources/carbon-cycle

National Oceanic and Atmospheric Administration. (2013). ESRL News: Carbon Dioxide at Mauna Loa reaches new milestone: Tops 400 ppm. Retrieved February 9, 2019, from https://www.esrl.noaa.gov/news/2013/CO2400.html

Navasky, B. (2016, August 11). Robert F. Kennedy Jr. on the Environment, Election, and a "Dangerous" Donald Trump. Retrieved March 24, 2019, from https://www.vanityfair.com/news/2016/08/robert-f-kennedy-jr-on-the-environment-election-and-donald-trump

O'Rourke, T. P., Sr. (2017). RE: Yurok Comments to Draft Revisions to the Licensed Indian Traders Regulations, 25 CFR Part 140 [Letter written October 26, 2017 to Office of the Assistant Secretary of Indian Affairs]. Retrieved February 3, 2019, from https://www.bia.gov/sites/bia.gov/files/assets/as-ia/raca/pdf/31%20-%20Yurok%20Tribe.pdf

Parker, L. (2019, March 5). Support is surging for teens' climate change lawsuit. *National Geographic.* Retrieved April 1, 2019, from https://www.nationalgeographic.com/environment/2019/03/youth-climate-change-lawsuit-grows-support/

Peng, S., Huang, J., Sheehy, J. E., Laza, R. C., Visperas, R. M., Zhong, X., Centeno, G. S., Khush, G. S. & Cassman, K. G. (2004). Rice yields decline with higher night temperature from global warming. *Proceedings of the National Academy of Sciences* 101(27), 9971-9975. https://doi.org/10.1073/pnas.0403720101

Plumer, B. (2018, November 14). Part of the Answer to Climate Change May Be America's Trees and Dirt, Scientists Say. The New York Times. Retrieved from https://www.nytimes.com/2018/11/14/climate/climate-change-natural-solutions.html

Polin, R. & Hansen, T. (2019). Economics and Climate Justice Activism: Assessing the Fossil Fuel Divestment Movement. Political Economy Research Institute. University of Massachusetts Amherst. *Working Paper Series, 462.* Retrieved from https://www.peri.umass.edu/economists/robert-pollin/item/1076-economics-and-climate-justice-activism-assessing-the-fossil-fuel-divestment-movement

Popovich, N., Albeck-Ripka, L. & Pierre-Louis, K. (2017, October 5). 78 Environmental Rules on the Way Out Under Trump. *The New York Times.* Retrieved from https://www.nytimes.com/interactive/2017/10/05/climate/trump-environment-rules-reversed.html

Postelnicescu, C. (2016). Europe's new identity: the refugee crisis and the rise of nationalism. *Europe's Journal of Psychology*. 12. 203-209. doi: 10.5964/ejop.v12i2.1191.

Prud'Homme, A. (2011). Drought: A creeping disaster. *The New York Times.* Retrieved from http://www.nytimes.com/2011/07/17/opinion/sunday/17drought.html

Riebeek, H. (2005). The Rising Cost of Natural Hazards. *NASA Earth Observatory.* Retrieved from https://earthobservatory.nasa.gov/features/RisingCost

Roberts, D. (2012, August 14). Obama's stimulus package was a ginormous clean energy bill, says Michael Grunwald.

Grist. Retrieved March 31, 2019, from https://grist.org/politics/obamas-stimulus-package-was-a-ginormous-clean-energy-bill-says-michael-grunwald/

Roberts, D. (2019, March 30). The Green New Deal, explained. *Vox.* Retrieved March 31, 2019, from https://www.vox.com/energy-and-environment/2018/12/21/18144138/green-new-deal-alexandria-ocasio-cortez

Rogers, C. A., Wayne, P. M., Macklin, E. A., Muilenberg, M. L., Wagner, C. J., Epstein, P. R., & Bazzaz, F. A. (2006). Interaction of the onset of spring and elevated atmospheric CO2 on ragweed (Ambrosia artemisiifolia L.) pollen production. *Environmental Health Perspectives, 114*(6), 865-9. doi: 10.1289/ehp.8549

Rothschild, D. (2007). *The live earth global warming survival handbook: 77 essential skills to stop climate change—or live through it.* Emmaus, Pennsylvania: Rodale Books.

Samaras, C. (2019, January 2). Encourage electric vehicles. In Post Opinions Staff (eds) Here are 11 climate change policies to fight for in 2019. *The Washington Post.* Retrieved from https://www.washingtonpost.com/news/opinions/wp/2019/01/02/feature/opinion-here-are-11-climate-change-policies-to-fight-for-in-2019/?noredirect=on&utm_term=.a39fd0487101#2

Saulny, S. (2006). Clamoring to Come Home to New Orleans Projects. *New York Times, June 6.*

Schiermeier, Q. (2018). Droughts, heatwaves and floods: How to tell when climate change is to blame. *Nature,* 560(7716), 20-22. doi:10.1038/d41586-018-05849-9

Schulman, J. (2017, June 23). How 19 big-name corporations plan to make money off the climate crisis. *Mother Jones.* Retrieved February 9, 2019, from https://www.mother-jones.com/environment/2015/12/climate-change-business-opportunities/

Sloan, K. & Hostler, J. (2011). Yurok Tribe and Climate Change: An Initial Prioritization Plan. Report prepared for the Yurok Tribe. Yurok Tribe Environmental Program. Retrieved from http://www.yuroktribe.org/departments/ ytep/documents/YurokTribeandClimateChangePrioriti-zationPlan_Final.pdf

Solomon, C. G., & LaRocque, R. C. (2019). Climate Change — A Health Emergency. New England Journal of Medicine, 380(3), 209–211. https://doi.org/10.1056/ne-jmp1817067

Specia, M. (2019, February 15). Students Skip School Across Europe to Demand Climate Action. The New York Times. Retrieved from https://www.nytimes.com/2019/02/15/ world/europe/student-climate-protest-europe.html

Springmann, M., Clark, M., Mason-D'Croz, D., Wiebe, K., Bodirsky, B. L., Lassaletta, L., … Willett, W. (2018). Options for keeping the food system within environmental limits. Nature, 562(7728), 519–525. https://doi. org/10.1038/s41586-018-0594-0

UN Climate Change. (2017). Sweden plans to be carbon neutral by 2045. *UNFCCC*. Retrieved March 24, 2019, from https://unfccc.int/news/sweden-plans-to-be-carbon-neutral-by-2045

Union of Concerned Scientists. (2019). Nuclear Power & Global Warming. Retrieved April 3, 2019, from Union of Concerned Scientists website: https://www.ucsusa.org/ nuclear-power/nuclear-power-and-global-warming

United Nations Environment Programme. (2018). Emissions Gap Report. Retrieved from http://wedocs.unep.org/bit-stream/handle/20.500.11822/26895/EGR2018_Full-Report_EN.pdf

United Nations Permanent Forum on Indigenous Issues. (2008). Climate Change and Indigenous Peoples. Retrieved from https://www.un.org/development/desa/in-digenouspeoples/climate-change.html

U.S. Global Change Research Program. (2018). *Impacts, Risks, and Adaptation in the United States: Fourth National Climate As-*

sessment, Volume II [Reidmiller, D.R., C.W. Avery, D.R. Easterling, K.E. Kunkel, K.L.M. Lewis, T.K. Maycock, and B.C. Stewart (eds.)]. U.S. Global Change Research Program, Washington, DC, USA. doi: 10.7930/NCA4.2018.

Vinik, D. (2018, March 27). How Trump favored Texas over Puerto Rico. *Politico.* Retrieved February 3, 2019, from https://www.politico.com/story/2018/03/27/donald-trump-fema-hurricane-maria-response-480557

Wackernagel, M., Schulz, N. B., Deumling, D., Linares, A. C., Jenkins, M., Kapos, V., Monfreda, C., Loh, J., Myers, N., Norgaard, R. & Randers, J. (2002). Tracking the ecological overshoot of the human economy. *Proceedings of the National Academy of Sciences* 99 (14), 9266-9271. https://doi.org/10.1073/pnas.142033699

Wall, D. (2009). Indigenous Perspectives on Climate Change. *Institute for Tribal Environmental Professionals, Northern Arizona University, Native Voices newsletter,* Spring 2009. Retrieved from http://www7.nau.edu/itep/main/tcc/docs/tribes/tribes_IndigenousPers.pdf

Ward, P.,D. (2010). *The flooded earth: Our future in a world without ice caps.* New York: Basic Books.

Warlenius, R. (2018). Decolonizing the atmosphere: The climate justice movement on climate debt. *The Journal of Environment & Development,* 27(2), 131–155. https://doi.org/10.1177/1070496517744593

Warren, R., Price, J., Graham, E., Forestenhaeusler, N. & Vanderwal, J. (2018). The projected effect on insects, vertebrates, and plants of limiting global warming to 1.5°C rather than 2°C. *Science,* 360(6390), 791-795. doi: 10.1126/science.aar3646

Watts, N., Amann, M., Arnell, N., Ayeb-Karlsson, S., Belesova, K., Berry, H., . . . Costello, A. (2018). The 2018 report of the Lancet Countdown on health and climate change: Shaping the health of nations for centuries to come. *The Lancet.* doi:10.1016/s0140-6736(18)32594-7

Westerling, A. L., Hidalgo, H. G., Cayan, D. R. & Swetnam, T. W. (2006). Warming and earlier spring increase western U.S. forest wildfire activity. *Science* 313(5789), 940-943. doi: 10.1126/science.1128834

Wigley, T. M., & Santer, B. D. (2013). A probabilistic quantification of the anthropogenic component of twentieth century global warming. *Climate Dynamics,* 40(5-6), 1087-1102. doi:10.1007/s00382-012-1585-8

Willett, W., Rockström, J., Loken, B., Springmann, M., Lang, T., Vermeulen, S…. Murray, C. J. L. (2019). Food in the Anthropocene: the EAT–Lancet Commission on healthy diets from sustainable food systems. *The Lancet,* 393(10170), 447-492. https://doi.org/10.1016/S0140-6736(18)31788-4

Wilson, S. (2008). *Research Is Ceremony: Indigenous Research Methods.* Black Point, Nova Scotia & Winnipeg, Manitoba, Canada: Fernwood.

Wootson, C. R., Jr. (2018, November 26). The deadliest, most destructive wildfire in California's history has finally been contained. *Washington Post.* Retrieved November 30, 2018, from https://www.washingtonpost.com/nation/2018/11/25/camp-fire-deadliest-wildfire-californias-history-has-been-contained/?utm_term=.5686779981dd

World People's Conference on Climate Change and the Rights of Mother Earth. (2010, April 22). Peoples Agreement. Retrieved April 2, 2019, from https://pwccc.wordpress.com/support/

Yale Program on Climate Change Communication (2019). What we do. *Yale.* Retrieved from http://climatecommunication.yale.edu/

Yurok Tribe, [n.d.]. Culture. Retrieved on January 17, 2019 from http://www.yuroktribe.org/culture/

Zaelke, D. (2019, January 2). Be smart about your air conditioner. In Post Opinions Staff (eds) Here are 11 climate change policies to fight for in 2019. *The Washington Post.* Retrieved from https://www.washingtonpost.com/news/opinions/wp/2019/01/02/feature/opinion-here-are-11-climate-change-policies-to-fight-for-in-2019/?noredirect=on&utm_term=.a39fd0487101#2

Zhang, D. D., Brecke, P., Lee, H. F., He, Y. & Zhang, J. (2007). Global climate change, war, and population decline in recent human history. *Proceedings of the National Academy of Sciences* 104(49), 19214-19219. doi: 10.1073/pnas.0703073104

Zhu, K., Chiariello, N. R., Tobeck, T., Fukami, T., & Field, C. B. (2016). Nonlinear, interacting responses to climate limit grassland production under global change. *Proceedings of the National Academy of Sciences*, 113(38), 10589–10594. doi:10.1073/pnas.1606734113

8

Heroic Acts of Extraordinary People

SAMUEL P. OLINER

There's a light in this world: a healing spirit more powerful than any darkness we may encounter. We sometimes lose sight of this force when there is suffering, too much pain. Then suddenly, the spirit will emerge through the lives of ordinary people, who hear a call and answer in extraordinary ways.
- Richard Attenborough, from the film *Mother Teresa*

They did not ask any questions, and I did not think that they thought of themselves as doing anything heroic when they saved my life. They did it out of love.
- A Jewish Holocaust Rescued Survivor

One of the Holocaust rescuers that I interviewed said, "Without love and care, what have you got? A world without a heart." What do we know about altruistic love and compassion? Under what conditions will individuals or groups regard others as true neighbors deserving of their concern, care, and love? What are the reasons that millions of people remain bystanders and witness others suffer or men perish? In the 1940s and 1950s, the great sociologist Pitirim Sorokin was concerned with a crisis of divisiveness and dehumanization in Western civilization. His antidote to a divided and troubled world was altruistic love, or agape, which can be manufactured or instilled in millions of people if society as a whole and the various institutions in particular could model altruism and compassion.

Behavior can be described as altruistic when it: (1) is directed toward helping another, (2) involves a high risk or sacrifice to the actor, (3) is accompanied by no external reward, and (4) is voluntary. In the following discussion, I regard altruism as a continuum. At one end is heroic altruism, involving greater risk to the helper, and at the other is conventional altruism, not normally life threatening to the helper. In this chapter I include: (1) *heroic Gentile rescuers of Jews during the Holocaust,* comparing them with nonrescuers; and (2) *hospice volunteers,* who fall at the conventional end of the continuum, comparing them with nonhospice volunteers and nonvolunteers in general.

The data were gathered over several years. The research on rescuers of Jews in Nazi-occupied Europe consisted of a sample of bona fide rescuers, recognized by Yad Vashem, who were compared with bystanders and rescued survivors.[1] Ninety-three hospice volunteers and 73 nonhospice volunteers were interviewed using both open and closed-ended questions in order to learn the salient factors that motivated them.

In addition to asking questions about respondents' backgrounds, upbringings, and values, we were interested in the triggering mechanisms that moved these individuals to help. We identified three categories of rescuers/helpers. Those individuals who took part in rescue/helping activities and had internalized highly valued norms—the expectations of social

---

1. For a detailed discussion of methodology, see Oliner and Oliner (1988). Yad Vashem is the Holocaust Martyrs and Heroes Remembrance Authority, established in 1953 by an act of the Israeli Knesset in order to commemorate the 6 million Jews murdered by the Nazis.

groups, their moral community, or leadership of a highly regarded authority—we term *normocentric*. Rescuers/helpers who responded to external events that arouse a heightened sense of empathy, were considered empathic. Rescuers/helpers who responded to their own overarching moral principles (mainly autonomously derived), who were moved to action by external events that they interpreted as violations of social justice and human rights principles, were deemed *autonomous/principled*.[2]

Looking closely at the two groups, one can discern common triggering mechanisms for acting on behalf of others. My discussion focuses on the common motivating factors of the two groups and draws conclusions about the implications.

Gentile Rescuers During the Holocaust

The study of rescuers was guided by the following three questions: (1) Was rescue or helping primarily a matter of opportunity, that is, external circumstances or situational factors (recognizing that help was needed (awareness); having hiding places, food, and so forth)? (2) Was rescue or helping primarily a matter of individual character, that is, personal attributes such as empathy, caring for others, and so forth, and if so, what were those traits and how were they acquired? (3) Was rescue or helping a matter of moral and ethical values?

The study, which was undertaken in the early 1980s, included Gentile rescuers residing in Poland, France, Germany, Italy, and Norway and rescuers who had immigrated to the United States and Canada after the war. It involved the use of scales for self-esteem, social responsibility, locus of control, empathy, and a commonality scale developed by

---

2. For further discussion of empathic, normocentric, and principled motivations, see Oliner and Oliner (1988) and Reykowski (1987).

Oliner and Oliner (1988)[3,4]; also, importantly, in-depth taped interviews were conducted with more than 700 respondents. In addition, there was a comparison group of bystanders. A group of rescued survivors were also interviewed because it was felt that they might have insights into why the rescuers helped them during these trying times. The comparison of the rescuers and bystanders showed that both had *equal opportunity to rescue* and both were *equally aware of the tragedy and plight of Jews*. Whereas rescuers took action, bystanders refrained from helping. We can say with a degree of confidence that opportunity may have facilitated rescue somewhat but did not by any means determine it.

Of the several reasons expressed by the rescuers for their actions, at least one ethical or humanitarian reason or value was cited by an overwhelming majority (87%). The ethical reasons cited included justice and fairness; Jewish victims were deserving of help and persecution of the innocent could not be justified. However, the ethic that mattered most was the *ethic of care and compassion*. Most of the rescuers' helping

---

3. The Social Responsibility Scale was developed by L. Berkowitz and K. Luterman (1968); see Oliner and Oliner (1988, p. 376). The Internal/External Locus of Control Scale was developed by J. B. Rotter (1966); I used an adaptation developed by G. Gurin, P. Gurin, and B. M. Morrison (1978). The Self-Esteem Scale I used was developed by M. Rosenberg (1965); see Oliner and Oliner (1988, p. 378). The Empathy Scale was developed by A. Mehrabian and N. A. Epstein (1972).
4. Oliner and Oliner (1988). Using a Likert scale, we asked respondents whether they have something in common with diverse other people. The question asked was: "Some people think that they have things in common with others. Please tell me if you have very much in common with the following groups, something in common, not very much in common, or nothing at all in common." This commonality scale was originally developed for the research on the rescuers of Jews in Nazi-occupied Europe, so the groups identified were rich people, poor people, Catholics, Protestants, Jews, Turks, Gypsies, and Nazis. For purposes of the hospice volunteer study, the list was amended to: rich people, poor people, Catholics, Protestants, Jews, Native Americans, Mexican Americans, Black Americans, and homosexuals.

was rooted in a need to assume personal responsibility to relieve suffering and pain. While some felt a particular affection toward Jews they knew, most felt an obligation *toward others in general*. Pity, compassion, concern, and affection made up 76% of the reasons rescuers gave for extending help to strangers. More than 90% said they had helped at least one stranger, as well as a friend. Typical expressions of rescuers were the following: "Our religion says we are our brother's keepers." "I sensed I had in front of me human beings who were hunted down like wild animals. This aroused a feeling of brotherhood with the desire to help." "I was always filled with love for everyone, for every creature, for things. I infuse life into every object. For me, everything is alive."

Caring compelled action. Rescuers assumed responsibility—not because others required them to but because failure to act would destroy innocent people: "I knew they were taking them and that they wouldn't come back. I didn't think I could live knowing that I could have done something."

Acquisition of Caring Values

Many values of caring and social responsibility were acquired directly from parents.[5] Although parents played an important role for both rescuers and nonrescuers, significantly more rescuers perceived them as benevolent figures who modeled moral and spiritual values conducive to forming close, caring attachments to other people. The values rescuers learned from their parents—and from other significant people in their lives—differed significantly from those learned by nonrescuers. One value was related to ethics and

---

5. By values, I mean an enduring organization of beliefs concerning preferable modes of conduct and/or states of existence, along with continued values of importance and a collective conception of what is considered good, desirable, and proper, or bad, undesirable, and improper in a culture. Schulman and Mekler (1985) define moral values as consisting of empathy, kindness, and responsibility.

ethical behavior. Significantly more rescuers said that they owed an obligation to *all people*. We term an orientation of caring for all living things *extensivity*.[6] The extensive-personality predisposition comprises emotionally healthy attachment to family and inclusion of diverse others as deserving of care: "They taught me to respect all human beings." "I have learned from my parents' generosity to be open, to help people. I learned to be good to one's neighbor ... to be responsible, concerned, and considerate. To work and to work hard. But also to help—to the point of leaving one's work to help one's neighbor." "He taught me to love my neighbor—to consider him my equal whatever his nationality or religion. He taught me especially to be tolerant." "She taught me to be responsible, honest, to respect older people, to respect all people not to tease or criticize people of other religions. She taught me to be good."

Significantly more rescuers felt a sense of responsibility toward others—feeling an obligation to help even when nothing could be gained for themselves. In contrast, many nonrescuers felt exempt from such obligations. Nonrescuers often were unaffected by such suffering, more detached, and less receptive to other people's helplessness and pain. "I could not comprehend that innocent persons should be persecuted just because of race. We all come from the same God." "They believed in humanity and were incredulous that people were being killed simply because of their Jewishness." "They are very noble, very fine people. They felt that people should not be hurt for no reason at all. When they saw injustice, they felt they should do something.... Whether it was religion or their sense of justice they didn't mind paying the price for this."

---

6. For a detailed discussion on extensivity, see Oliner and Oliner (1988). For an excellent discussion on caring and compassion, see Wuthnow (1991).

Modes of discipline were also important in inculcating ethical behavior. As children, rescuers were more likely to have been disciplined by reasoning and explanation of the consequences of their misbehavior, rather than by verbal or physical punishment, as was common among nonrescuers.

Normocentric Motivation

For some rescuers, witnessing arrest or persecution of Jews triggered a response based on the norms of the social group with whom they strongly identified and to which they looked for moral guidance. Their motivations arose not from their connection with the victim but from feelings of obligation to their group or community—the implicit and explicit rules of which they felt obligated to obey. Thus, for normocentric rescuers, inaction was a violation of the community's religious and moral norms of behavior. For them, feelings of obligation or duty were frequently coupled with anticipation of guilt or shame should they fail to act. The norms of the community, its habits and culture, encouraged tolerance and helping. For certain Italian rescuers—military officials, religious leaders, and diplomats—such social norms legitimated and encouraged them to sabotage, thwart, slow down, and resist deportation of Jews. Approximately 52% of our respondents said they were motivated by obligations that fell into the normocentric category.

Such an internalized *normocentric* orientation characterized a Danish rescuer who began his rescuing activities in this way:

> In 1943, on the twenty-ninth of August, we heard that the Nazis were going to make a razzia and put Danish Jews into German concentration camps. Together with friends from the police department, we organized a refugee organization—it had no name. We ferried by taxi, and even by police cars, down to the commercial fishing

harbor and arranged for people to go over to Sweden. The harbors were controlled partly by the German Navy but also by the Coast Police—a special department of the Danish police force. We had to be rather careful to do our "shipment" from places where controllers would not stop fishing boats and where we knew German Navy patrol boats would not be present. After a week's time, we managed to get all people of Jewish extraction out of the country-7,000 of them.

Empathic Motivation

Empathic motivation involves concern with the fate of another in distress; compassion, sympathy, and pity are its characteristic expressions. Reactions may be emotional or cognitive and frequently contain elements of both. The following account demonstrates an instance in which empathy was the major motivator of rescuer behavior:

In 1942, I was on my way home from town and was almost near home when M. came out of the bushes. I looked at him, in striped camp clothing, his head bare, shod in clogs. He might have been about thirty or thirty-two years old. And he begged me, his hands joined like for a prayer—that he had escaped from Majdanek and could I help him? He joined his hands in this way, knelt down in front of me, and said: "You are like the Virgin Mary." It still makes me cry. "If I get through and reach Warsaw, I will never forget you." Well, how could one not have helped such a man? (A Polish rescuer)

Human compassion. When someone comes and says "I escaped from the camp," what is the alternative? One alternative is to push him out and close the door—the other is to pull him into the house and say, "Sit down, relax, wash up. You will be as hungry as we are because we have only this bread."

Empathic reactions create overpowering feelings that lead people to react spontaneously: Some rescuers could not stand by when seeing people in pain, could not withstand the agony and grief it caused them. The direct face-to-face encounter with a distressed person further heightened the impulse to act. Thirty eight percent of rescuers said that they were moved empathically to their first helping act.

Principled Motivation

People with *principled* motivation, autonomously derived, interpreted persecution of Jews as a violation of their own moral precepts. Unlike normocentric motivation, which prescribed a certain group behavior, *principled* motivation involved acting on one's own. The main goal of such behavior was to reaffirm and apply the individual's personal moral principles, even when their actions on behalf of others might prove futile. An Italian rescuer, responding to the statement that what rescuers did was extraordinary (i.e., that rescuing a great number of people was a truly remarkable act), answered that it really was something simple. He did it without considering risk or thinking about being either lauded or maligned. He did it because it had to be done, and he didn't even weigh the danger. Persecution was unacceptable; justice had to be done.

> No, no. It was all something very simple. Nothing grandiose was done. It was done simply without considering risk, without thinking about whether it would be an occasion for recognition or to be maligned, it was in effect done out of innocence. I didn't think I was doing

Samuel P. Oliner

anything other than what should be done, or that I was in any special danger because of what I was doing. Justice had to be done. Persecution of the innocents was unacceptable.

Principle-motivated rescuers felt challenged in fundamental ways by the acts they were observing—they felt that allowing such acts was tantamount to condoning such behavior. Only a small minority of rescuers, approximately 11%, fell into this category.

The Religious Factor and Rescuers

Although no officially organized bodies in the top echelons of religious leadership advocated rescue of Jews, there are examples of religious institutions that were deeply involved. Ewa Kurek (1997) studied convents and orphanages in Poland, interviewing nuns in various orders and the children who survived because of them. The nuns had no central authority to coordinate common action and no communication between orders; they performed these heroic acts on their own. When asked what motivated them to rescue the children, they usually gave a dual response: (1) they rescued for missionary reasons—to convert them to Catholicism, and (2) for purely humanitarian reasons, dictated by Christian ethics. They asked Jesus for advice and always concluded that rescue was what He would have wanted. These nuns now look at their deeds with great pride; the Jewish children (now adults) express great appreciation for the nuns' heroism.

The Huguenot congregation in Le Chambon, France, under the strong leadership of Pastor Andre Trocme and his assistant Edouard Theis, were by sheer determination able to rescue 5,000 Jews in the Le Chambon area. This was a moral community; it knew its own history of suffering, had internalized well the parable of the Good Samaritan, and acted upon it (Sauvage, 1985–1986).

Father Ruffino Niccacci of Assisi, Italy, saved about 5,000 Jews. This Franciscan monk operated a refuge and underground escape route in Nazi-occupied Italy that began in the summer of 1943 when nine Jews appealed for sanctuary, and his bishop charged him with the task of saving Jews. Eventually, the Nazis suspected that Father Ruffino and other friars were hiding and transporting Jews, and they mounted sudden raids. Had they discovered the victims, they would probably have been executed along with the friars and innocent citizens. Father Ruffino eventually organized several hundred priests and half the townspeople: local porters, cleaning women, and even hangers-on at Nazi police headquarters coalesced into an efficient counterespionage service. When danger threatened, they gave the priests advance warning (Fischman, 1964).

Although we cannot say that religiosity determines rescue, there are religious individuals who internalized the value of compassion and helping from their parents. Douglas Huneke (1985–1986), examining the backgrounds of major righteous rescuers of Jews, showed that they were often motivated by religious beliefs. Herman (Fritz) Graebe, a German rescuer of many Jews in the Ukraine, was greatly influenced by his profoundly religious mother, who constantly preached the ethic of helping as one of the most important aspects of human behavior.

In the homes of some religiously oriented rescuers, there were discussions about Jews—that they were God's people—which simultaneously emphasized an ethic of care. I reached the conclusion that parental values and culture were importantly correlated with rescue behavior. Religion, in this context, was a lesser factor than other aspects of living and relating, but it was embedded in the whole of living, in which trust and mutuality, nurtured by parental caring, were reenacted in religious expressions.

Moral and Political Climate Conducive To Rescue

Yahil (1969), Zuccotti (1987), Ramati (1978), Carpi (1977), Chary (1972), Flender (1964), Friedman (1978), and Baron (1988) have addressed climates in which social, cultural, and political conditions were more conducive to rescue of Jews and in which anti-Semitism was less rampant. Partly because of such a climate, most of the Danish Jewish population was shipped to Sweden and rescued. In Italy, 85% of the Jewish population was rescued, which is attributed to a general lack of antiSemitism and an absence of sharply drawn distinctions between Jewish-Italians and other Italians. Fleischner (1988), Kurek-Lesik (1992), and Huneke (1985) concluded that a major factor for rescue was compassion for Jewish victims. Others found that Christian charity and other religious factors help explain rescue. Among these are Baron (1992), Sauvage (1986), Huneke (1986), Fleischner (1988), Zeitoun (1988), and Oliner and Oliner (1988 and in their latest analysis of their data).

Hospice Volunteers

Volunteerism can be defined as a nonspontaneous helping behavior for which one receives no material compensation. It can be parochial, within one's own social group, or nonparochial. Nonparochial volunteerism is a form of conventional altruism in that it is directed at others beyond the parochial group and is accompanied by no external reward. It has been established in the literature that volunteers generally score high on measures of *empathy, social responsibility, and moral development* (Allen & Rushton, 1983). Piliavin (1990) states that individuals are more likely to volunteer if their parents did; their parents modeled volunteerism. The work of hospice volunteers can be said to be nonspontaneous, nonparochial, prosocial behavior that fits the definition of conventional altruism.

In 1967 Dr. Cicely Saunders, a British physician, established St. Christopher's, a medical facility for the care of the terminally ill in London. The hospice model of care developed by Saunders and others was less an innovation in health care than it was a return to an earlier model. The name "hospice" comes from the Latin word hospes, meaning guest. Like other derivations of the root word, such as hospitality, host, hotel, and hospital, it connotes the ideas of kindness and generosity to strangers and travelers. Ancient and medieval hospices were sanctuaries for poor travelers, the sick and the dying, and religious pilgrims. In the medieval period, hospices were generally run by religious orders who saw the care of the poor and sick as part of the Lord's work. For many centuries hospices and hospitals were one and the same. Life was thought of as a journey from this world to the next, and all travelers were in need of comfort, whether they were journeying from one land to another or from one life to the next.

During the past century, the care of the sick and dying ceased being a private and religious function and became a governmental one (Buckingham, 1983, p. 12). Advances in medical science and technology resulted in a total transformation of medical science from a palliative model to an aggressively therapeutic one. However, in the post World War II years, some health care professionals began to suggest that although the system was well equipped to deal with acute life-threatening situations, it was ill equipped to meet the special needs of terminally ill patients. Indeed, the terminally ill patient was considered a sign of medical failure and frequently shunned by medical personnel, who were at a loss to deal with patients to whom they could not offer any hope of recovery. This medical avoidance of death was accompanied by an increasing aversion to death because it was no longer so visible. No longer was death a part of everyday life. Few people died at home, and many died alone in hospitals, separated from their families.

St. Christopher's Hospice set out to address these problems by seeking to combine the old concept of hospitality with the medical skill and technology of the modern hospital (Buckingham, 1983,p 13). Emphasis was placed on control of pain and other adverse symptoms. Families were incorporated into the care plans for each person of the patient, staff continued bereavement care for the patient's families.

Both Saunder's writings and those of Dr. Elisabeth Kübler-Ross (1997) were well received in the United States; by 1974 the first hospice program was operating in this country in New Haven, Connecticut. Since that time, approximately 2,000 hospice programs have been established in the United States. Hospice programs in this country vary considerably in design, ranging from those that rely on volunteer care and charge nothing for their services, to institutionalized programs with staff who are paid by third-party payers (Medicare, private carriers, state and local government). Although there are some in-patient hospices in this country, home care is the norm (Buckingham, 1983, p. 13).

That hospice programs have been able to provide a high level of personal care, is due in no small part to the effort of volunteers. Nearly every hospice program employs both laypersons and health professionals as volunteers in their programs. These volunteers are interviewed by hospice staff and, if accepted, undergo orientation and training before being assigned to patients and their families. Volunteers meet regularly with each other and with staff to discuss both patient care and the problems they themselves may be facing as part of their interaction with the terminally ill and their families.

My study had a twofold purpose: to identify the characteristics and motivations of hospice volunteers in comparison with nonvolunteers and to compare these findings with other research on volunteerism. The study was guided by two considerations Was the decision to become a hospice volunteer a matter of opportunity, that is a result of particular facilitating external circumstances, or was it the result of character, that is a result of particular values and attitudes?

To answer this question, 93 hospice volunteers from Humboldt and Marin Counties in California and from the Boston area were interviewed by trained interviewers. These interviews were recorded and transcribed. Seventy-three non-hospice volunteers (who may have volunteered in other settings) and nonvolunteers were given an abbreviated version of the hospice volunteer questionnaire, which they completed by themselves. This group was categorized by level of volunteering. Forty-three respondents, who volunteered substantially more than 6 hours per week, were classified as high-level volunteers. The other 30 individuals either volunteered occasionally or not at all.

The questionnaire consisted of three sections, which included both open-and closed-ended questions. Section A dealt with the characteristics of the family milieu during the respondents' childhood and the relationship between family members. Section B explored the respondents' parental, educational, and occupational background, their political beliefs, religiosity, values, and the disciplinary techniques used on volunteers. Section C focused on such matters as the respondents' degree of closeness to parents and significant others; religious background and relative health of parents and significant others; whether parents or significant others volunteered; and how parents felt about their own volunteer experience. Also included in Section C were 42 personality items comprising four psychological scales:"(1) the Social Responsibility Scale, developed by Berkowitz and Luterman (1968); (2) the Internal/External Locus of Control Scale, developed by Rotter (1966) and modified by Gurin, Gurin, and Morrison (1978); (3) the Self-Esteem Scale, developed by Rosenberg (1965); and (4) the Empathy Scale, developed by Mehrabian and Epstein (1972) and modified by E. Midlarsky (1981). In addition, we included Oliner and Oliner's Diversity Scale, which measures identification with nonparochial groups.

In addition to the categorization of nonhospice volunteers by amount of time spent in volunteer activities, this sample was also separated into two groups based on the nature of volunteer activity, that is, parochial and nonparochial volunteer behavior. Nonparochial volunteers were those who volunteered beyond their own social group, whereas parochial volunteers limited their volunteer activities to their children's schools or their churches, clubs, or political groups. The responses to closed-ended questions were analyzed by computer, and open-ended questions were assessed and coded into categories for comparison.[7] The nature of the sample did allow for simple correlations and percentages.

The hospice sample was 73% female with 88% of the sample being 40 years old or older. It was overwhelmingly Caucasian (96.9%), and, although only 57% identified with a Judeo-Christian religious tradition, 85% described themselves as "very" or "somewhat" religious. Within the hospice sample, 97% had prior volunteer experience. Seventy-five percent reported that their mothers had volunteered and 49% that their fathers had done so.

Within the high-level volunteer group, 63% were female, 58% were over 40, and 83% were Caucasian. Seventy-six percent identified themselves as Protestant, Catholic, or Jewish, and 83% described themselves as "very" or "somewhat" religious. Of the high-level volunteers, 58% reported

---

7. For example, for question B19, which asked, "What was the most important thing you learned from your mother?" responses could be grouped under headings such as religion, compassion, kindness, independence, getting ahead, and so forth.

that their mothers had volunteered, and 49% that their fathers were volunteers. Within the low-level and nonvolunteer group, which was 58% female, 36% were over 40 and 80% were Caucasian. Ninety-two percent were either Protestant or Catholic, and 76% described themselves as "very" or "somewhat" religious.

Comparisons of hospice volunteers and nonhospice volunteers demonstrated no significant difference with regard to self-esteem or internal/external locus of control. Hospice volunteers and high-level volunteers scored significantly higher on measures of empathy and social responsibility, and hospice volunteer scores were higher than those of high-level volunteers on these two measures. Hospice volunteers scored significantly higher on measures of intrinsic religiosity, that is, religiosity that is implicit in its nature and in the personal orientation by which one lives as opposed to an extrinsic religious orientation that is utilitarian, explicit, and self-justifying in nature.

In response to the question, "What is the most important thing you learned from your mother?", the most frequent response among hospice volunteers was religion, followed by kindness, compassion, and empathy. Religion was also found to be the most frequent response in the nonhospice group.

Hard work and honesty were the most frequent responses in both samples to the question, "What is the most important thing you learned from your father?"

There was little difference between the two groups when asked who they most admired, parents and spouses being the most frequent response of those who cited individuals known personally. The next most frequent response among hospice volunteers was hospice workers and administrators or hospice patients.

Another question, which sought to illustrate the respondents' values and beliefs, asked what advice they would give to young people about what things are important in life.[8] The most frequently cited advice by hospice volunteers was to be true to oneself and respect others, followed by advice to "follow your heart," to be aware of self and others, and to recognize one's connection to others. High-level volunteers' most frequent responses were similar, whereas low-level volunteers' and nonvolunteers' most frequent responses were to have faith in God, enjoy life, and be responsible.

The responses to this question were then classified as to extensivity, that is, whether they referred to the respondent's connection to others in terms of service, care, respect, and acceptance. Half of the hospice volunteers and high-level volunteers gave extensive responses, whereas among the low-level volunteers and nonvolunteers extensive responses were found in 25% or less of the responses. This tendency toward extensivity was also found to correlate with type of volunteering when the nonhospice volunteers were categorized on that dimension. Forty-five percent of nonparochial volunteers gave extensive responses, whereas only one third of the parochial volunteers mentioned connection to others and putting the welfare of others before their own.

By their responses to the diversity scale, hospice volunteers and high-level volunteers demonstrated that they felt they had more in common with diverse groups of people than did the low-level or nonvolunteer group. This included more favorable attitudes toward African Americans, Jewish Americans, homosexuals, and so forth.

That hospice volunteers appeared to value acceptance of others is also indicated by their response to a question regarding what groups they have strong negative feelings toward. Of the 52 hospice volunteers who admitted strong

---

8. This was question C35: "If you had an opportunity to speak to a group of young people, what kinds of advice would you offer them? That is, what would you consider the most important thing about life?"

negative feelings toward a group, 95% identified groups such as the Ku Klux, Aryan Nation, religious fundamentalists, bigots, or polarizing and intolerant groups.

Although there was no apparent difference in history of discipline as children among the groups, with over 95% in all groups responding that they were disciplined as children, there did appear to be a difference in the type of discipline reported. Thirty-nine percent of the hospice volunteers reported being physically disciplined, whereas 60% of the high-level volunteers and 78% of the low-level and nonvolunteers reported physical discipline.

Motivations for Volunteering

The responses to the question regarding motivations for volunteering were placed within four categories: (1) self-enhancement, (2) empathic, (3) normocentric, and (4) principled. No hospice volunteer gave only a single motive for volunteering, and many gave several.

Sixty-eight hospice volunteers gave responses that can be categorized as self-enhancing, including responses describing a need to confront or learn more about death, a desire to feel needed and useful, a need to develop a sense of connection to the community, and a desire for job-related experience: "I was probably trying to fill a personal need. I was looking for something meaningful to do." "I sought it out to become involved in something where I was needed."

Others wanted to feel better about themselves, fill up time, or feel less lonely. Eleven individuals described their motives as "selfish." "I had a purely selfish motive in that I thought it would be a good way to get into the community. ...I needed to get away from the rather shallow, glitzy life I lived in New York."

Still, others described how this motivation was transformed by the hospice experience: "When I first went in as a volunteer, I was trying to fill a lot of stuff in me, and now I feel like I'm more sure of who I am, and I'm able to be there as a true person, to really be there."

But the most frequent response concerned the need to confront death, either because of fear or simply lack of knowledge. Many of these individuals also remarked on how working with hospice had led to an acceptance of death: "I think that part of our message is that dying is part of our whole life journey. The media tells us that we never have to grow old if we use certain products, we are told we can live forever if we have enough money ... whatever they do, it's just not accepting this wonderful rite of passage that is ours. It's a gift. We've lost it." "I've lived most of my life, but I still have some time to go... but identifying what's around the corner feels good to me, seeing that death is really not such a terrible thing, that it's really the last stage in life."

A similar percentage of both high and low-level nonhospice volunteers gave responses that could be categorized as self-enhancing. Most frequent were responses that referred to enjoyment, fulfillment, and reward, followed by references to a desire to feel helpful and needed.

Seventy percent of the hospice volunteers gave responses that could be characterized as empathic, that is, they reflected an identification with hospice patients and their needs. This figure compares with 12% for the high-level volunteers and 5.5% for the low-level volunteers.

The most frequent of all motivations given for becoming a hospice volunteer was the death of a parent, spouse, or close friend. Thirty-seven percent of the hospice volunteers included this as a motivation. Those respondents who indicated that the experience was a negative one and who wished to spare or mitigate that negative experience for others were categorized as empathic. One woman whose husband had died of cancer commented on how the painful experience led her to volunteer: "I felt I could do something for someone that I wished I could have had when my husband died. I wanted to offer what I would have liked to have had."

Three of the hospice volunteers were cancer patients themselves and related that they knew how it felt to suffer alone and wanted to spare others. Others had had bad experiences with cancer patients and wanted to prevent the same bad experiences from happening to others. One woman spoke of being in the hospital for her own cancer treatment and encountering a woman who was being forced to accept treatment against her will: "I felt so sorry for this woman. She seemed so alone. And I remembered going in there not knowing if I could do anything. ... She was in a situation that nobody understood. Nobody even cared what she was feeling."

Another volunteer, a registered nurse, related an experience from her early nursing career: "I would see nurses virtually ignoring dying patients. Giving them their medication, changing their beds, but avoiding any real contact. I thought, what good are we if we can't give comfort to these people? Whenever I had a patient who was dying I would really try to spend whatever free time I had, giving them sips of water, back rubs ... just holding their hand. But I always had to leave knowing the next shift would ignore them again."

Those who cited a personal experience with the death of a significant person in their lives were equally divided between the aforementioned categories: those who wished to spare others the difficulty they themselves had experienced and those whose experience had involved hospice and who volunteered out of a sense of gratitude and a desire to share that positive experience: "I felt I owed them an obligation to contribute whatever I could ... I wanted to continue my association with those marvelous people who did so much for her and me too."

As previously stated, volunteering is a widely accepted social norm in the United States, perhaps more so than in any other Western country. Thus it can be said that many volunteer because of social expectations and pressure, that is, for normocentric reasons. Forty-four percent of the hospice volunteers gave responses that were considered to be normo-centric. Only 7% of high-level volunteers gave normocentric responses, and none of the low-level volunteers gave responses that could be interpreted as normative.

Hospice volunteers often referred to the importance of volunteering, reflecting societal norms: "I think as you get older, you start thinking, what am I doing for my community, and you start feeling the need to just do something, to put something back." Still others stated that they were directly re-cruited: "Some people that I knew were volunteers, and they recruited me. They told me I would be good at it and they needed volunteers."

The fourth category, principled responses, were those that reflected underlying principles or beliefs and that were cited by 30% of the hospice volunteers as compared with 5% and 11% of the high- and low-level volunteers, respectively. The responses arise out of abstract, ethical principles, which hold that all humanity is deserving of justice, fairness, and equity and that caring and compassion should be available to all-friends and family, as well as other diverse groups. It is difficult to extract purely "principled" responses from nor-mocentric or empathic forces, but generally they indicate a more autonomous or axiological nature than normocentric responses.

The most frequent response was a strong belief in the hospice concept, as seen in the following statements: "I had seen on several occasions how inadequate the health care system was in taking care of dying patients. I felt there had to be a better way. Hospice has a philosophy that I am very comfortable with, that is, that people have a right to live until the second they die ... a right to live as well as we can pos-sibly make it for them." "I guess I thought I could make a difference in the way people died and the way they went out of this lifetime, make it a little less difficult maybe ... It's nice to have someone there when you need them. I'm strong, I can help." "I believe we all need a hand getting into life and we all need a hand getting out of life."

Other responses included in this category reflected a more generalized belief in the role of service that, in contrast to the normocentric responses, indicated an autonomous belief in the importance of service to others: "I think it is important for people to know they are part of a society. So many people think that what they do doesn't affect other people. There isn't anyone like that. You affect everyone, every person who touches you or the groups you touch."

Hoffman (1983) has said that the development of the caring, altruistic individual requires setting boundaries between right and wrong, moral and immoral, and deviant and normative behavior. In childhood, the hospice volunteers were more likely to have been disciplined by reasoning and less by physical means than the non-volunteers, a finding that reflects our findings on rescuers and nonrescuers in Nazi-occupied Europe. In addition, there appears to be a cultural theme in America that we have an obligation, even a divine obligation, to contribute to the betterment of the community (Adams, 1990). Throughout U.S. history, the truest form of charity in volunteering is found in local, one-on-one relationships. Adams (1991) examined 159 articles from 19 popular magazines between 1980 and 1989 focusing on motivation for volunteering and charitable giving. He found that Americans give because they want to help other people, especially those with whom they share communities.

Summary and Implications

Based on the data on the two groups, there is no single motivating explanation that triggers people to behave compassionately for the welfare of others. Rather, there are a variety of factors that converge to motivate them to help. We found that Gentile rescuers risked their lives because they had learned *compassion, caring norms, and efficacy* and could assume *responsibility for diverse others.* This increased extensivity is demonstrated by higher acceptance of diverse groups and increased awareness of the connectedness with all humankind. They had also acquired a *moral code of justice* and fairness from parents, significant others, and institutions, which dictated to them that the innocent must not be persecuted. Religious factors are evident; and although religiosity per se did not determine rescue, those who had learned religious principles of love and responsibility in a caring home were among the rescuers.

In the hospice volunteer study, we discerned factors such as *empathy*, including the need for *affiliation, reciprocal helping, self-enhancement, and an internalized norm of care.* Although there exist no profound differences between hospice volunteers and other volunteers, the former group has been shown to be more extensive in its outlook. Hospice volunteers also exhibit a higher degree of intrinsic religiosity, despite a lower incidence of affiliation with mainstream religious traditions. These differences can partially be explained by the role models and discipline styles of the volunteers' backgrounds and, in the case of hospice volunteers, the experience of the loss of a significant individual prior to their decision to volunteer for hospice. It should be pointed out that the assessment of hospice volunteers' attitudes occurred after the decision to volunteer and after one or more experiences with hospice. It is difficult to separate previous beliefs and attitudes from those shaped by the hospice experience. In fact, some participants referred directly to the transformation of beliefs and attitudes as a result of their experience.

Motivations were found to be varied, with most hospice volunteers citing self enhancement and empathic motives, whereas nonhospice volunteers overwhelmingly cited self-enhancement reasons. The findings of other motivational studies of volunteering were reinforced-individuals seek out volunteer experiences that meet their particular needs for self-esteem, education, and social responsibility. The hospice organization was found to be remarkably effective in retaining volunteers, and this success was felt to be the result of the organization's ability to provide support, affiliation, and self-actualization for its volunteers.

So what can we say from studying these two groups of individuals? First, acts of heroic or conventional altruism are not the exclusive province of larger-than life figures. Rather, they are usually the *deeds of ordinary people* whose moral courage arises out of the routine of their daily lives; their characteristic ways of feeling; their perceptions of what authority should be obeyed; the rules and models of moral conduct they learned from parents, friends, schools, religion, political leaders, co-workers, and peer groups; and what kind of moral code is to be followed. What we see is that these two groups at various times of their lives were engaged in moral behavior in general.

As Iris Murdoch (1970/1985) has observed, the moral life is not something that emerges suddenly in the context of traumas. Rather, it arises piecemeal in the routine business of living. It begins with parents who emphasize broadly inclusive ethical values, including caring and social responsibility, which they teach in the context of loving family relationships. Thus, assuming caring roles seems to require pre-rehearsed scripts and previously learned skills acquired in ordinary activities. If we are serious about cultivating these characteristics associated with helping others, then we cannot leave the job to parents alone. Other social institutions religious, educational, and workplace-need to seriously reconsider their roles, their responsibilities, and their routine behaviors. Until social institutions accept responsibility to nurture inclusive ethical commitment in a context of caring environments, it is likely that no more than a fragment of the population can be counted on to engage in heroic and conventional altruism. It is my firm conviction that caring and social responsibility can be nurtured in individuals and groups and that kindness and helping is rewarding and empowering not only for those helped but also for those who help.

Albert Schweitzer said it best: "One thing I know: The only ones among you who will be truly happy are those who have sought and found how to serve."

Reprinted by permission of Stephen G. Post, Lynn G. Underwood, Jeffrey P. Schloss, William B. Hurlbut. Eds. *Altruism and Altruistic Love*

Notes

I especially want to acknowledge Kathleen M. Lee for her participation with me on the research on hospice volunteers. In addition, I wish to gratefully acknowledge Kia Ora Zeleny, a Humboldt State University sociology graduate student, for her assistance with this chapter.

References

Adams, D. S. (1990). Issues and Ideas in the Culture of American Volunteerism. Paper presented at the American Sociological Association meeting, Washington, DC.

Adams, D. S. (1991). Why Should Americans Volunteer? A content analysis of popular magazines. Paper presented at the North Central Sociological Association meeting, Dearborn, MI.

Allen, N., & Rushton, J. P. (1983). Personality Characteristics of Community Mental Health Volunteers: A review. Journal of Voluntary Action Research, 12(1), 36–49.

Baron, L. (1988). The historical context of rescue. In P. M. Oliner & S.P. Oliner (Eds.), *The Altruistic Personality: Rescuers of Jews in Nazi Europe* (pp. 13–48). New York: Free Press.

Baron, L. (1988). The historical context of rescue. In P.M. Oliner & S.P. Oliner (Eds.), *The Altruistic Personality: Rescuers of Jews in Nazi Europe* (pp. 13-48). New York: Free Press.

Baron, L. (1992). The Dutchness of Dutch rescuers: The National Dimension of Altruism.In P. M. Oliner, S. P. Oliner, L. Baron, L. A. Blum, D. L. Krebs, & M. Z. Smolenska (Eds.), *Embracing the Other: Philosophical, psychological and historical perspectives on*altruism (pp. 306–327). New York: New York University Press.

Berkowitz, L., & Luterman, K. (1968). The Traditionally Socially Responsible Personality. Public Opinion Quarterly, 32, 169–185.

Buckingham, R. (1983). The Complete Hospice Guide. New York: Harper & Row.

Carpi, D. (1977). The rescue of Jews in the Italian zone of occupied Croatia. In Y. Gutman & E. Zuroff (Eds.), Rescue attempts during the Holocaust: Proceedings of the Second Yad Vashem International Historical Conference, April 8–11, 1974 (pp. 465–525). Jerusalem: Yad Vashem.

Chary, F. B. (1972). The Bulgarian Jews and the final solution, 1940–1944. Pittsburgh: University of Pittsburgh Press.

Fischman, W. I. (1964, December 1). The Friar Who Saved 5,000 Jews. Look Magazine.

Fleischner, E. (Ed.). (1988). Can the few become the many? Some Catholics in France who saved Jews during the Holocaust. In *Remembering for the future: Jews and Christians during and after the Holocaust* (Theme 1, International Scholars Conference, Oxford, England, July 10–13, 1988). Oxford: Pergamon.

Flender, H. (1964). Rescue in Denmark. New York: Manor Books.

Friedman, P. (1978). Their Brothers' Keepers. New York: Holocaust Library.

Gurin, G., Gurin, P., & Morrison, B. M. (1978). Personal and Ideological Aspects of Internal and External Control. Social Psychology, 41(4), 275–296.

Hoffman, M. L. (1983). Affective and Cognitive Processes in Moral Internalization: An Information Processing Approach. In E. T. Higgins, D. Ruble, & W. Hartup (Eds.), Social Cognition and Social Development: A socio-cultural perspective (pp. 236-274). New York: Cambridge University Press.

Huneke, D. K. (1985). The Moses of Rovno: The stirring story of Fritz Graebe, a German Christian who risked his life to lead hundreds of Jews to safety during the Holocaust. New York: Dodd, Mead.

Huneke, D. K. (1986). Lessons of Herman Graebe's life: The origins of a moral person. Humboldt Journal of Social Relations, 13(1&2), 320-332.

Kübler-Ross, E. (1997). On Death and Dying. New York: Simon & Schuster.

Kurek, E. (1997). Your life Is Worth Mine. New York: Hippocrene Books.

Kurek-Lesik, E. (1992). The Role of Polish Nuns in the Rescue of Jews, 1939–1945. In P. M. Oliner et al. (Eds.), Embracing the Other: Philosophical, psychological and historical perspectives on altruism (pp. 328–334). New York: New York University Press.

Mehrabian, A., & Epstein, N. A. (1972). A Measure of Emotional Empathy. Journal of Personality, 40(4), 525–543.

Midlarsky, M. I. (1981). Helping during the Holocaust: The role of political, theological,and socioeconomic identifications. Humboldt Journal of Social Relations, 13(1&2), 285-305.

Murdoch, I. (1985). The Sovereignty of Good. London: Ark. (Original work published 1970) Oliner, S. P., & Oliner, P. M. (1988). The Altruistic Personality: Rescuers of Jews in Nazi Europe. New York: Free Press.

Piliavin, J. A. (1990). Give the Gift of Life to Unnamed Strangers: A review of research on *blood donors since Oswalt (1977). Transfusion, 30, 444-459.*

Ramati, A. *(1978). The Assisi Underground: The priests who rescued Jews. New York: Stein &* Day.

Reykowski, J. (1987). Dimensions of Development in Moral values: Two approaches to the development of morality. In N. Eisenberg, J. Reykowski, & E. Staub (Eds.), Social and M*oral Values: Individual and Societal Perspectives. Hillsdale, NJ: Erlbaum.*

Rosenberg, M. (1965). Society and the Adolescent Self-image. Princeton, NJ: Princeton University Press.

Rotter, J. B. (1966). Generalized Expectancies for Internal Versus External Control of Reinforcement. Psychological Monographs, 80, 1.

Sauvage, P. (1986). Ten things I Would Like to Know About Righteous Conduct in Le Chambon and Elsewhere During the Holocaust. Humboldt Journal of Social Relations, 13*(1&2), 252-259.*

Schulman, M., & Mekler, *E. (1985). Bringing Up a Moral Child: A New Approach for Teaching Your Child to be Kind, Just, and Responsible. Reading, MA: Addison-Wesley.*

Wuthnow, *R. (1991). Acts of Compassion: Caring for Others and Helping Ourselves. Princeton,* NJ: Princeton University Press.

Yahil, L. (1969). The Rescue of Danish Jewry: Test of a Democracy (M. Gradel, Trans). Philadelphia: Jewish Publication Society.

Zeitoun, S. (1988). The Role of Christian Community in Saving Jewish children in France During the Second World War. *In E. Fleischner (Ed.), Remembering for the Future: The Impact of the Holocaust and Genocide on Jews and Christians (supplementary vol., International Scholars Conference, Oxford, England, July 10-13; pp. 505-525). Oxford: Pergamon.*

Zuccotti, *S. (1987). The Italians and the Holocaust: Persecution, Rescue, and Survival. New* York: Basic Books.

9

Sorkin's Vision of Love and Altruism

SAMUEL P. OLINER AND JEFFREY R. GUNN

The Russian-born Pitirim Sorokin (1889-1968) was a maverick in the field of sociology[1]. His abiding concerns in the last decades of his life were that sensate society, indulgent and materialistic, had led humanity to a crisis point. Recently, some scholars and commentators lament the fact that we find ourselves on the brink of spiritual bankruptcy. Sorokin's vision that only altruistic love will result in human consensus earned him the derogatory name of "philosopher of love," or "Christian anarchist" by mainstream sociologists in the 1950s. These positivistic sociologists were in turn accused by Sorokin as giving too much weight to their scientific method as the only way of knowing. He accused them of "quanto-phrenia" and "quantomania," and of indulging in the exercise of "fads" and "foibles."[2] Sorokin did not dismiss the scientific method, but felt that sociologists and sociological journals were filled with quantitative research that ultimately signified very little. Similar to Max Weber, he advocated a type of insightful understanding, a logico-meaningful approach to explain human behavior. In addition, Sorokin

---

1. For further discussion of Sorokin's scholarship, see Ford, Richard, and Talbutt 1996.
2. Samuel P. Oliner, "Sorokin's Contribution to American Sociology" Nationalities Papers, 4 no.2 (1976): 125-151; Barry V. Johnston, Pitirim A. Sorokin: An Intellectual Biography, (University Press of Kansas, Lawrence, KS, 1995).

dared to argue that value-relativity was an elusive product of an overripe sensate mentality and a root cause of the crises of our age. He further dared to take a position of value-advocacy. He was particularly insistent on the need for humanity to recognize and propagate the value and process of altruistic love. In our view, Sorokin was a visionary who has not only described his contemporary world, but also foresaw what we are experiencing currently. A glance at any newspaper, journal, movie, or television will quickly remind us that the symptoms of human degradation and separation are pervasive.

If we accept Sorokin's premise that our human relations are in a state of worsening crisis that can only be averted by an increase in altruistic love, and if we are concerned about the future of society, then the promotion of altruistic love becomes imperative. Successful promotion, however, requires effective understanding, and our understanding of altruistic love today has not advanced much beyond Sorokin's initial conceptualization. Contemporary theories of altruism and prosocial behavior miss the point of altruistic love, and contemporary research methods may in part miss its essence.

The purpose of this paper is twofold: to renew Sorokin's vision of altruistic love and to present research on rescuers of Jews in Nazi-occupied Europe that supports that view, having uncovered many living examples of this love, compassion, and courage. We hope to show that Sorokin's conceptualization means more than contemporary theories allow and that its understanding requires more than contemporary research methods can adequately yield. We also hope to show, through examples, that altruistic love is a tremendous force, which, if unleashed, could transform the character of human relations.

Sorokin's altruistic love is ideally boundless. It originates within itself and extends out to the cosmos. It makes no distinctions; it embraces all. It is unconditional and undaunted by disappointment and failure. It is compassionate and caring; it hurts when others hurt and suffers when they suffer. It is endlessly giving; it reaches out in the spirit of care, justice, and compassion. It is ennobling and exalted; it represents the highest in human potential, historically achieved by Buddha, the Dalai Lama, Christ, Gandhi, Albert Schweitzer, Mother Teresa, and many of the rescuers of Jews in Nazi Europe studied by the Oliners.[3,4]

Contemporary sociobiologists who attribute altruistic love to genetic programming miss the point. Sorokin's altruistic love is not the automatic "love" of the drone bee for its queen. Sorokin's love originates within itself and emanates from itself. It is not the barest of human predispositions but the highest of human achievements.

Contemporary psychologists who attribute altruistic love solely to developmental processes also miss the point. Sorokin's love does not depend on developed brain physiology or on the ability to differentiate self from others. It is not a Hobbesian egocentric love that occurs when the interests of self become identified with the interests of others. Altruistic love is a giving, sacrificial love; it often involves the sacrifice of very important interests, possibly one's life. Such sacrifices can never be based or justified on egocentric premises. As he said:

No logical ego-centered ethics can urge the individual to transcend his ego(s)...to sacrifice his interests. The major premises of such logic forbid any plea for sacrifice. If it does present such a plea, it becomes self-contradictory: "For the benefit of your egos and your ego-centered I; for

---

3. Pitirim A. Sorokin, The Ways and Power of Love: Types, Factors, and Techniques of Moral Transformation, (Boston, MA: The Beacon Press, 1954); Pitirim A. Sorokin, Fads and Foibles in Modern Sociology and Related Sciences, (Henry Regnery Company, Chicago,IL, 1956).
4. See Oliner and Oliner 1988, and Oliner 2003, 2005.

the benefit of your egos you have to sacrifice their very interests; for the benefit of your personal life you have to sacrifice your life." The second parts of these propositions deny what their first parts affirm.[5]

Sorokin's love is a selfless love attained by the primal human capacity to submerge self and others into a greater whole. He says:

Love...annuls our individual loneliness; fills the emptiness of our isolation with the richest value; breaks and transcends the narrow walls of our little egos; makes us co-participants of the highest life of humanity and the... cosmos; expands our true individuality to the...boundaries of the universe.[6]

Sacrifice is encouraged, not contradicted, by this love. The individual who accepts the ontological primacy of the Whole does not have interests or life; he or she has existence that is bestowed by the living Whole, an existence that cannot subsist apart from the Whole. Such individuals do not sacrifice interests or life; rather, they sacrifice subsistence for life of the Whole. "Love tends thus to destroy death and to replace it with eternal immortality."[7]

Sorokin's altruistic love cannot be fully comprehended by the scientific method, nor is it likely to be found in the contrivances and manipulations of the social sciences' laboratories. Sorokin eschewed the scientific encapsulation of

5. Samuel P. Oliner and Pearl M. Oliner, The Altruistic Personality: Rescuers of Jews in Nazi Europe, (The Free Press, New York, 1998).
6. Pitirim A. Sorokin, The Ways and Power of Love: Types, Factors, and Techniques of Moral Transformation, (Boston, MA: The Beacon Press, 1954).
7. Pitirim A. Sorokin, The Ways and Power of Love: Types, Factors, and Techniques of Moral Transformation, (Boston, MA: The Beacon Press, 1954).

altruistic love. Though he did use reason and observation to outline some of its contours, he argued that love could not be adequately captured or confined within a tidy conceptual scheme; to do so would be to lose its manifold essence. Citing P. Tillich, Sorokin maintained:

> I have given no definition of love. This is impossible, because there is no higher principle by which it can be defined. It is life itself in its actual unity. The forms and structures in which love embodies itself are the forms and structures in which life overcomes its destructive forces.

Martin Buber had a similar view about love. Altruistic love can only be distorted, not encountered or actively known by scientific analysis. "It is not the law that is afterwards derived from appearance but in appearance itself that being communicates itself."[8] Love is also positively associated with forgiveness.[9]

Philosophers, poets, and novelists have been concerned over the centuries with the processes called love and loving. Several reflected Sorokin's notion that in any genuine psychological experience of love, the ego or "I" of the loving individual tends to merge with and to identify with a loved "Thee" and that love is the justification and deliverance of individuality through the sacrifice of egoism. Both Aristotle and Plato suggested that love is a motivating force that gives incentive to justice and moral action. A number of philosophers have addressed the issue that the love by God toward humankind is agape, a kind of altruistic love, which is eternally powerful. Agape love, which some say is divinely inspired, moves human beings to care and help other human

---

8. Pitirim A. Sorokin, Explorations in Altruistic Love and Behavior: A Symposium, (The Beacon Press: Boston, MA, 1950).
9. Martin Buber, I and Thou, (Charles Scribner's Sons: NY, 1970).

beings. It also implies sympathy and compassion and the non-separation between self and others, as Max Scheler pointed out.[10]

Rescuers of Jews in Nazi-Occupied Europe

The authors have discerned clear manifestations of altruistic love envisioned by Sorokin in a study by Oliner and Oliner, "The Altruistic Personality,"[11]: in which they interviewed a sample of rescuers of Jews, bystanders, and rescued survivors in Nazi-occupied Europe. Samuel P. Oliner, Pearl M. Oliner, and their associates interviewed almost seven hundred people who lived in Nazi-occupied Europe. The sample consisted of authenticated Gentile rescuers, bystanders (a group of people who did not engage in rescue even though some were asked to help), and a group of rescued survivors. During the Nazi occupation, the respondents had lived in Poland, Germany, France, Holland, Italy, Denmark, Belgium, and Norway. The study sought answers to three key questions:

1. Was rescue primarily a matter of opportunity, that is, a question of external circumstances? If so, what circumstances?

2. Was rescue a matter of character, that is, personal attributes and values? If so, what attributes?

3. Were those attributes and values learned, and if so how?

The Oliners estimated that less than one percent of the population of Nazi-occupied Europe was engaged in the

---

10. Samuel P. Oliner, "Altruism, Forgiveness, Empathy and Intergroup Apology," 2005.
11. Max Scheler, The Nature of Sympathy: Sorokin's Vision of Altruistic Love as a Bridge to Human Consensus, (Yale University Press, New Haven, CT: 1954).

rescue of Jews during the Holocaust period. The rarity of this activity is somewhat understandable in view of its extreme danger. The occupied countries were saturated with Gestapo officers, German soldiers, and local collaborators. Persons caught sheltering or otherwise helping Jews were subject to arrest, torture, imprisonment, and/or death. One rescuer reported what he witnessed:

> It started before the war...I was in Germany, where I visited a family—a very nice family—that had two boys. One boy was gone every night. The mother told me, "He is in a club. The club is unbelievable." The boy was in the Hitler Youth movement. It was a secret. In the evenings the boys took lessons and then they got an animal, a rabbit or a pig or a mouse or a rat. He had to kill that animal. He learned to kill, and he learned to see blood.

Another rescuer said:

> I saw how they killed... I wanted flour for the bread. It was so quiet there, after-wards, I just saw in the street so many people killed —Jewish people. I was scared. I was really scared. I told my mother what I saw. My mother told me, "You are lucky they don't kill you."

Yet another said:

> Personal contacts were dangerous. A friend of mine was hung in a cell with a chain around his wrists. They hung him on the ceiling just so far from the floor. Then they killed him. I don't know if you have heard of the "bath" treatment—they put people underwater in a bath to suffocate.

Most of the rescuers knew the risks they were taking, and yet most of them persevered for long periods of time. They had to provide transportation, construct hiding places, avoid their neighbors and even some members of their families, procure food, forge identification papers, and sometimes lie and steal to carry out their rescues.

They lived in constant fear of detection. Many of the rescuers and their homes were searched. Some of them were arrested and beaten or tortured. Some lost loved ones who were also engaged in rescue. In Poland alone, 2500 Gentile Poles lost their lives when they were caught hiding Jews and other victims of Nazi extermination. A Polish rescuer said:

> The Germans caught me and almost beat me to death. They grabbed me and threw me to the basement. I opened my eyes and I saw the man hanging in front of me. I sat with him like that for almost one week.

Yet another said:

> The S.S. came and they killed my husband and one of the Jews. They came with a dog... My husband wouldn't say anything so they set the dog on him. It bit off his hand... Then the dog ran upstairs. We had the hiding place upstairs. They went after the dog and took my husband up. The guy, Farber...he was the worst S.S. He was sitting with me with a gun in his hand and he ran upstairs after the dog. Somebody was shooting upstairs. The dog had found the hiding place...My little girl was crying because she wanted to go upstairs to Daddy—because Daddy was screaming.

The rescuers included both males and females. They were from all occupied countries, from all social class backgrounds, and from all levels of education. The rescuers held a variety of religious beliefs, while some held no religious beliefs at all. They ascribed to various political ideologies; some were politically indifferent. They represented a broad range of occupational specialties and some were housewives or too young to hold any occupation at all. No gender, country, social class, level of education, religious belief, political ideology, or occupational specialty was predominant in the sample.

The rescuers reported having learned a number of values as they were growing up. These values tended to cluster around care, compassion, empathy, honesty, religiosity, social responsibility, risk-taking and industriousness. The rescuers were interviewed using an open-ended questionnaire that included attitude scales measuring empathy, social responsibility, religiosity, self-esteem, and social control. They were not singularly located on any of these scales. The rescuers reported a variety of reasons or motives for their actions, and some reported they had no conscious reason or motive at all. In comparison to bystanders (non-rescuers) in our sample, the rescuers scored higher on the empathy and social responsibility scale. They were typically more psychologically attached to their family as well as being able to extend their responsibility to diverse other groups and included them in the universe of responsibility. They exhibited sympathetic concern, justice, Christian duty, and, in a number of cases, prior friendship. Over 87 percent mentioned the ethic of caring for diverse others as a reason for helping.

The rescuers did exhibit two commonalties, both of which were emphasized by Sorokin. Most of the rescuers reported having been raised in a warm and loving family environment, and most showed a strong sense of attachment to their family as well as an extension of this attachment to others such as strangers, foreigners, and Jews.

While we cannot gain an active personal knowledge of altruistic love outside of the being of that love itself, we can catch a glimpse of that knowledge from those who have acted and lived that loving and caring reality. The rescuers of Jews saved lives. We discern the altruistic love of the rescuers from their stories. We provide excerpts from three stories. The first is from T.W., who lived in the Netherlands during the war. She was married and had five children, all less than ten years old in 1940. She told us that her father was the most influential person in her life as she was growing up. "From him, we learned that we were very poor, but if somebody knocked on the door, he would always give a few pennies. He told us to be kind to all people. Never point the finger." She related the following story:

> When we first were occupied by the Germans we really did not think too badly of it. We were young, and we did not know. They were very friendly. It came so quick...My girl friend came and said to me, "Tia, I got here a little girl. Her father was shot to death, her mother fled with her brother, and she crunched her in a closet." Then the mother said—and that struck with me—"Christians will come and help you, but don't cry."

J.D., the second of these rescuers, also lived in the Netherlands during the war. He was married and had two children. J.D. was a coal miner, and his wife was a housewife. He regarded his mother as the most important person in his life while he was growing up. From her he learned, "We were not allowed to lie, not allowed to steal... You had to help little children and older people when they needed your help. When you didn't, you were in trouble with Mamma." When asked about his rescue activity, he told us the following:

> It all started right in the beginning of the war. The Germans bombed Rotterdam pretty badly, and they sent children out. We ended up with a boy about my daughter's age... In 1942 they knew that we had a boy. So in 1942 a lady came. She heard we had a boy from Rotterdam, and asked if we would mind having another boy.

My wife said, "Sure, we can have another boy." She said, "But he is Jewish." My wife said, "Then I will have to talk with my husband."

I was a coal miner at the time... It was about midnight when I came home. We talked it over. I said, "Sure. They are little human beings. When she comes back tomorrow you tell her to bring the little boy." And so she did. The boy was about three and a half years old. They called him Bobby...My wife says, "I am glad we got this little boy and not somebody else."

Then he talked about his little sister. I...found out where his little sister was. She was only a year and a half. I...went to the people. I asked, "May I come with the little boy sometime and visit her." That was granted.

That was only one visit. It was a really beautiful to see how pleased these little kids were and how happy they were to see each other again. Right then and there I made up my mind. Them kids should not go apart from each other...So I came home and I told my wife the story. She looked at me and said, "I think the same as you do but it's risky for you. You are the head of the household." I said, "If they are going to shoot me for one, we may as well do two. It's the same bullet."

The next morning I got the little girl...After that they were always together. They grew up together. That time was a difficult time because there were so many Dutch people who moved over to the Germans. You didn't know who you could trust any more. So we didn't trust nobody...

The last couple they brought us was an elderly couple... They brought them over at one o'clock in the night.

After we were free this gentleman came back to thank us for what we did. My wife had chicken soup and we fed those people some warm food. And they had to have dry clothes. About three thirty or four o'clock I had everything washed and dried for them. I laid down for an hour and got some shut eye. It was a trying time but it was forty years ago and I was so much younger. When you are young you don't feel it so much. I never knew who was coming with who.

We had a kind of a knock that we knew who was at the door. I did not open up when I didn't know who it was. There were four or five people who would bring Jewish people for us to hide. Most of the time we had our two little kids as well as adults.

We went through the war that way. Sometimes when it was dangerous we got a warning from the police. I had a friend who was a policeman. He was head of the police, we never met. I knew him and he knew me. When there was talk about a raid he told a friend of mine to come and warn us...

One night when it became very dangerous my wife was in the cell of the police station with the children. A cell was the safest place they could find. We put them in jail!

The father was picked up right in the beginning and was killed. The mother was underground in Belgium or the south of Holland. A Catholic priest came with the mother..

A third rescue took place in Krakow, the ancient capital of Poland. For purposes of space, we shall abstract the story. In Krakow in 1942, the S.S. guards were leading approximately a thousand Jews out of the ghetto toward a railroad station for trans-shipment to Treblinka death camp. Many among the marching Jews, which consisted of men, women, and children, had a premonition that they were going to their deaths. One marcher among the Jews was a woman with a small, infant boy. In desperation, she was thinking of a way of saving her child, when she noticed a blond, young

Polish Catholic woman standing on the sidewalk among the other Poles who were simply onlookers to this tragedy. The Jewess sneaked away from the ranks of the marchers and rushed over to the Polish, Catholic woman and said to her, "Please, please, save my baby. I know that they are going to kill us." The woman on the curb took this infant into her arms and took it home. She was neither married nor pregnant, so the neighbors were curious how she got this Semitic-looking child.

Shortly thereafter, someone among the neighbors reported her to the local Krakow police, which was the Polish police in the service of the Nazis. Soon a Polish policeman came and arrested her, with the child. He sat her in a large room that contained at least a dozen desks, behind each sat a policeman. The captain walked in, sat down in front of the desk, and said to the woman, "This is not your child, is it? This is a Jewish child, isn't it? Do you know what the penalties for hiding a Jewish child are?" The woman burst into automatic, genuine tears, pounded the desk, looked the captain in the eyes and said, "You should be ashamed of yourself. Do you call yourselves Poles? Do you call yourselves gentlemen?" Then her eyes traversed the room and she said, "There is one among you who has fathered this child and who is willing to stoop so low, who is such a vicious human being, that he would rather see this child labeled as a Jew and have him exterminated than own up his responsibility and paternity in this matter." The captain proverbially straightened his tie, cleared his throat, looked around the room thinking who might be the father of this child, and let this woman go.

Many of the dozens of rescued survivors that the Oliners interviewed were asked the question, "Why do you think your people rescued you?" They responded that the rescuers "did it out of love, out of caring, out of compassion, and could not stand by and see the innocent die."

The rescuers' stories provide examples of a love that is neither determined nor selfish. It is a love that reaches out to care for others, even to those who are strangers. It is a love directed by conscious choice, a choice by persons who are both motivated and existentially free to do otherwise. The great majority of people in Nazi-occupied Europe did do otherwise; most people did nothing to help the Jews because of their fear or their indifference to the pain of others.

A salient concept derived from the Oliner study is the concept of extensivity, which has its roots partially in Sorokin's work on the dimensions of love. The rescuers, as they were growing up, felt attached to their family of origin in a psychologically healthy way. Their relationships with their families and also others deserving of their love and care, were not simply empty abstractions but involved action, and these relationships resulted in the motivation to aid and save others, often strangers. The Oliners assert that extensivity consists of several dimensions, including attachment to family of origin, inclusiveness of others, care, and so on.

If altruistic love is neither self-interested nor determined, then what is it, and where does it come from? It is more than anything a state of mind, a state of mind that cannot easily differentiate or separate self from the Whole, and where separation does occur. It is a state of mind that prompts action to be taken for the good of the Whole rather than for the good of the self. It regards all people as deserving of love. They feel responsible for all people, not just friends and family members.

We do not know exactly where this state of mind comes from. Most of the rescuers were raised in loving family environments, where caring for others was common practice. And most rescuers were taught to be tolerant, to regard everyone in the same caring light. But these environmental factors alone do not guarantee altruistic love, nor does their absence necessarily preclude it.

While the definition of love is complex, we can clearly discern its positive consequences. As Sorokin argued, altruistic love may be the most important key to the survival of humanity. In recent decades social science has opened new fields of altruism and love to its exploration and use. The probing into the subatomic world and the harnessing of atomic energy are but two examples. Perhaps the latest realm to be explored is the mysterious domain of altruistic love. Though now in its infancy, its scientific study is likely to become a most important area for future research. The topic of unselfish love has already been placed on today's agenda of history and may become its main business.[12] We see the field of social psychology, apology and forgiveness, positive psychology, evolutionary biology, and other disciplines have become interested in the nature of goodness that may lead to a more caring world.[13]

The Oliners, in their altruistic personality research, suggest that we must teach and tell the stories of altruistic heroes because our young people should use these rescuers and others as moral role models. The understanding and disseminating of altruistic love is the most important item on the agenda today. Fyodor Dostoyoevsky was once asked whether we should fight evil with force or with humble love. Humble love, he argued, is the most powerful force in the world, and was the only answer to evil.[14] Just as love is important in the survival of newborn babies, so it is crucial for the survival of the planet. Altruism and altruistic love may be the antidote to war. This was precisely Sorokin's vision. © *Oliner and Gunn*

---

12. 1988
13. Pitirim A. Sorokin, Pitirim, "The Mysterious Energy of Love." Transcripts of lectures recorded by Campus World, Inc., 1960.
14. Samuel P. Oliner, Altruism: Intergroup Apology and Forgiveness. (In progress), 2006.

References

Buber, Martin. 1970. I and Thou. New York: Charles Scribner's Sons.

Johnston, Barry V. 1995. Pitirim A. Sorokin: An Intellectual Biography. Lawrence, KS: University Press of Kansas.

Matter, Joseph Allen. 1974. Love, Altruism, and World Crisis: The Challenge of Pitirim Sorokin. Chicago, IL: Nelson-Hall Company.

Oliner, Samuel P. 1976. "Sorokin's Contribution to American Sociology." Nationalities Papers 4 (2):125-151.

Oliner, Samuel P. 2005. *"Altruism, Forgiveness, Empathy and Intergroup Apology." Humboldt* Journal of Social Relations. 29 (2): 8-39.

Oliner, Samuel P. 2008. Altruism, Intergroup Apology and Forgiveness. MN: Paragon House

Oliner, Samuel P. and Pearl M. Oliner. 1988. The Altruistic Personality: Rescuers of Jews in Nazi Europe. New York: The Free Press.

Scheler, Max. 1954. The Nature of Sympathy: Sorokin's Vision of Altruistic Love as a Bridge to Human Consensus. New Haven, CT: Yale University Press.

Sorokin, Pitirim A. 1950. Explorations in Altruistic Love and Behavior: A Symposium. Boston, MA: The Beacon Press.

Sorokin, Pitirim A. 1954. The Ways and Power of Love: Types, Factors, and Techniques of Moral Transformation. Boston, MA: The Beacon Press.

Sorokin, Pitirim A. 1956. Fads and Foibles in Modern Sociology and Related Sciences.Chicago, IL: Henry Regnery Company.

Sorokin, Pitirim A. 1960. "The Mysterious Energy of Love." Transcripts of lectures recorded by Campus World, Inc.

10

Altruism in Different Religions

SAMUEL P. OLINER

Judaism

The basic source of Jewish belief is the Hebrew Bible, called the Old Testament by Christians, which consists of three major works: The Torah (the five books of Moses) and the First and Last Writings; together they form the Tanakh. The Torah was traditionally regarded as the primary revelation of God and his laws to humanity; it is considered valid for all time. Its laws were clarified and elaborated in the oral Torah, or the tradition of the elders, and were eventually written down in two other works, the Mishnah and Talmud. These traditions consist of legal, ethical, philosophic, mystical, and devotional issues, and they are impressive in their length.

The goal of Judaism lies in strict obedience to God. The philosophy perceived in Judaism is that humankind has two impulses: good and evil. One can alleviate the plight of the individual and of society by being compassionate, just, forgiving, and by loving and obeying God. Or, one can rebel and be influenced by Satan, who caused God's creation to go astray. To follow God's law is the highest morality, which includes among many other good things—justice, charity, ethics and honesty, and being true to the one true God, Yahweh. The Ten Commandments propose desirable relationships with one's neighbor, one's father and mother, and God.

Judaism is the mother religion of both Christianity and Islam, and Christianity has inherited main religious ideas and ritual practices from Judaism. Jews do not belong to any one race or people in the anthropological sense. They were expelled from their homeland, ancient Palestine, and today are found in most parts of the world.

Despite dispersal, Jews have retained a sense of people-hood, and in great part this is due to their religious prac-tices. Jews claim a special relationship to God and believe that by receiving the Torah, which contains the Ten Com-mandments, that He has ordered them to be righteous. The prophet Micah made the famous declaration that God re-quires all humankind to do good, which means to practice loving kindness and to walk humbly with God.

During Rosh Hoshanna, observant Jews recall their deeds towards other human beings over the preceding year. Ten days later on Yom Kippur, the Day of Atonement, ob-servant Jews are encouraged to think about the harm and offenses they have committed over the past year. They are asked to apologize to neighbors, and if they do not apolo-gize, to try to do better for their fellow human beings. Acts of loving kindness are the best means of making amends. As the rabbis have said, "whoever has sinned, let him go and do a good deed, and he or she will be forgiven" (Ross and Hills 1956: 120).

Tzedakah is the Hebrew word for charity. It means giv-ing aid, assistance and money to the poor or to worthwhile causes, and it includes the responsibility to give a portion of one's personal substance for the common good (Degroot 2005). A mitzvah includes 613 commandments Jews are ob-ligated to observe, and, more generally, refers to any good deed. One often reads of the "mitzvah of tzedakah." Tze-dakah is more than just giving money to the poor. In the writings of Maimonides, whoever gives tzedakah to the poor with a sour expression and in a surly manner, even if he gives a thousand gold pieces, loses his merit. One should instead give cheerfully and joyfully, and empathize with his sorrow.

The command to love one's neighbor, found in the book of Leviticus, is central to the Jewish faith (Templeton 1999: 11). In fact, Templeton argues that in Judaism, "When one loves and cares for others, one is loving God" (1999: 11). The Bible portrays a God who loves all people: the rich and the poor, the weak and the powerful. God's love is unconditional.

One of our interviewees, a man who has helped in the Jewish community for many years, said:

> My own feeling about being spiritual is that I'm a person that other people can look up to. I consider two main qualifications: one, that you do good [in Hebrew, tikun olan – fix the world), that you're a constructive person in your family, in your community, and in your country. Secondly, that you have goals and beliefs and activities that are bigger than yourself. (Respondent 013)

Another, a woman who identifies herself with the culture of being Jewish and of helping:

> Just being Jewish influences a me lot.... I mean there's such an infusion of persecution throughout Jewish cultural history that there is always a sense of helping out in communities for people who don't have as much, through thick and thin, you know, helping people more.

The Bible holds many references to altruism. In Leviticus: "And when you reap the harvest of your land, you shall not reap all the way to the edges of your field, or gather the gleanings of your harvest. You shall not pick the vineyard bare, or gather the fallen fruit of your vineyard; you shall leave them for the poor and the stranger; I am the Lord your God" (Leviticus 19:9-10). In Deuteronomy, God commands the faithful: "If, however, there is a needy person among you, do not harden your heart and shut your hand against your needy kinsmen. Rather, you must open your hand and lend him sufficient for whatever he needs" (Deuteronomy 15:7-8).

It is considered more credible by some to develop a habit of giving regularly rather than giving large sums infrequently. Placing a pushke—a tin can where coins may be donated—in the house represents one way people can express a commitment to helping their communities philanthropically. By collecting money in one's home regularly, whether for a specific or the community's general good, one is fulfilling an obligation to neighbors. The use of a pushke is meant to further the spirit of philanthropy and righteousness in the home and in the community.

Charity has been defined in many ways. It may consist of offering help to the poor, or almsgiving. It may be a general benevolence or generosity toward others or toward humanity, or indulgence or forbearance in judging others.

Helping your neighbor can manifest itself in many ways. One such way for Jews is through MAZON, a citizens' movement, which is the outgrowth of tens of thousands of American Jews who have stepped forward to try to solve hunger, one of the world's most devastating—and most preventable—problems. With their support, MAZON works around the globe to bring critical relief to millions of hungry families. MAZON also funds emergency food providers, food banks, multi-service organizations and advocacy groups both in this country and abroad.

Like all other religions, Judaism teaches about the importance of ethics, love, kindness, caring, and social responsibility. Yet it is important to realize that the faiths that we discuss in this chapter have an ideal level and a real level. By ideal level, we mean they preach these things; however, they fail to live up to the ideals in their sacred books.

Chief Rabbi Jonathan Sacks, a major Jewish scholar who represents an ecumenical spirit in his writings, emphasizes the importance of responsibility. In his book *To Heal a Fractured World* (2005), he speaks about responsibility as one of the major ethical virtues. He speaks about charity as justice and the importance of love that must translate into compassionate deeds. He feels that human beings are capable of repairing the world now. He addresses the universality of all human beings and emphasizes strongly the importance of kindness towards strangers and society.

Rabbi Sacks maintains that Judaism is a complex faith, but that Jewish ethics are down to earth and practical. It is not enough to speak about help, caring, and compassion: it matters to the Jewish God only when he sees action on the part of one to another. Sacks stresses the concept of inclusiveness among human beings. He cites Rabbi Abraham Kook (100 1935) who said, "The narrow-mindedness that leads one to see what is outside the bounds of one's people ... is ugly and defiled, is a terrible darkness that causes general destruction to the entire edifice of good, the light of which every refined soul hopes for" (Sacks 2005: 10). Judaism also stresses the importance of righteousness.

Deuteronomy 16:18 tells people, "Do not stand by idly by the blood of your neighbor." In other words, don't be a bystander to murder or injustice. Jewish writings have much to say about justice. Isaiah 1:17 says "Learn to do good, seek justice, aid the oppressed, uphold the rights of the orphan, defend the cause of the widow." Dr. Sacks disagrees strongly with Karl Marx, who famously called religion "the opium of the people." Rather, he maintains that religion, in its most authentic form, is actually quite practical and helpful, because it includes, among other deeds, helping others to obtain justice. Within Judaism, justice is a form of caring or altruism; it is considered a form of charity. A Tzedakah is a kind of deed, intended not to humiliate the recipient, but to render him aid and return him to a condition in which he can stand on his own two feet. Charity as loving kindness has many manifestations in Judaism. For example, when King Alfonso V of Portugal captured 250 African Jews and sold them as slaves throughout the Kingdom of Portugal, Portuguese Jews formed a representative committee of 12 members and traveled throughout the country redeeming the Jewish slaves, often at a very high price. These ransomed Jews were clothed, lodged, and maintained until they had learned the language of the country and were able to support themselves (Sacks 2005).

Jews believe, at least at the ideal level, that the world is reparable by loving thy neighbor. Using a vast body of literature and learning, Rabbi Sacks speaks about the singleness of the human soul—and it is not simply a Jewish soul but inclusive. Great emphasis is stressed on the treatment of strangers. Rabbi Sacks concludes that even the smallest good deed can change someone's life, and that religions reach their highest level when they stop worrying about other people's souls and care instead for the needs of their bodies. The ability to give to others is a gift. Judaism, like other religious traditions, has great and lofty teachings in its sacred texts, although not all Jews live up to those ideals.

Christianity

Christianity is based on the teachings of Jesus of Nazareth some 2,000 years ago. It is the world's largest religion, followed by Islam. Scriptures in the Christian Bible consist of the Old Testament (39 books of the Hebrew Bible) and the New Testament. There are three major sects of Christianity: Catholicism, Eastern Orthodox, and Protestantism, which has splintered into many denominations. Like Judaism and Islam, Christianity is monotheistic. The goal of Christians is to gain eternal life with God in heaven, which is considered a perfect existence of bliss. The path of attainment is obedience to God. As in some other major religions, Christians believe that man is born a sinner and can receive salvation only from God. For them, this salvation comes through belief in Jesus Christ as savior. Some Christians have an unshakable belief that Christianity is the only true religion, the only path to salvation, and that only "good Christians" will be saved, which is somewhat problematic; but the other side of Christianity emphasizes love, compassion, and caring. Christianity, like Judaism, adheres to the Ten Commandments. Also, as in Judaism, Christianity teaches the Golden Rule: "Do unto others as you would have them do unto you."

Jesus is the central figure of the Christian religion. Stories about Jesus are numerous; probably the best known come from the first four books of the New Testament, known as the Gospels. Each of the books is separately written and presents Jesus's life in a way that would appeal to a wide group of people. The main point emphasized in Christianity is that Jesus was born to the Virgin Mary, is the Son of God, and that God loved humankind so much that he sacrificed his own son, Jesus, in order to absolve humanity from its sins. Though Jesus was a Jew and some of the teachings of the two religions overlap, Jesus's teachings were never accepted by the Jews. Even though Jesus's disciple Peter insisted upon keeping the movement exclusively Jewish, Paul was able to persuade Peter and others to admit non-Jews into the group (Ross and Hills 1956: 137). It was not long before non-Jews outnumbered Jews in the Christian movement.

Christianity, like other faiths, strongly emphasizes that its believers should clothe the naked and feed the poor, but to Christians, caring for other human beings reflects the essence of the love of Christ for humanity. Christianity preaches love for one's fellow human beings and peace and justice for all. It also teaches that there is no greater love for a man than to give up his life for another man. Christians manifest caring and altruism on a global scale through establishing charities that assist the needy around the world. In fact, there is a worldwide Catholic charitable institution called Caritas, which stands for altruism, charity, and compassion for others.

A recent example of Christian charity was manifested in Mother Teresa of Calcutta, who dedicated her life to helping the poor and afflicted in India. In Macedonia, where she grew up, statues and shrines of the Madonna and Child impressed her, moving her to become increasingly involved with the activities of the local Sacred Heart Church. One of the most influential priests in her life was Franjo Jambernkovic, a Croatian who encouraged her; it was he who pushed her toward missionary work in India.

In 1928 she traveled to Ireland and entered the Order of the Sisters of Our Lady of Loretto and was subsequently sent to Darjeeling, India for her training. She then studied for a teaching certificate at Loretto Entally in Calcutta, taking her final religious vows in 1937. Every time she left the convent and ventured out into the city, she was moved by the plight of the sick and the dying who were always to be found on the streets.

In 1946, on a train trip to Darjeeling, she received the call from God that transformed her life, thus beginning her quest for permission to minister to the sick and dying. In 1948 she was allowed by the Vatican to leave her post at the convent. She founded the Missionaries of Charity in 1950, and a number of nuns trained and worked with her. During the day the nuns taught, and during the evening they cared for the poor in the slums of Calcutta. Their creed and purpose was:

> To fulfill our mission of compassion and love to the poorest of the poor we go: seeking out in towns and villages all over the world even amid squalid surroundings the poorest, the abandoned, the sick, the infirm, the leprosy patients, the dying, the desperate, the lost, the outcasts;

taking care of them; rendering help to them; visiting them assiduously; living Christ's love for them; and awakening their response to His great love 9.

In 1952, Mother Teresa opened the Nirmal Hriday (or "Pure Heart") Home for Dying Destitutes in Calcutta and subsequently extended her work onto five continents. In recognition of her efforts, she was awarded the Nobel Peace Prize in 1979. In presenting the prize, Chairperson John Sanness said of her: "Can any political, social, or intellectual feat of engineering, on the international or on the national plane, however effective and rational, however idealistic and principled its protagonists may be, give us anything but a house built on a foundation of sand, unless the spirit of Mother Teresa inspires the builders and takes its dwelling in their building?"10

In 1990 Mother Teresa became ill and was forced to scale down her activities; in 1997, after a long and selfless life, she died. Mother Teresa represents the ultimate example of how altruism is exhibited through Christian love and caring, although recently Hitchens (1995) has pointed out that she has not been a perfect human being.

Just as all Jews do not subscribe to Mazon or practice Tzedakah, not all Catholics support Caritas, and not all Christians dedicate their lives to the poor and dying. But many do involve themselves in this faith-based form of helping others. There are common themes in Judaism and Christianity: the Golden Rule, loving one's neighbor, clothing the naked, and feeding the hungry. This similarity can be traced back to the Abrahamic roots of both religions.

Islam

Muslims believe that their religion, founded in the early seventh century, is the restoration of the original religion of Abraham (Judaism) through the Prophet Muhammad. It is the second largest religion after Christianity with approximately one billion believers, primarily in the Middle East, Pakistan, Bangladesh, Africa, China, Indonesia, Central Asia, and India, although many adherents can be found in Europe and the Western Hemisphere as well. There are two main divisions within Islam: The Sunnis are followers of the political successors of Muhammad. The Shiites are followers of Muhammad's family successors, Iman Ali and others, all of whom were martyred at an early age. The major scripture is the Qur'an.

The primary goal of Islam is to enjoy eternal spiritual life in heaven with Allah (God). Heaven is a paradise in which all the joys and pleasures abound, and man is the noblest creation of God, ranking above the angels. To attain this state, Muslims believe that they must observe the virtues of truthfulness, temperance, and humility before God, and that the practices of fasting, pilgrimage, prayer, charity, and acts of altruism to the Muslim community—and other creatures of God—are most necessary to please Allah.

In the Qur'an, it was explained that while Judaism and Christianity also had prophets who revealed the truth, Muhammad was the latest prophet who proclaimed the truth to humanity. One of Muhammad's major biblical functions was to try to convince other tribes that there was but one God, Allah, and that Muhammad was God's prophet. He drew up a constitution for his people, who were trying hard to unite, and made them into a close-knit fellowship. The people had to protect each other against enemies and help with other difficulties. Muhammad expected that the Jews and the Christians would accept him as the next prophet because of all they hold in common. He was prepared to be very patient with his Jewish followers. In Medina, he asked his followers to pray facing Jerusalem as Jews do currently, and emphasized the common elements of their traditions. When it became clear that the majority of the Jews had no intention of calling Muhammad their prophet, and some of the Jews violated the terms of the agreement they had with Muhammad, he demanded that they convert to Islam or leave.

In Islam there is a Day of Judgment, such as in Judaism and Christianity, when Allah judges everyone for their deeds and for having followed the precepts of Islam. Islam's contribution to altruism is its belief that Allah is goodness and its central teaching is that men should help each other. One of the five pillars of Islamic faith is the obligation of charity, *zalat*, the admonition to aid the less fortunate. The Qur'an instructs those who would follow God not only to do for others what they would have others do for them but to "give in full what is due from you, whether you expect or wish to receive full consideration from the other side or not" (Templeton 1999: 37). The emphasis on giving and helping within the Abrahamic religions is a primary reason prosocial behavior is considered a social norm and a moral imperative in Western culture.

The Qur'an is filled with messages ordering people to behave ethically. Muhammad forbade gambling and intoxication. Donations and alms to the poor are strong precepts, as are kindness, compassion, and caring for one's neighbors.

"What is the purpose of being good?" asked Islam scholar Aminah Assilmi. "As a Muslim, I believe that there is a God, Creator of the universe. We should judge what is good by what the Creator has said. Good is something that changes with time. Islam goes through the relationships between parents and children, brothers and sisters, and so on; and these guidelines will never change or be outdated. However, the understanding of Islam by different people may change." Assilmi noted the unique nature of the basic value structure of Islam. "If we could just learn more about these guidelines, we could make the world a better place." She notes the differences in the concept of altruism from Islam to other religions. "Every religion requires you to be kind, but Islam goes down to the minutest details. For example, Muslims are supposed to know their neighbors well enough to be able to help them out with their problems" (Khan 2003). Koran, Sura al-Hashr (The Gathering 59:9), "But those who, before them, had homes (in Medina) and had adopted the Faith, show their affection to such as came to them for refuge, and entertain no desire in their hearts for things given to them, but give them preference over themselves, even though poverty was their own lot. And those saved from the covetousness of their own souls; they are the ones who achieve prosperity."

In Islam it is not considered enough to only have noble beliefs and principles. One must work for the economic upliftment of the less fortunate and needy. The Qur'an states (The Gathering 59:9) "Those saved from the covetousness of their own souls; they are the ones that achieve prosperity."12 The Qur'an also says (The Gathering 39): "So give the kinsman his due, and to the needy, and to the wayfarer. That is best for those who seek the favor of Allah, and it is they who prosper." In this verse the Qur'an uses the Arabic word which means "present" instead of "give," indicating that when a Muslim gives charity to his poor brother, he is not doing a favor but rather discharging the obligation he owes him-returning to him what is his due. According to the Prophet Muhammad, if the right hand gives charity, the left hand should not know to whom he gives. Islam requires that not only should the material needs of the poor be fulfilled, but also that their dignity be maintained.

Kindness is another very important attribute of the Islamic religion. Muhammad said, "God is kind and loves kindness in all things." He also said, "God is kind and loves kindness, and grants kindness but is most granted to harshness, and what is not granted to anything else." He also said, "Anything is beautiful by the inclusion of kindness and is marred by its lack" (Cleary 2001: 130).

Buddhism

Buddhism is about 2,500 years old and is based on the teachings of Gautama Siddhartha Buddha. The main goal of Buddhism is to attain nirvana, which is defined as the end of change and the end of birth and rebirth. One can reach nirvana through various practices, including meditation, leading a moral life, and detaching oneself from possessions and the struggle for wealth.

Buddha adapted the Vedic and Brahmanic concepts of rebirth and dependent origination. According to these theories, the next life is dependent upon the good and bad that one does in the present. In order to leave behind the cycle of death and rebirth, and thus also leave behind suffering, one must follow the precepts of Buddhism. In Buddhism the causes of suffering include the force of desire. Cessation of suffering comes from completely giving up the desires that lead to suffering; only after detaching ourselves from desire can we end the cycle of birth, pain, and rebirth. There are eight paths that one can follow to end suffering: right thought/aim; right speech; right action; right livelihood/occupation; right effort/endeavor; right mindfulness—which includes caring, love, and right meditation. Another very important step is to give love and show compassion toward other creatures.

There are at least two major sects in Buddhism: Mahayana and Theravada. Mahayana Buddhists emphasize the ideal of the unselfish bodhisattva, a living being committed to awakening. The bodhisattvas, because of their compassion for suffering beings, have delayed entering Nirvana even though they are capable of reaching enlightenment. The bodhisattva remains instead in this world to help others attain enlightenment.

Buddhism views altruism as an expression of one's awakening to one's true self and explains that it stems from compassion, appreciation, and a sense of interconnection. Buddhism encourages a holistic view of self, a view that transcends selfishness. Robert Ruffner Chilton (1992) notes that the essence of Buddhism, according to the Dalai Lama, consists of loving kindness and compassion; these are the two cornerstones upon which all of Buddhism rests. The core of Buddhist doctrine is to practice altruism: one should refrain from harming others and help others whenever possible. The most important practice is the *lojong* tradition (mind training), which implies ethical behavior on psychological grounds and accounts for why bodhisattvas act for the benefit of others and abstain from self-cherishing.

In Tibet, an Indian known as Atisa (980–1054) was involved in *lojong* instruction. Atisa traveled through parts of Southeast Asia including Sumatra, where Mahayana Buddhism—under the patronage of the Sailindra Empire—was introduced. Much of the teachings of Atisa focused on generating bodhicitta, which means an equal exchange of oneself in others. Atisa said, "Whenever I meet a person of bad nature who is overwhelmed by the negative energy and intense suffering, I will hold such a rare one dear and as if I found a precious treasure" (Geshe Tsultrim Gyeltsam quoted in Chilton 1992: 12).

The practice of bodhicitta is simply letting go of the feeling of indifference toward others and maintaining a sincere and loving mind towards all (Chilton 1992: 14). His Holiness the Dalai Lama said the bodhicitta is the ultimate state of mind that will allow us to accomplish our own welfare as well as the welfare of all other sentient beings (Chilton 1992: 15).

According to Chilton, there are five steps in generating bodhicitta by way of practices that equalize the exchange:

1. Viewing the equality between oneself and others
2. Contemplating the faults of self-cherishing
3. Contemplating the advantage of cherishing others
4. Exchanging oneself for others
5. Engaging in the practice of giving and taking

Thus, the essential spirit of altruism in these *lojong* teachings can be summarized as recognizing that self-concern is a true enemy of others' happiness and that others are true friends, worthy of our concern (Chilton 1992: 34).

Self-cherishing is one of the problems in the world today, by which we mean that a person looks out for "number one" and is not concerned with "the other." By cherishing another you are benefiting from it, and that may result in being cherished yourself. Having perceived emptiness, as compassion arises, there is no self or other. When there is no self or other, you will bring about the well being of all living beings (Chilton 1992: 24).

The Buddha, as he was about to die, was questioned by some of his students. They were concerned that after the master's death, people might begin propounding doctrines that had not been spoken by the Buddha himself, and these people might tell others that these doctrines were the actual words of Buddha. In reply, the Buddha told them "Whatever is well spoken is the word of the Buddha." If teaching results in greater peace, compassion, and happiness, and if it leads to a lessening of negative emotions, then it can be safely adopted and practiced as dharma, no matter who originally propounded it.

The Dalai Lama's contribution toward the promotion of global peace was formally recognized in 1989, when he won the Nobel Peace Prize. According to the Nobel Committee, he "consistently has opposed the use of violence...and advocated peaceful solutions based upon tolerance and mutual respect in order to preserve the historical and cultural heritage of his people" (Dalai Lama 1989). The Dalai Lama exhibits his love of humanity and warmth. He does not speak bitterly against the Chinese who continue to oppress Tibet, his homeland. Instead, he stresses a positive focus on human rights and the preservation of Tibetan cultural values. He has a great desire and need not only to hold onto faith and spirituality but also to seek truth. He believes that truth leads to understanding, inspiration, and a full liberation from ignorance and the suffering that we impose upon each other; these in turn will help bring about world peace. Buddhists believe that suffering can then cease and that lasting peace can be achieved—both peace of mind and peace in the world. "The path to such peace," the Dalai Lama says, "begins with the development of a calm abiding." He believes people need to have faith that they can achieve a more enlightened state of existence, even when the material world seems to deny such a possibility. There must be an ongoing interaction between reason and faith, between analysis and the growing conviction that one can find ways to live for the betterment of all human beings.

The Dalai Lama also maintains that there is another aspect of spiritual wholeness—compassionate action. Just as reason and faith interact to enhance conviction, so too do reflection and action interact to determine our spiritual faith. He further maintains that all religious thought points toward loving kindness and compassionate action. We must not believe that we are isolated, totally independent actors in this world. Rather, it is important that we keep our interdependence in mind, and remember that we are woven together by spiritual life. If we can maintain faith and conviction that such an understanding is the foundation on which we build our lives, then we must treat all human beings and other living things with respect and love. We may not succeed, but it is important to try our best. Then we will have at least made an attempt to form a better human society.

The Dalai Lama says that all the religious faiths, despite their philosophical differences, share an emphasis on human improvement, love and respect for others, and compassion. Prejudice and intolerance are afflictions of human society. When altruism is practiced, we are not angry at our enemies but are kind to them. When we are altruistic, we not only have inner happiness but can work toward social understanding, cooperation, unity, and harmony. Buddhism has historically sought a solution to suffering in inner transformation and a corresponding commitment to the highest ethical ideals, unlike science, which has sought a solution through knowledge (Davidson and Harrington 2002).

Kenneth Liberman (1985) concludes that the Tibetan people have developed a cultural praxis for the generation of altruism which operates on a mass scale and which is soundly based on a philosophical logic. In the Tibetan system of bodhicitta thought training, epistemology interacts with ethical practices: "method" and "wisdom" mutually affect each other. Just as one is said to be incapable of achieving enlightenment through altruistic compassion alone, it is held to be impossible to attain Buddhahood with only wisdom. Compassion and wisdom are mutually influential consciousnesses. Each augments, activates, and sets the tone for the other at every stage of the path. Bodhicitta is the seed for all higher mental and spiritual development. In this fashion, the Tibetans undertake ethical training that is philosophical, and conduct philosophical investigations that are ethical, in their orientation and their consequences (Liberman 1985: 125). Meditation is another attribute of Buddhism. Some perceive that meditation is a form of self-absorption, an Eastern relaxation technique. But some scholars feel that meditation is "better considered as a powerful means of engaging a universal psychological process, that of shifting one's preoccupation with self to a sense of interconnectedness with others." Jean Kristeller and Thomas Johnson

(Kristeller and Johnson 2005) compare the Buddhist tradition of loving kindness meditation, Judeo-Christian means of cultivating compassion and altruistic behavior, and the resurgent Catholic interest in contemplative prayer; all stress this idea of interconnectedness (Kristeller and Johnson, in press: 18–19). In effect, all religious traditions seek to encourage what Kristeller and Johnson term "a universal capacity for altruistic experience, love, and compassion" (2).

However, Catholic scholar Mathew Fox sees some differences between Buddhism and the Judeo-Christian traditions:

> Buddhism is explicit about compassion, for example, although I think that the Jewish and Christian traditions are more explicit about justice—but justice is a part of compassion. The Western prophets bring a kind of moral outrage, what I call "holy impatience," whereas the East brings serenity and an emphasis on patience. I think there's a time for both, but I think we are in a time now of holy impatience. (Van Gelder 2006: 22)

Hinduism

Hinduism is considered to be the oldest organized religion in the world. Hindus accept other religions with respect and do not look down on them. Hinduism teaches that all reality is ultimately one, in being and in function. Thus, if all are one, then the only way to treat others is with agape, respect, kindness, justice, and compassion. In a Hindu context, agape is the byproduct of *bhakti yoga*, which is the realization of God through love—compassionate love is the highest vehicle to union with God. Agape follows as a natural expression of purifying one's motives and being of service. In pursuing God, one becomes more like God, and agape follows as a natural result.

There are a number of gods in Hinduism; the supreme one being Brahman, creator of the world. Unlike Christianity or Judaism, many of the gods are personalized and have human characteristics. The largest percentage of Hindus worship three main gods: Brahman; Vishnu, the savior; and Shiva, the destroyer and restorer.

Hindus believe that the creation of the world is a continuous process and is not finished. The world is a living entity with human beings reincarnated into various stages in life, depending upon their deeds in previous lives. A complex religion, Hinduism seeks answers to questions about the meaning of life and about aspects of living a moral and ethical life. Hindus seeking to live a good life have several goals. They should participate in the good life and material goods can be important—but while one is making a living, one should not strive to accumulate wealth for its own sake. Each person has an important obligation to himself and to society to help all living things. Hindu teachings emphasize the idea of moral duty; selfishness is frowned upon, while selflessness is perhaps the most important moral precept.

The ideas of justice, caring, and nonviolence were emphasized in the Hindu religion by Rama Krishna (Ross and Hills 1956: 42), who is considered by some to be the reincarnation of the supreme Lord Vishnu (Ross and Hills 1956: 44). Rama Krishna attempted to combine the great spiritual values of Buddhism, Islam, and Christianity. He is remembered as one who sought the unity of all religions. One of the main values of Hinduism is peace, and its most famous representative among Hindus is Mahatma Gandhi, who was known worldwide as an advocate of peace and nonviolence. In fact, in the areas of human rights and social activism, there is no greater moral exemplar than Mahatma Gandhi. Gandhi's persistent passive resistance helped liberate India from years of oppression, and his Satyagraha ("truth-force"), acts of nonviolent resistance in the service of moral truth, were among the most influential events of the twentieth century. In 1948, India gained its independence largely through nonviolent resistance. Gandhi's ideology of nonviolent resistance on behalf of freedom and human dignity is his most durable legacy. Martin Luther King, Jr., employed Gandhi's techniques to change the face of a segregated nation. Likewise, Nelson Mandela inspired South Africans to work persistently against centuries of racism, terrorism, and oppression in that country and on the African continent. Both of these men saved lives and gained freedom for their oppressed people. Gandhi's philosophy has been planted in the minds of people all over the world and is perhaps the most powerful and inspirational force in modern history. The following statement by Gandhi offers us deep insight into his worldview: "Mankind is one, seeing that all are equally subject to the moral law. All men are equal in God's eyes. There are, of course, differences of race and status and the like, but the higher the status of a man, the greater is his responsibility" (Brinkley 1999).

Gandhi did not believe in the doctrine of the greatest good for the greatest number. He felt that the only real, dignified, human doctrine is the greatest good for all (Shepard 1987). When all his arguments in favor of the moral path proved futile, his answer was to voluntarily invite suffering in his own body to open the eyes of those determined not to see the light. Gandhi's perseverance and influence have been far reaching, and his life and death have touched and inspired some of the world's most influential spiritual leaders who continue to spread messages of nonviolent disobedience, affecting social change through empathy, compassion, inspiration, and love.

Theodore M. Ludwig (1996) notes that Hinduism, unlike Christianity and Islam, does not appear to be a missionary religion. The fundamental belief of Hinduism is that there are many spiritual paths appropriate to different people, dependent upon their own path, past karma, and spiritual perfection, and the idea of converting others to Hinduism does not fit this concept at all.

Hindu sages classify their values into four groups: physical, economic, moral, and spiritual. The final destiny of Hinduism is, as in Buddhism, union with the supreme god. Hindus believe in reincarnation, being held accountable for one's deeds (karma), and depending on those deeds; that is, if they are moral, just, and compassionate, their reward is a higher status upon rebirth. Thus, altruistic behavior is directly rewarded.

Taoism

Taoism began about 2,500 years ago in China. The Tao Te Ching (or Book of Reason and Virtue) is the shortest of all scriptures, containing only 5,000 words. The primary goal of Taoism may be described as realizing the mystical intuition of the Tao, which is the way, the undivided unity, and the ultimate reality. Tao is the natural way of all things, the nameless beginning of heaven and earth, and the mother of all things. All things depend upon the Tao, and all things return to it. Yet it lies hidden, transmitting its power and perfection to all things. He who has realized the Tao has arrived at pure consciousness and sees the inner truth of everything. Only one who is free of desire can apprehend the Tao, thereafter leading a life of "actionless activity." There is no personal god in Taoism and thus no union with a god. There is a strong ethic of caring for others.

According to Ross and Hills, Lao Tse, founder of Taoism, lived in China about 600 BCE, and the world would be poorer without him. He taught that "the world moves according to a divine pattern, which is reflected in the rhythmic and orderly movements of nature. The sum of wisdom and of happiness for man is that he adjust himself to this order and himself reflect the way the world moves. You seek wisdom, goodness, and contentment. In the ways you are trying to attain them, you are blind and foolish. Can you not see that wisdom is trust, goodness is acceptance, and

contentment is simplicity? This is the way of the world"
(Ross and Hills 1956: 76).

"Tao" means "way" or "way to go," or possibly as "nature" or "way of nature." The Tao is the source of all created things, even the Chinese gods. It existed before there
was any universe. Rise and fall, flow and ebb, existence and
decay, the Tao simply operates. The early Taoists frequently
referred to a past "Golden Age," when men lived in peace
and harmony because they were free from artificiality and
were simple. The "Man of Tao is described by them:

> He is cautious, like one who crosses a stream in winter;
> He is hesitating, like one who fears his neighbors;
> He is modest, like one who is a guest;
> He is yielding, like ice that is going to melt.
>   (Ross and Hills 1956: 80)

It is this person who sees that his true welfare is good for
all men. The good for all men is his good, too. This is what
Lao Tse meant by loving. The man of Tao trusts the world,
and the world can be entrusted to him.

Taoism is the indigenous religion of China and may be
defined as the Chinese philosophical and religious tradition
dedicated to achieving harmony with salutary forces inherent in the cosmos. Taoism teaches how to live life wisely, have
a quiet mind, and detach oneself from self-serving motives
and senseless activity. The avoidance of conflict allows actions of agape and charity to spontaneously flow through believers. The hope of attaining immortality for the masses not
adept in the practices of Taoism lies in merit—doing good
works such as building roads, performing acts of charity, and
extending compassion to living things.

In some ways Taoism appears to be the opposite of Confucianism. Confucianism seeks to perfect men and women
in the world. Taoism tries to turn away from society to the

contemplation of nature, seeking fulfillment in the spontaneous. The Tao, metaphysical absolute, appears to have been
a philosophical transformation of an earlier personal God.
Taoism is not just a passive contemplation, rather it serves
a later generation of religious-minded thinkers anxious to
transcend the limited conditions of human existence. "Their
ambition was to 'steal the secret of Heaven and Earth, to
wrench from it the mystery of life itself, in order to fulfill
their desire for immortality" (Beaver et al 1982: 251). Taoism
can be distinguished from Confucianism in that its goal is
the quest for freedom. For some it was freedom from political and social constraints of the emerging Confucian state,
while for others it was a more profound search for immortality. The Tao was the sum total of all things, which are and
which change, for change itself was a very important part of
the Taoist view of reality. "The Tao is complete, all embracing, the whole; these are different names for the same reality
denoting the One" (Beaver et al. 1982: 252). Lao Tse says,
"The ways of men are conditioned by those of Heaven, the
ways of Heaven by those of the Tao, and the Tao came into
being by itself. The Tao is therefore the principle of the universe and is also a pattern for human behavior, often called
uncontrived action" (Beaver et al 1982: 252).

Because as the Taoist tradition values self-perfection as
an imperative, many critics thought it was useless when trying to help others. But Lao Tse counseled against just such
an attitude, warning "One who cultivates himself while neglecting others has lost sight" of the path. He said, "The sage
is always adept at saving others, so that no one is rejected,
and is always adept at saving things, so that nothing is aban-
doned" (Kirkland 1986: 22). Taoists had lived in the hope of
a savior who would come to redress the evils of the world.
However, as noted by Russell Kirkland, Taoists soon realized
that "if one waits for someone else to save the world, the
task will never be accomplished. Hence the Taoist religion

enjoined its adherents to take aiding others and assisting in edification as their ambition" (Kirkland 1986: 22).

Confucianism

Confucius, the founding sage of Confucianism, was born in 551 BCE and died in 479 BCE. He was a contemporary of Lao Tse, the founder of Taoism. One important source of its major beliefs is the Analects (ca. 500 BCE) compiled by the students of Confucius after his death (Confucius c. 500 BCE). Because it was not written as a philosophy, it contains frequent contradictions and is therefore somewhat ambiguous. Besides the Analects, there is the Doctrine of Means, Great Learning, and the writings of Mencius, all of which are regarded as sacred texts.

The primary goal of Confucianism is to create true mobility through proper education and the inculcation of the Confucian virtues. It attempts to formulate an expanded definition of self "until it encompasses all others" (Czíkszentmihályi 2005: 184). Confucianism is described as a return to the ways of one's ancestors; the classics are studied to discover the ancient ways of virtues. Ethics are important, as is social propriety, especially the principle of reciprocal propriety in the five relationships; that is, in the relationships between ruler and subject, father and son, husband and wife, older brother and younger brother, and friend and friend. These reciprocal relationships are important because they help sustain the moral order of the society. There is a belief in the supreme ruler in Heaven as the ethical principle, whose law is order, impersonal and yet interested in all humankind. Confucianism offers the "Silver Rule": "What you do not want done to yourself, do not do to others" (Hume 1959: 121). Similar statements in Judaism and Christianity tend to take the positive, or "Golden Rule" form.

Confucianism's ethical teachings include *Li* (ritual, propriety, etiquette), *Hsiao* (love within the family; parent for children, children for parents, siblings), *Yi* (righteousness), *Xin* (honesty and trustworthiness), *Jen* (benevolence, humanity towards others; the highest Confucian virtue), and *Chung* (loyalty to the state). Confucian morality emphasizes the hierarchical structure of social relationships. As such, the social context determines what is morally proper. Discipline in the Chinese classroom does not come downward from a harsh teacher to submissive students but rather goes upward from respectful students to an admired teacher. There is a combination of high motivation and a strong sense of cooperation that exists in the absence of any externally imposed constraints. Education flowers easily in such an environment. This is possibly one of the chief differences between East and West: in the West we struggle for freedom and individual expression, which inevitably results in competition and feelings of alienation.

In traditional China, the struggle for selfless consideration of others (Confucian humanism) and collective achievement often results in strong feelings of identity at home, at work, and in the classroom. The Confucian principles are best exemplified by the concepts of *Yi*, the principle of reciprocity, and *Chung-shu*, conscientious altruism expressed by empathy and moderation (Ziniewicz 1996). The Confucian concepts of virtue, goodness, charity, and love are integrated into an ideal of love that finds that all forms of love are one and the same; the more we love one another, the more we are capable of loving one another.

As one major distinction between Western and Eastern religions is the difference in defining self, so is there a major distinction in addressing the concept of altruism. In Confucianism, the concept of altruism can be described as "impartial caring." As Czíkszentmihályi describes it, "goodness is defined at the level of the society as a whole, not in terms of the individual or the clan... [and] the moral rightness of an act is determined solely by the goodness of the act's consequences" (Czíkszentmihályi 2005: 181). Czíkszentmihályi introduces Mozi, a Chinese philosopher (470 BCE-390 BCE), whose ideology displayed a clear preference for altruistic behavior. The collective good underlies it all, and there is not much separating the idea that, "One must treat one's friend's parent as if he or she were one's own; one must treat one's friend's body as if it were one's own." Mozi continues, "If it were truly the case that the people of the world cared for each other impartially, then one would care for others (*ren*) as one cares about one's own self (*shen*)" (Czíkszentmihályi 2005: 182).

Confucianist thought on altruism points out the tension between intention and consequence. Some Confucianist thinking focuses on consequence, other passages focus on intentions. This raises the question: Should an action that has good consequences for others, but is undertaken for the wrong reasons, be considered good? It is easy to get tied up in philosophical knots when we address altruism, considering the subjectivity that such an examination inevitably involves.

Native American Traditions

The native people of the North American continent are composed of hundreds of tribes that share many spiritual ideas. Their traditions are not a religion in the Western sense (Jack Forbes, quoted in Weaver 1998: ix-x), but it has been observed that for the indigenous people of the Americas, religion is

> The Native American religious tradition is not similar to Christianity or Islam. There is no belief in proselytizing. Rather, one tribe has its instruction from the Creator and respects the fact that other tribes have their instructions as well. There is no need for one group to convert another group, thus Native American religious traditions are pluralistic. There is no religious conflict among tribes.

But what is found to be almost universal among the many hundreds of Northern American tribes is a common belief in something that is termed *Usen*, which loosely translates to "holy spirit" or "creator." Chief Seattle of the Suwamish Tribe tried to explain this in a letter to President Franklin Pierce in 1854: "Whatever befalls the earth befalls the sons of the earth. Man did not weave the web of life; he is merely a strand in it. Whatever he does to the web, he does to himself."

Joseph Marshall (2001) explains that life demands much from Native Americans. "We are all called upon to make sacrifices for ourselves and more often for others" (Marshall 2001: 105). In Native American traditions, acts are equally important, whether small or large:

We may not wake up to a war in our residential neighborhood, or find ourselves caught up in social or political upheaval, but some measure of sacrifice is often necessary nonetheless; such as parents working two jobs to enable their children's dreams, whether it's a college education or a pair of Nikes for basketball.... The acts are the gift of self (Marshall 2001: 106).

Native Americans find altruistic acts important. Courage and sacrifice and everyday examples of thoughtfulness are signs of being in balance, and those acts serve as examples for the rest of us:

Sacrifices come in all shapes and for every reason under the sun, and there are times when we can be unaware that someone has made one for us or because of us. Tough and extraordinary circumstances will always bring extraordinary individuals to the top with their acts of selfless courage and sacrifice. History has its crazy horses, spotted tails, and buffalo calf roads. We will never forget their deeds or their sacrifices. Ordinary, everyday people also make sacrifices and remind us that it is within human nature to do so. We stand and offer our seats on the bus or the subway, or we step back to let someone ahead of us in line. We help the elderly travelers near us in line carry their bags.... These are simple acts, but they can give us all a sense of dignity and an example to follow. (Marshall 2001: 108–9).

Native American Studies scholar Martin Brokenleg (1999) says that altruism is inborn and that the rudiments of empathy are apparent even in a newborn. An apology to one we have offended can be a form of generosity, because such an act places the offender in a position of humility. More powerful is the generosity of forgiveness extended to those who have hurt us. The less the offender deserves it, the greater the gift. Such generosity heals hurts and hatred. *Mitakuye oyasin* means "for all my relations" in Lakota Sioux. It is a prayer of harmony with all forms of life: other people, animals, trees and plants, and even rocks. Most Indians hear this phrase thousands of times a year in native ceremonies, and for many the phrase seems to be a liturgical blessing that includes all other forms of life in human ceremonial activities.

Dennis McPherson cites the observations of Christopher Columbus in 1492:

[The native people) are so ingenuous and free with all they have, that no one would believe it who has not seen it; of anything that they possess, if it be asked of them, they never say no; on the contrary, they invite you to share it and show as much love as if their hearts went with it, and they are content with whatever trifle be given them, whether it be a thing of value or of petty worth.

I forbade that they be given things so worthless as broken crockery and of green glass and lacepoints, although when they could get them, they thought they had the best jewel in the world (McPherson 1998: 79–80).

Another foreigner, Jesuit Paul Lejeune, writing a report in 1632, refers to the Huron people in what is now Quebec as "savages," but still notes that they do have some "rather noble moral virtues." Their selfless hospitality particularly struck LeJeune:

...their hospitality toward all kinds of strangers is remarkable; they present to them, in their feasts, the best of what they have prepared, and, as I have already said, I do not know if anything similar, in this regard, is to be found anywhere. They never close the door upon a stranger, and once having received him into their houses, they share with him the best they have; they never send him away, and when he goes away of his own accord, he repays them with a simple "thank you" (quoted in McPherson 1998: 80).

Historian Robert Bremner noted that the first American "philanthropists" came from Native American tribes. Although there are only Western records of early contact between Europeans and Native Americans, they describe the interconnectedness of tribal members. The Blackfeet tribe based their religion and philosophy on sharing, giving, and receiving. Some tribes engaged in a regular philanthropic ceremony where individuals gave away their possessions to others. Although only a few tribes had specific philanthropic ceremonies, the underlying values of giving and sharing are universal to America's native peoples (Bowden 2006).

As the contemporary Native American poet Chrystos (1991) sums up in her poem, "Shame On":

Samuel P. Oliner

... We've been polite for five hundred years
and you still don't get it
Take nothing you cannot return
Give to others, give more
Walk quietly
Do what needs to be done
Give thanks for your life
Respect all beings
Simple
And it doesn't cost a penny...

Commonality Among World Religions

"Truth is One-Paths are Many"

Of the several religious traditions discussed in this chapter, two of the oldest are Hinduism and Judaism, both approximately 4,000 years old. During thousands of years of human history, people searched for God for many reasons, resulting in a great diversity of religious expressions. Most of the religious prophets and philosophers reached the same truth—often it is only the language in which it is uttered that differs. All the traditions reviewed teach morality, reverence for truth, honesty, justice, dignity, freedom, and brotherhood. Thomas Oord's (2008) edited volume addresses the importance of love in both ancient and contemporary religions. Most contributors in the book see love as an important component of altruistic behavior. The fact that religions teach peace and love remains true despite the many wars and the terrible cruelty committed at times in our history among and between religious groups. There is no doubt that much blood has been shed in the name of religion.

Most religions contain three basic elements: philosophy, mythology, and rituals. Reviewing the various religious traditions, we find that they have in common a basic ethical behavior in the brotherhood of all people and in the idea of love for others. It is also true that sometimes these ethical ideals are not practical. The major differences are found mainly in rituals, and these differences may be due to the fact that religions developed in different places, within different cultural settings. Thus you have some religions that question birth control, how many wives a man should have, whether divorce should be permissible, and so forth. Robert E. Hume, in his book *The World's Living Religions* (1959), looks at the major religious traditions in the world and makes some notable comparisons. Hume sees many similarities between Christianity, Buddhism, and other faiths. All emphasize a moral and ethical life. Christianity emphasizes morality, linking it to the character of God. Buddhism also links its moral framework to a universal god. Both Christianity and Buddhism condemn selfishness, which seems to be responsible for so much human misery. Christianity says that the cure for human misery is positive love for others. Both religions teach the possibility and importance of salvation, and both have produced monastic institutions. Although many religious traditions stress the underlying equality of all human beings in their teachings, Hume sees a particular focus on equality in Buddhism. It puts emphasis on a person's inner attitude, as well as containing a certain noble earnestness in its ethics. Renunciation, conditional salvation, successful repudiation of the caste system, a major attribute of the Hindu tradition, differentiate Buddhism from Hinduism.

Within Confucianism one must compensate injury with justice, just as kindness repays kindness. On the other hand, in Taoism, as in Christianity, one forgives the harm-doer, implying that we must treat others better than they deserve. There is no *quid pro quo* in human relations. Other similarities include the fact that there is a Supreme Being and a claim of divine incarnation. There is also a claim of the supernatural origin of the founder, as well as a belief in divine revelation. Hume writes that within Hinduism, we find "the immanence of the divine in the world; human society, a divinely ordained structure; union with the divine, the goal of existence." In Buddhism, we see "selfishness as the root of misery; salvation through inner purity and self-discipline. Confucianism sees "the essential goodness of human nature as divinely implanted; religion as exercised in proper social relationships." In Taoism, religion is "exercised in humbly following the serene divine 'Way." In Judaism, "Superlative satisfaction [is] to be obtained through obedience to a God of righteousness," while in Islam, that satisfaction "is to be obtained through submission to an omnipotent God, who is not only a sovereign, but also a judge and a rewarder" (Hume 1959: 273-274).

All of these traditions make claims to being based upon divinely inspired scriptures or the ideas that informed their recording. In Hinduism there are the Vedas or "Books of Knowledge." In Buddhism, there is the Tripitaka or "Three Baskets" of teachings. Confucianism has The Five Classics and The Four Books. Judaism claims a divinely inspired "Law," "Prophets," and the "Sacred Writings." Islam has the Qur'an or "The Reading" or "The Recital." Christianity claims the Bible or "The Book" (Hume 1959: 275). In many of the traditional faiths, there are reports of miracles appearing, and the Golden Rule prevails.

Shah (1994) compares Indian and Western religions; Western religions tend to see the universe as a creation, while Indians look at the universe as an ongoing, cyclical process. Western religions have one absolute God, and the existence of God is proved through direct communication with Him. Indian religions tend to think in terms of receiving liberation or God's grace through experience on many paths, according to their understanding, temperament, and maturity; God is pure love and consciousness. In the West, there tends to be one true path to God; in Indian religions, man is on a progressive path that leads from ignorance to knowledge, from death to immortality. For Western religions, evil is a real, living force opposed to God's will, but in Indian religions there is no intrinsic evil.

Human values and conduct are viewed similarly in some ways. Western religions tend to be based on ethical and moral conduct, for the opposite leads one away from God. Indian religions also stress moral living, and in both the virtuous life is upheld as central. Salvation in the West comes at the end of the world, at the end of time, and has nothing to do with enlightenment. For the Indian religions, the goals of enlightenment and liberation are to be found in this life, within the context of time and within man himself. Saintly behavior in the West is based on good works, but in the East, it is based on moral ideals.

We should note here that not only religious background motivates altruistic behavior; altruistic behaviors found in cultures around the world are also motivated by identification with a definite moral community. According to Yablo (1980), there is a clear difference in the manner that Thais and Americans approach altruism; Thais showed a greater altruistic orientation than people in the United States. Thai behaviors were associated with charity and service work, and helping in ways that do not necessarily require wealth, yet require some degree of constant commitment over time. American subjects appear to most often offer help in ways associated with wealth or possessions. Thais also seem to donate more frequently to charities than American subjects. Although Thais reported that their helping behavior was influenced by Buddhism to some extent, it was due more to the collective nature of Thai culture than specifically to religion. There seemed to be much greater concern among the Thais for matters related to the heart, to such emotions as compassion, empathy, and a desire that others suffer less and experience happiness—all of which share roots in Thai culture, as well as in the Buddhist doctrine. American subjects rarely mentioned religion as a motivating factor for their responses, and their responses were very individual. Among American subjects, there seemed to be little sense of belonging to a whole. A sense of alienation is highlighted when comparing the United States to other cultures. There is a pervasive sense of alienation from society in Americans compared to Thais. American society's focus on an individualistic, "looking out for number one" attitude toward others may have short-circuited the likelihood of altruistic helping behavior (Yablo 1980: 139).

Reprinted From: Samuel P. Oliner, Altruism, Intergroup Apology, Forgiveness and Reconciliation, *Manifestations of Altruism in Different Religious Traditions,* (St. Paul MN: Paragan House, 2008)

References

Beaver, R. Pierce, Jan Bergman, Myrtle S. Langley, Wuff Metz, Arild Romarheim, Andrew Walls, Robert Withycombe, and R. W. F. Wootton. 1982. *Eerdmans' Handbook to the World's Religious.* Grand Rapids, MI: Wm.B Eerdmans Publishing Co.

Brokenleg, Martin. 1999. "Native American Perspectives on Generosity. *"Reclaiming Children and Youth 8 (2): 66-68*

Chilton, Robert Ruffner. 1992. "A Buddhist Practice of Altruism: Equalizing and Exchanging Oneself and Others." Master's Thesis, Department of Religious Studies, University of Virginia.

Chrystos. 1991. "Shame On". Dream On. Vancouver, BC: Press Gang Publishers.

Cleary, Thomas. 2001. Wisdom of the Prophet: The saying of Muhammad. Boston: Shambhala Publications, Inc.

Czikszentmihalyi, Mark. 2005. Altruism in Chinese Religions" in Altruism in World Religions, edited by Jacob

Neusner and Bruce Chilton: pp. 179-90. Washington, DC: Georgetown University Press.

Davidson, Richard J. and Anne Harrington, eds. 2002. Visions of Compassion: Western Scientists and Tibetan Buddhists Examine Human Nature. New York: Oxford University Press.

Degroot, Jacquelyn. N.d. "Jewish Philanthropy – The Concept of Tzedakah." Retrieved Oct. 6, 2005 (http://www.learningtogive.org/papers/index.asp?bpid=66

Hitchens, Christopher.1995. The Missionary Position: Mother Teresa in Theory and Practice. New York: Verso

Hume, Robert E. 1959. The World's Living Religions. New York: Charles Scribner's Sons.

Khan, Taimur. 2003. "Lecture Discusses Virtues of Altruism and Islam." Daily Pennysylvanian.com, University of Pennsylvania. Retrieved Aug. 18, 2005 (http://dailypennsylvanian.com/vnews/display./ART/2003/10/06/3f8112704d8bf)/

Kirkland Russell. 1986. "The Roots of Altruism in the Taoist Tradition." Retrieved Oct. 25, 2005 (http://www.arches.uga.edu/-kirkland/rk/pdf/pubs/ROOTS.pdf).

Kristeller, Jean L. and Thomas Johnson. 2005. "Cultivating Loving Kindness: A Two-Stage Model of the Effects of Mediation on Empathy, Compassion, and Altruism. "Zygon: Journal of Religion and Science. In press

Lama Surya Das. 1997. "Love and Forgiveness." A talk delivered in Cambridge, MA on January 27. Dharma Talks. Retrieved March 21, 2006 (http://www.dzogchen.org/teachings/talks/love.html).

Liberman, Kenneth. 1985. "The Tibetan Cultural Praxis: Bodhicitta Thought Training, Humboldt Journal of Social Relations 13 (1,2):113-26

Ludwig, Theodore M. 1996. The Sacred Paths: Understanding the Religions of the World. Upper Saddle, NJ: Prentice Hall.

Marshall, Joseph M. III. 2001. The Lakota Way: Stories and Lessons for Living, New York: Penguin Compass.

Mcpherson, Dennis. 1998. A Definition of Culture: Canada and first Nations" in Native American Religious Identity: Unforgotten Gods, edited by Jace Weaver: 77-98. Maryknoll, NY: Orbis Books.

Oord Thomas. 2008. The Altruism Reader: Selections from Writings on Love, Religion, and Science. Conshohocken: Templeton press.

Ross, Floyd H. and Tynette Hills. 1956. The Great Religions by which Men Live. Greenwich, CT:Fawcett Publications.

Sacks, Rabbi Jonathan: 2005. To Heal a Fractured World. New York: Schocken Books.

Shah, Parvin K.1994. " Essence of World Religions: Truth is One, Paths are Many." Retrieved Oct.11,2005 http://www.ibiblio.org/jainism/database/WORLDR/worldr.doc)

Shepard, Mark. 1987. Gandhi Today. Arcata, CA: Simple Productions.

Templeton, John Mark. 1999. Agape Love: A Tradition Found in Eight World Religions. Philadelphia, PA: The Templeton Foundation Press.

Van Gelder, Sarah Ruth. 2006. "Holy Impatience- An interview with Matthew Fox. "Yes! A Journal of Positive Futures, winter 4-5

Weaver, Jace, ed. 1998: Native American Religious Identity: Unforgotten Gods. Maryknoll, NY: Orbis Books

Yablo, Paul. 1991. "A Cross-Cultural Examination of Altruism and helping Behavior: Thailand and the United States. "Microfilm."

11

Ecumenism of the Deep Well

PAT DEVINE

Down through the ages the Western world has been influenced by three monotheistic religions considered part of the Abrahamic tradition: Judaism, Christianity and Islam. Judaism is the oldest of the religions having originated with the people of ancient Israel and Judea, and its teachings are embodied in the Torah and other sacred texts. It was followed later in the First Century by Christianity, which is based on the life of Jesus of Nazareth, whose teachings are embodied in the New Testament of the Bible. Lastly, there is the religion of Islam in the 7th Century A.D. which is based on the teachings of the prophet Mohammed and the Qur'an, which contains his revelations. These three religions have managed to coexist together, for better or for worse, for over two thousand years. Each of them had their own path, or their own way to God, which is embodied in their specific belief systems, sacred texts, dogmas, rituals, and spiritual practices. Unfortunately, all too often their belief systems have separated them from each other, rather than united them in living out related compassionate spiritual callings. At their core, the Abrahamic religions, as all the major world religions do, have a deep wisdom of love, caring, compassion, patience, understanding, forgiveness, mercy, generosity and justice. The question is: How do we tap into and share this core wisdom in the post-modern world? Is ecumenism the answer? If it is, how do the Abrahamic religions work together in the spirit of ecumenism with each other? How do they relate to religions such as Buddhism and Hinduism? How do they relate to indigenous spiritualities such as Native American traditions and historic/present pantheism practices?

The word ecumenism comes from a family of classical Greek words: *oikos*, meaning a "house," "family," "people" or "nation;" *oikoumene*, "the whole inhabited world" and *oikoumenikos*, "open to or participating in the whole world." From its beginning, it is a word infused with Christian meaning. Both Matthew and Luke refer to some form of *oikos* or *oikoumene* in their writings. This theme of unity, however, also is referred to in the Hebrew Scriptures, which talk about the Hebrew people gathering the disparate tribes into one religious nation called Israel as a way of reconciling God's people. Ancient Judaism was based on the unitive idea of one people of God (Ecumenical movement 2017).

Reaching the unitive state of *oikos* has been an elusive concept throughout the history of Christianity. From its inception, Christianity was diverse, and it has been a challenge to create this special home, family, or people centered around the life of Jesus, the Jewish itinerant peasant from the Galilee, who travelled the countryside speaking in parables about a new way of living. At the time, different segments of the Jewish community had experienced this Jewish peasant firsthand; they had heard him preaching or witnessed his miraculous acts. After his death, they tried to discern the meaning of his life and works and to create a narrative that could be incorporated into their lives. What followed was not a single narrative but varying interpretations rendered by the community regarding the life and works of Jesus of Nazareth.

As the narrative moved beyond Judaism to include gentiles, Christians struggling with the idea of how to become a unitive people was an ongoing process. Various perspectives were debated and eventually a canon of beliefs was adopted and Christianity became a state religion under the Roman Emperor Constantine. Later, major schisms and breakaways took place, but none were as divisive as the Reformation of the 16ᵗʰ Century, which fragmented the Church of Rome into a number of small Christian sects. It has taken until the 21ˢᵗ Century before Christianity could begin to heal the wounds inflicted by this tumultuous period in church history.

The early ecumenical movement is a child of the Reformation. The first ecumenical endeavor involved the organization of the overseas missions as well as small church settings. It was not until after the Second World War, in 1948, that representatives of 147 Christian churches assembled in Amsterdam to form an official organization called the World Council of Churches. The Council became the first official body responsible for promoting ecumenism, or Christian unity, in the world. The 1948 conclave was the beginning of the modern ecumenical movement. Because of the efforts of the World Council of Churches, there are Christian churches on every continent that are working to bring about Christian unity (World Council of Churches, n.d.).

In the decade of the 1960's, the ecumenical movement became filled with the energy and passion characteristic of this period of great social change in America. Ecumenical efforts started out simple and grew. Initially, Catholic and Reform clergy began to socialize together. Priests and ministers began to educate their parishioners and congregants about a new idea called ecumenism. Later, Protestant ministers and Catholic priests were invited to give joint lectures about their respective traditions and to speak at length about the worship styles, liturgies and belief systems associated with each tradition. Communities began to sponsor interfaith dinners. Interfaith services began to be held. These were all positive developments for Christian faith traditions that, a few years earlier, had barely tolerated each other.

In addition to ecumenism evolving in Christian communities, the decade of the 1960's was breaking down barriers and posing new religious challenges; for example, the Anti-War Movement, the Women's Movement and the Environmental Movement to name a few. Americans soon saw people dressed in orange robes who called themselves Hare Krishna, chanting and dancing at airports and in the downtowns of major US. cities. They heard about a peaceful looking man called the Dali Lama who had just lost his home in some far away land. They nightly watched on their television sets Buddhist monks in crimson robes who were setting themselves on fire in protest over the Vietnam War. An Eastern group calling themselves Moonies tried to enlist converts on American city streets. An eastern spiritual community settled into life in rural Iowa. The Beatles traveled to the East to visit a spiritual master. An Eastern guru opened a commune in rural Oregon. Young women, calling themselves Wiccans, established collectives embracing the spirituality of the Goddess. New groups who worshiped nature, calling themselves Pagans, came to the fore. A Zen retreat center on the coast of California became a desired destination. Meditation and yoga began to be incorporated into the lifestyles of many Americans. The American Indian Movement along with other Indigenous supporters took over Alcatraz one year to draw attention to their movement. They wanted their lands back and later they wanted their spirituality back as well. Eastern spiritual traditions were becoming ever more popular in the West; Indigenous spiritualities were getting noticed in positive ways by popular culture; earth based spiritualities were coming to the fore. Where did Christian ecumenism fit in with the other Abrahamic traditions of Judaism and Islam? Where did it fit in with the Eastern traditions such as Buddhism and Hinduism? Where did it fit in with Native American spirituality as well as with the reemerging nature-based spiritualities? To find an answer to these questions, let us look to two sources: Christian Theologian Matthew Fox and to a leader in the interfaith community.

Fox gives us a new way of looking at ecumenism in his book *One River, Many Wells* (2000). He introduces the concept of Deep Ecumenism in the following passage:

> There is one underground river—but there are many wells into that river: an African well, a Taoist well, a Buddhist well, a Jewish well, a Muslim well, a goddess well, a Christian well, and aboriginal wells. Many wells but one river. To go down a well is to practice a tradition, but we would make a grave mistake (an idolatrous one) if we confused the well itself with the flowing waters of the underground river. Many wells, one river. That is Deep Ecumenism (Fox 2000, p. 5).

According to Fox, Deep Ecumenism is a model not just to learn about other traditions but also a model to go deeper into one's own tradition. He quotes the Dali Lama as saying: "the biggest obstacle to interfaith sharing is people's unhealthy relationships to their own faith" (Fox, 2000, p. 7). Thus, the term Deep Ecumenism, or what one could call Ecumenism of the Deep Well, is a paradigm shift that more aptly addresses the religious pluralism of the present day and leads one into the world of interfaith, which is the practical application of Deep Ecumenism at work in the world.

According to Rev. Will McGarvey, a Presbyterian minister who heads an Interfaith Council in northern California, the dialoguing and mutual sharing that took place between the various Christian groups in the decade of the 1960's, laid the groundwork for the interfaith movement that emerged later in the decade of the 1970's. The goal of interfaith work is the living out of shared values as people representing the various faith traditions and to speak from these common values, especially in protecting the vulnerable in society states Rev. McGarvey (McGarvey, 2018).

Today the religious landscape in the U.S. reflects Christians, Jews and Muslims joining with the Eastern faith traditions of Buddhism and Hinduism, as well as with other traditions, in the sharing of core values and in working towards establishing relationships based on mutual respect and understanding. Since the early 1970's, an interfaith movement has grown up. It has progressed from its beginnings, through an intermediate phase, and into maturity. Its growth has been an exponential blossoming, not only on the national level, but on an international level as well. There is now an interfaith infrastructure in America that is made up of networks of interfaith organizations on the regional, state and national levels. Interfaith settings are diverse and encompass every aspect of life; for example, youth and young adult programs; airport, hospital, hospice and nursing home interfaith chaplaincies; an Interfaith Worker Justice Program; an Interfaith Power and Light Program; an Interfaith Democratic Rights Program to name a few (The Pluralism Project n.d.-c).

Presently there are many organizations committed to advancing interfaith cooperation in the world. However, the following two organizations, the United Religions Initiative (URI) and the Parliament of the World's Religions, stand out not only because of their unique histories and present-day endeavors to advance interfaith understanding, but also because of their advocacy efforts to bring Native American, Wiccan, Neopagan and other spiritualities to the interfaith table and to give them a voice (Frey 2012).

The United Religions Initiative (URI) was founded by Episcopal Bishop William Swing in San Francisco in 1995. At the time when the city was celebrating the 50th anniversary of the United Nations, Bishop Swing asked the question "If the nations of the world are working together for peace through the UN, then where are the world's religions?"

(United Religions Initiative, n.d.). The answer to this question took the form of the signing of a UN Charter whereby the United Religions Initiative (URI) was born. In addition to having official representation at the UN, the URI sponsors Cooperation Circles that bring faith traditions together, at home and abroad, around local and global initiatives designed to help communities in conflict resolution and reconciliation, environmental sustainability, education, women and youth programs, as well as advocacy for human rights to name a few (United Religions Initiative 2017, Spring).

Parliament of the World's Religions was birthed one hundred years ago in 1893 when the World's Parliament of Religions held its first interfaith conclave at the World's Fair in Chicago, Illinois. At the time, it brought together a diverse group of national and international figures representing the spiritual traditions of both the East and the West. It was the first gathering of its kind to take place centered around formal interreligious dialogue. One hundred years later in 1993 the Parliament returned and is now a major voice in promoting the concept of interfaith understanding and cooperation. Today, under the name of Parliament of the World's Religions, it works to address a variety of societal issues; for example, promoting climate action, supporting women's dignity, combating hate on many different levels to name a few. It continues its commitment to interreligious dialogue by hosting interfaith conclaves every three years in some part of the world (Parliament of the World's Religions n.d.).

Religious Diversity

When one looks at the religious landscape of modern-day America, one can see that the paradigm shift to Deep Ecumenism is an appropriate one. We have become a nation of many wells. Presently, America is quickly becoming a multifaith country. For an understanding of the present religious landscape in America, let us look to the recent studies done by the Pew Research Center.

The most salient feature that stands out when looking at the current religious makeup in America is that we are a very different society religiously than we were 50 to 100 years ago. Just how much America has changed religiously was the impetus behind two relatively recent Pew Research Center Religious Landscape studies. The first study was conducted in 2007 and a second follow-up study took place in 2014. The Pew studies revealed that even though the Christian portion of the U.S. population is going down, the United States continues to be *oikos* or home to more Christians than any other country on the planet. According to the study, around seven-in-ten Americans continue to call some branch of the Christian faith their religious home. However, both mainline Protestants and Catholics have declined approximately three percentage points from 2007 to 2014. During the same time period, the number of Americans who call themselves religiously unaffiliated (atheist, agnostic or no identification) has increased more than six points from 2007 to 2014 from 16.1% to 22.8%. Moreover, the study revealed that the number of Americans who identify with non-Christian faiths (Jews, Muslims, Buddhists, Hindus and other faith traditions) has also moved ahead from 2007 to 2014 rising 1.2 percentage points from 4.7% to 5.9% (Pew Research Center 2015).

Based on these research findings, the spiritual paradigm Deep Ecumenism more accurately reflects the current-day religious diversity in American society. The following quote from the Harvard Pluralism Project reflects how members of the Christian tradition are embracing the idea of interfaith understanding and cooperation:

> There has also been a concurrent re-examination of the relation of Christianity to other world religions that has been strong, positive, and biblically-based. The

Roman Catholic Church and most of the major Protestant denominations have given new emphasis to interfaith dialogue as essential to the relation of Christians to people of other faiths.

Documents like the Catholic *Nostra Aetate*, the Presbyterian "Interfaith Relations Denominational Principles and Policies," and the United Methodist "Guidelines for Interreligious Partnerships" provide a new sense of direction for Christians seeking to be good neighbors in a multi-religious society (The Pluralism Project, n.d.-a).

Communities of Faith Develop Interfaith Models

The Neighbor-to-Neighbor (N2N) partnership, founded by Elder Terence Clark of Lafayette- Orinda Presbyterian Church in northern California, is an inspiring program that was developed at the community level. Clark brought members of his church, the local synagogue, and the local Islamic Center together to create an interfaith community. What followed was the founding of the Neighbor-to-Neighbor (N2N) partnership whereby the three faith traditions mutually share in sponsoring a wide variety of social, educational, social justice programs and women's support groups (Clark, 2018). Similarly, in western Omaha, negotiations over sharing a parking lot led to Christians, Jews and Muslims crossing the faith divide and engaging in dialogue. This process eventually led to the founding of the Tri-Faith Neighborhood Project which later evolved into the development of an interfaith center to promote the scholarly study of the religious traditions as well as a social and cultural center to foster interfaith relationships (The Pluralism Project n.d.-d). The Neighbor-to-Neighbor (N2N) partnership and the Tri- Faith Neighborhood Project serve as templates for the development of other interfaith communities. In addition to sharing core values, these programs work hard to educate the participants in cross-faith understanding and

Pat Devine

to create environments which facilitate social bonding (The Pluralism Project n.d.-d).

Interfaith Model Adapts to Complex Environment

In addition to faith communities developing interfaith programs, interfaith efforts have been able to adapt to modern-day complex environments. Since 1982, the Hartsfield-Jackson Airport serving Atlanta, Georgia has embraced the interfaith model of airport chaplaincy based on the three Abrahamic faith traditions as well as Buddhism. The four faiths come together to share core values and to bring caring and compassion to travelers for a brief moment on their journeys. In between arrivals and departures, interfaith clergy minister to the needs of the diverse transient population that makes up this large metropolitan airport. In addition, neutral sacred space is provided where travelers can spend quiet time and practice their spiritual traditions. The Hartsfield-Jackson Airport is a wonderful example of how interfaith ministries are adapting to the complex environments that make up the modern-day world (The Pluralism Project, n.d.-b).

Interfaith Model Supports Native American Rights and Lands

There are interfaith models of faith traditions coming together to help and support indigenous peoples in their fight for their lands and their rights. A recent example of such an endeavor took place on November 16-17, 2017 when Christian clergy and Jewish rabbis joined in coalition with environmentalists and representatives from the various Indian tribes (Hopi, Pueblo of Zuni, Ute, Mountain Ute and the Navajo Nation) to help save Bears Ears, a 1.35 million-acre protected area in southeast Utah that was being threatened by Government development (Larkman 2017). On another occasion, June 19, 2017 marks the first time that religious leaders representing twenty-one countries as well as the Christian, Muslim, Jewish, Hindu, Buddhist, and Taoist religions came together to work in unison with indigenous people to end deforestation and protect the planet's tropical rainforests (World Council of Churches 2017). Such interfaith initiatives typify a grassroots energy that is beginning to surface in recent years whereby faith traditions are embracing environmental, climate and indigenous rights issues.

Interfaith Models in the Middle East

On the nightly news we are bombarded with stories from the Middle East where conflict among people representing one or more of the Abrahamic faith traditions is involved. However, there is an alternate narrative that is developing that does not fit into news sound bites. The seeds of the interfaith model were planted in February of 2018 in Vienna, at a conference sponsored by the Vienna-based International Dialogue Centre (KAICIID). It was a time when 200 religious leaders from the Middle East met to affirm social cohesion and peaceful coexistence in the Arab region between Christians, Jews and Muslims. The conference was a first step in what is hoped to be a continuing dialogue between the Abrahamic faith traditions to promote unity in the Middle East (World Council of Churches 2018).

Another major effort in the Middle East is in the planning stages for an interfaith project on the Arabian Peninsula. On September 20, 2019 in New York City, the Higher Committee of Human Fraternity unveiled plans for a unique complex called Abrahamic House. The project will include a mosque, church and synagogue on Saadiyat Island in Abu Dhabi. It came out of Pope Francis and Dr Ahmed Al Tayeb, the Grand Imam of Al Azhar jointly signing the Document on Human Fraternity in Abu Dhabi in February 2019, which called for the reconciliation of people from all faith traditions in service of peace in the world. The Committee intends for

Abrahamic House to stand for religious tolerance and education and be a place where all faiths can come together in mutual respect and understanding (Higher Committee of Human Fraternity 2019).

Interfaith Religious Education

Whether preparing for life as part of the Christian clergy or for life as a Rabbi, the theological and rabbinical education involved is broadening to include interfaith. The future priest, minister or rabbi will need to be versed in the other major religious traditions of the world in addition to being a good counselor and spiritual leader.

Many seminaries foster interfaith dialogue in hopes of engendering compassion, tolerance, and understanding among those who will later enter education and the clergy. Although such programming generally addresses only Christian-Jewish dialogue, in recent years leaders of the involved organizations have come to the realization that Muslims have just as crucial a voice. Many predict that within the next ten years monotheistic "trilogies" will develop more and more frequently (The Pluralism Project, n.d.).

The Crossing of Age-Old Divides

Deep ecumenism is at work in the area of intergroup apology, forgiveness and reconciliation. Age-old divides are being crossed between Christian denominations as well as between major faith traditions. A recent example of the former is the 500th anniversary of the Reformation in 2017, when not only the gifts of the Reformation were celebrated but the pain and suffering perpetrated by all sides was lamented. Catholics, Lutherans and other reform churches are now facing the future together (Underwood 2017).

In the book by Samuel P. Oliner, (2008) *Altruism, Intergroup Apology, Forgiveness and Reconciliation*, he delineates some of the religious divides that have been crossed in recent years. A small sample involving faith traditions includes the following: (1) The Evangelical Lutheran Church apologized for the antisemitism of Martin Luther and the harm perpetrated against the Jews over the past five hundred years; (2) The Pope apologized for centuries of Catholic prejudice and intolerance against the Jewish people as well as against the Muslim people—at the same time, he also apologized for the Crusades and slavery; (3) Cardinal John O'Connor of the Catholic Church apologized for all the pain imposed on the Jewish people by many Catholics over the past thousand years; (4) France's Catholic clergy apologized to the Jewish people for the Church's silence at the time of the Holocaust; (5) The United Methodists apologized to the Cheyenne and Arapaho tribes for the role that one of their ministers played in the 1864 massacre of their people (Oliner, 2018, pp 245-249).

Ecumenism and Forgiveness

There is a close relationship between forgiveness and ecumenism. According to Oliner, "Precisely because of the potentially divisive nature of organized religion, ecumenism is a desirable attribute and may be strongly associated with forgiveness" (Oliner, 2008, p.134). Thus, it is because of the conflict associated with religion that the spirit of ecumenism needs to be developed by our faith traditions. It is through healing the wounds of the historical past, and taking part in the process of forgiveness, that our faith traditions can come together and move forward to an ecumenical future of working together in interfaith cooperation.

The Catholic-Jewish Divide

One of the most significant divides that has been crossed in recent years is the divide separating the Roman Catholic Church and the world-wide Jewish community. Pope John Paul II, during his reign, crossed a divide that went back

Pat Devine

2000 years when in 1986 he visited Rome's synagogue to embrace Christianity's Jewish past. Later, Pope Francis used the occasion of his first visit to the synagogue to celebrate the 50th anniversary of the Vatican Council document *Nostra Aetate*. The original document sought to put to rest the accusation that has been perpetuated for centuries; namely, that the Jews were responsible for the death of Christ. Francis reiterated at length in a new document how Christianity is rooted in Judaism and renewed a pledge of cooperation. Also, Francis has put great emphasis on the idea that the institutional church should not try to convert Jews (Gruber 2016).

One of the positive signs of this new relationship between the Roman Catholic Church and the Jewish community, is the recently signed historic agreement between the Vatican and the Jewish organization World ORT. In 2017, World ORT and the Pontifical International Law Foundation, Scholas Occurrentes, signed a joint agreement to bring together 500 young people from all over the globe, with differing religious and socioeconomic backgrounds, to Buenos Aires in 2018, to participate in open, meaningful and multicultural dialogue. The overall goal of the gathering was to plant seeds of respect for differences that exist and to share in commonalities (ORT America 2017).

The Dali Lama on Living in an Interdependent world

On the subject of interfaith understanding, His Holiness the Dali Lama, from the Tibetan Buddhist tradition, addresses the fact that we now live in an interdependent world where there is no room for divisions as human survival depends now on cooperation. He stresses that dialogue and interfaith understanding is the only path for a world that is now truly interdependent. "In reality, the survival of one region of the world depends on that of others. Therefore, the world has become much closer, much more interdependent. As a result, there is much more human interaction on a larger scale. Under such circumstances, the acceptance of pluralism among the world's religions is very important" (Dali Lama 2003, p. 49).

Religious Pluralism

Living with religious pluralism is not an easy task. However, in this interdependent world, it is what is being asked of us. Just as in other areas of life, such as in marriage or in the political arena, one is required to negotiate differences; it is through healthy, constructive dialogue with our faith partners and respecting their perspectives that religious unity out of diversity can be achieved. Admittedly, working through differences is not an easy task. Just as living in a democracy can sometimes be messy, so too living with faith differences can sometimes be messy as well. However, it is through accepting a degree of healthy conflict and working to respect differences, that accompany religious diversity and pluralism, that humanity has the best chance of creating a more peaceful world (Kazanjian 2018).

Summary

Three questions were asked at the beginning of this writing: How do the Abrahamic faith traditions work together in the spirit of ecumenism? How do they relate to the other major faith traditions of the world? How do they relate to Native American spirituality and to the new re- emerging nature-based spiritualities? To find an answer to these questions, we examined the roots of ecumenism. We started with the early modern history of Christianity. We learned how the Reformation of the 16th Century birthed an early ecumenical effort to unite the Christian churches, which later matured into a modern ecumenical movement after World War II. In following the social changes of the 1960's, the limitations of Christian ecumenism were pointed out. At this point, we looked to two sources: Christian Theologian Matthew Fox and to a leader in the interfaith community for the paradigm shift to Deep Ecumenism. We learned how the interfaith model of interreligious cooperation is Deep Ecumenism at work in the world today. What followed were present-day examples of Deep Ecumenism, or interfaith work involving the Abrahamic faith traditions in joint efforts with other faith traditions as well as with other present-day spiritualities. We also learned how the idea of Deep Ecumenism was impacting the way we educate our religious leaders. We learned of efforts in the area of apology, forgiveness, and reconciliation where age-old divides have been crossed and how ecumenism is closely related to forgiveness. We learned the thoughts of a major religious leader of the Tibetan Buddhist tradition on living in an interdependent world. Finally, we learned how religious diversity and pluralism requires the ability of faith traditions to engage in healthy conflict and dialogue in order to respect differences. The narratives that were included in this writing are a small sampling of the world's religions working together and sharing core values in new ways. They are a bellwether projection of how Deep Ecumenism or interfaith work will define the religious landscape of the future.

His Holiness the Dali Lama reminded us how we now live in an interdependent world and that the quality that is needed in order for the human species to survive is cooperation. Modern-day physics tells us, that on a subatomic level, all of life is interconnected. Modern-day economists tell us the world's economies are all interwoven. Modern-day democracies seek unity out of diversity. Modern-day technology has created a world-wide web of connectivity— cooperation, interconnectedness, interwoven, unity out of diversity, connectivity—these are the qualities we also need today when speaking of our faith traditions. Just as the interweaving of modern-day economies bodes well for a more peaceful world, so too does the interweaving of our faith traditions. The arc of human progress is a long one, and despite present day religious intolerance and violence both at home and abroad, it appears to be pointing to a species that is evolving towards being interconnected and to faith traditions that are evolving towards being interconnected as well. The bellwether signs are pointing to the fact that people of all faith traditions are being called to be an intra people and an inter people. They are being called to be an ecumenical people and a people of Deep Ecumenism; to be an *oikos* people and a people of the deep well; to a new religious pluralism that is not only a pathway to peace between religious traditions but a pathway to peace in the world.

we are an *intra* people and an *inter* people;
we are an *oikos* people and a people of the *well*;
we are an *ecumenical* people and a people of *deep ecumenism*;
we will sit in each other's sacred spaces;
we will drink from the wisdom of each other's wells;
we will walk together in each other's footsteps;
we will treat each other with kindness and compassion;
we will unite together in the underground river of love.
                                                    Pat Devine

References

Clark, T. Interview by Pat Devine March 17, 2018. Lafayette-Orinda Presbyterian Church, Walnut Creek, CA.

Dalai Lama [Tenzin Gyatso]. (2003). *The compassionate life*. Wisdom Publications. Ecumenical movement. (2017). In P. Lagassé (Ed.), *The Columbia encyclopedia* (7th ed.). Retrieved January 25, 2018, from https://search.credoreference.com/

Fox, M. (2000). *One river, many wells: Wisdom springing from global faiths.* Jeremy P. Tarcher; Putnam.

Frew, D. (2012, March 15). *Wicca, Indigenous traditions, and the interfaith movement.* The Interfaith Observer. http://www.theinterfaithobserver.org/journal-articles/2012/3/15/wicca-indigenous-traditions-and-the-interfaith-movement.html

Gruber, R. E. (2016, January 16). *What Pope Francis synagogue visit says about Catholic–Jewish relations.* The Times of Israel. https://www.timesofisrael.com/what-pope-francis-synagogue-visit-says-about-catholic-jewish-relations/

Higher committee of human fraternity unveils design for the Abrahamic Family House. (2019, October 3). SteelGuru. https://steelguru.com/infra/higher-committee-of-human-fraternity-unveils-design-for-the-abrahamic-family-house/549873

Kazanjian, V. (2018, January 15). *Why religious diversity is the pathway to peace.* The Interfaith Observer. http://www.theinterfaithobserver.org/journal-articles/2018/1/12/why-religious-diversity-is-the-pathway-to-peace

Larkman, C. (2017, November 20). *UCC clergy, interfaith leaders join Native People to protect sacred site in Utah.* United Church of Christ. https://www.ucc.org/news_ucc_clergy_interfaith_leaders_join_native_people_to_protect_sacred_site_in_utah_11202017

McGarvey, W. Interview by Pat Devine, February 1, 2018. Interfaith Council of Contra Costa County, Walnut Creek, CA.

Oliner, S. P. (2008). *Altruism, intergroup apology, forgiveness, and reconciliation.* Paragon House.

ORT America. (2017, November 2). *Pope Francis facilitates initiative with ORT* [News release]. https://ortamerica.org/pope-francis-facilitates-initiative-with-ort/

Parliament of the World's Religions. (n.d.). Retrieved March 15, 2018, from https://parliamentofreligions.org/

Pew Research Center. (2015, May 12). *America's changing religious landscape* [Report]. https://www.pewforum.org/2015/05/12/americas-changing-religious-landscape/

The Pluralism Project. (n.d.-a). *From diversity to pluralism.* Retrieved January 31, 2018, from http://pluralism.org/encounter/todays-challenges/from-diversity-to-pluralism/

The Pluralism Project. (n.d.-b). *Interfaith Airport Chaplaincy, Inc.* http://pluralism.org/promising-practice/interfaith-airport-chaplaincy-inc/

The Pluralism Project. (n.d.-c). *The interfaith infrastructure: Citizenship and leadership in the multireligious city: Summary report of pilot study (2011–2012).* Retrieved March 15, 2018, from http://pluralism.org/interfaith/report/

The Pluralism Project. (n.d.-d). *An invitation to a Tri-Faith neighborhood* [Case study]. http://pluralism.org/case-study/an-invitation-to-a-tri-faith-neighborhood-b/

The Pluralism Project. (n.d.-e). *Jewish interfaith endeavors: Academic programs (2004)* [Report]. http://pluralism.org/research-report/jewish-interfaith-endeavors-academic-programs/

Underwood, K. (2017, October 31). *Catholics and Protestants commemorate the Reformation.* The Trumpet. https://www.thetrumpet.com/16392-catholics-and-protestants-commemorate-the-reformation

United Religions Initiative. (n.d.). *Charter.* https://uri.org/what-we-do/charter

United Religions Initiative. (2017, Spring). A special United Nations issue: International Day of Peace and World Interfaith Harmony Week [Special issue]. *Interaction.* https://uri.org/sites/default/files/media/document/2017/resource_files-InterAction_Spring2017_WEB.pdf

World Council of Churches. (n.d.). *About us.* https://www.oikoumene.org/en/about-us

World Council of Churches. (2017, June 19). *Religious leaders join interfaith rainforest initiative in Oslo today*. https://www.oikoumene.org/en/press-centre/news/religious-leaders-join-interfaith-rainforest-initiative-in-oslo-today

World Council of Churches. (2018, March 1). *Christian, Jewish and Muslim leaders in Vienna affirm social cohesion and peaceful coexistence*. https://www.oikoumene.org/en/press-centre/news/christian-jewish-and-muslim-leaders-in-vienna-affirm-social-cohesion-and-peaceful-coexistence

12

Apology and Forgiveness

SAMUEL P. OLINER

The one who pursues revenge should dig two graves.
-Chinese proverb

If we practice an eye for an eye and a tooth for a tooth, soon the whole world will be blind and toothless.
-Mahatma Gandhi

He that cannot forgive others breaks the bridge over which he must pass himself, for every man has a need to be forgiven.
-Lord Herbert

The importance of forgiveness cannot be underestimated. Indeed, a large body of work has grown up around the concept. The teachings and literature of all world religions are filled with persuasive suggestions that apology and forgiveness lead to both emotional and spiritual growth and healing. Many argue that apology and forgiveness ought to be implemented in our educational systems because scientific evidence indicates that they do make a difference in people's lives, helping to reconcile transgressor evildoers with those who have been victimized or hurt. We should perhaps take encouragement from the wide spectrum of research being conducted into the benefits of the forgiveness process in both interpersonal and intergroup relations. These studies are being conducted in evolutionary biology, philosophy, and within virtually every social science.

Religious scholars have addressed the manifestations of altruism and forgiveness in different religious traditions. What one derives from their discussions is that forgiveness is consistent with most or all world religions but it is addressed in different ways. Christian and Jewish scholars have indicated that forgiveness is central to their traditions, while forbearance and compassion is central to Buddhism. In Islam, personal forgiveness is valued, but Allah's forgiveness is considered to be of paramount importance. Christianity, Islam, and Buddhism all appear to encourage forgiveness irrespective of whether the offenders apologize or express regret. In Judaism, on the other hand, God is not anxious to forgive a sinner unless the sinner seeks forgiveness from those who have been harmed. Buddhist scholars inform us that within Buddhism, compassion and reconciliation are closely related, although one can be compassionate in the absence of reconciliation. In Christianity, forgiveness must always allow for the possibility of reconciliation, even though reconciliation may not always occur (Rye, Pargament, Amir, Beck, Dorff, Hallisey, Narayanan, and Williams 2000).25.

Secular scholars also have devoted considerable thought to altruism and forgiveness. Philosopher Joanna North defines forgiveness as "a willingness to abandon one's right to resentment, negative judgment, and indifferent behavior toward one who unjustly injured us, while fostering the undeserved qualities of compassion, generosity, and even love toward him or her" (Enright, Freedman, and Rique 1998: 46–47). According to North, forgiveness does not remove the fact of the wrongdoing, but rather relies on the recognition of the wrong having been committed in order for the process of forgiveness to be made possible. The act of forgiveness does not annul the crime itself but the "distorted effect that this wrong has upon one's relation with the wrongdoer and perhaps with others (North 1998: 17-18).

Forgiving is not condoning or excusing wrongdoing, nor does it necessarily have any legal status. Robert Enright, Suzanne Freeman and Julio Rique state that forgiveness is not the same as legal pardon. Some are concerned that when we forgive we will open all jail-cell doors, letting the lawbreakers free to further their destructive aims" (1998: 48). The authors go on to argue that forgiveness must be distinguished from reconciliation:

> The basic philosophical distinction between forgiveness and reconciliation is this: Forgiveness is one person's response to injury. Reconciliation involves two people coming together again. The injurer must realize his or her offense, see the damage done, and take steps to rectify the problem. When both parties are guilty of injustice toward the other, both may need to forgive and realize one's own failures, with intent to change. When already in a strong relationship with someone who offends, a forgiver usually reconciles (Enright, Freedman, & Rique 1998: 49).

There is a wide spectrum of opinion on the essence of forgiveness. Enright, Freedman, and Rique note that Robin Casarjian's approach equates forgiving with "the offer of moral love and acceptance to include one's 'forgiveness of arthritic hands or a less-than-healthy body. We understand and appreciate her attempt to help a person to achieve a certain inner peace in regard to a failing body. Yet, equating forgiveness with a generalized acceptance brings construct away from the interpersonal, and thus away from the moral qualities of generosity and/or moral love" (Casarjian, cited in Enright, Freedman, and Rique 1998: 51).

Forgiveness cannot be commanded. However, it can be taught as a way of healing not only the victim but also the victimizer. In 1991, Enright and the Human Development Study Group developed four phases of psychological variables that may be involved when we forgive. Phase one, termed "uncovering," consists of examining one's anger and confronting it, admitting the shame, being aware of the offense, gaining the insight that the injured parties may be comparing themselves with the injurer, realizing that one may be permanently and adversely changed by the injury, and being open to the possibility that the world is just. The second phase, called the decision phase," includes a change of heart and a new insight that old resolution strategies are not working, a willingness to consider forgiveness as an option, and being committed to forgiving the offender. The third phase is called the "work phase," which addresses reframing through role taking, identifying and viewing the wrongdoer in context, having empathy toward the offender, being aware of compassion as it arises toward the offender, and accepting and absorbing the pain. The last phase is the "deepening phase," which implies that we must find meaning for self and others in the suffering and forgiveness process. The self has needed the forgiveness of others in the past, and it is aware that we are not alone in this situation. We need to realize that the self may have a new purpose in life because of the injury, and we need to become aware of the decreasing negative effects and the possible increase in positive effects toward the injurer if this occurs. Finally, we must develop an awareness of our internal emotional release (Enright, Freedman, and Rique 1998: 53).

Scholars agree that there are important bases to the forgiveness process. Lewis Smedes (1996) outlines the stages of forgiveness. First, we forgive when we discover the humanity of the person who hurt us. Then, we surrender our right to vengeance. Finally, we reconcile our feelings toward the person we forgive.

Everett Worthington, a psychologist who has studied

apology and forgiveness for many years, concludes that those who find the weight of past wrongs to be oppressive must decide to "REACH." In Worthington's model of forgiveness, each of these letters stands for a specific step in the forgiveness process: "R" involves *recalling* the hurt, "E" stands for practicing *empathy* towards the one who has hurt us, "A" stands for giving the *altruistic* gift of forgiveness to another, "C" stands for publicly *committing* to work for forgiveness, "H" is for working on *holding* oneself to forgiveness. Many people see that empathy is the crucial step in the process of forgiveness. If one is not capable of empathizing with the wrongdoer, understanding why he has done harm, knowing his background and what prompted him to do that, it would be difficult to forgive (Worthington 1997; 2004).

Worthington is his own best example. On New Year's Eve 1995, two men broke into Worthington's mother's house and murdered her. At first, Worthington was full of rage. He felt that he could not forgive the people who took his mother's life. It took a great deal of empathy and compassion to try to understand why this tragedy occurred. Being a spiritual person, he thought of the words Jesus spoke on the cross, "Forgive them for they know not what they do." In an effort to be empathetic, Worthington decided that the socioeconomic background of the people who broke in must have seriously impacted their inner world. After soul searching, he decided to forgive the murderers.

Forgiveness helps relieve the pain we felt due to the offense (Hartwell 1999). When we forgive, we take an important step toward mending and rebuilding our relationship with the wrongdoer. We remove the burden that weighs us down. Forgiveness helps us go on with our lives, instead of holding onto the past. It makes us into better people and improves our overall mental and emotional health (McCullough, Rachal, Chris, Sandage, Worthington, Brown, Hight 1998: 1595).

Forgiveness refers to the process people go through when they no longer find it necessary to carry hurt or harm on their shoulders or in their hearts. Donald W. Shriver Jr. (1995) relates the story of a contemporary Native American, a Lakota:

> After my five-year vision quest, I was tempted to go out and shoot every white man... I thought about Sand Creek and Wounded Knee, and I got angrier and angrier... I wanted to grab a gun and start shooting. Then, I thought, my ancestors might honor me...but then I saw the beauty of the moon and the morning star, and I knew that the only way I could live was to forgive... I work on that now every day. If one doesn't work on forgiveness, one will die on the road someday (Shriver 1995: 151).

True forgiveness often requires an emotional or spiritual transformation. It is an exercise in compassion and is both a process and an attitude. "Lack of forgiveness is giving others power over you" (Parachin, 2006: 3). Through the process of forgiveness, we transform suffering into psychological and spiritual growth; through the attitude of forgiveness, we attain serenity by letting go of the ego's incessant need to judge others and ourselves. To make amends, we must apologize, acknowledge the harm we have done, make appropriate restitution, and change our behavior toward the other person. Amends must be appropriate and should benefit all.

These themes are also present when considering intergroup forgiveness. Archbishop Desmond Tutu (1999), referring to the South African Truth and Reconciliation Commission, says that there is "no future without forgiveness" and that forgiveness is one of the key ideas in this world. Apology and forgiveness are not just nebulous concepts; they contain the realization of wrongdoing on the side of apologizers and empathic understanding on the part of forgivers that has the practical effect of allowing people to unite or reunite. Psychiatrist Richard Fitzgibbons maintains that forgiveness has remarkable healing power for those who are able to use it (1998). Whether it is for small wrongs or for great crimes and injustices, most people struggle to find a way to forgive. The failure of our society to teach young people the skills of dealing effectively with conflicts echoes loudly today in school violence, our high rate of divorce and domestic battering, drug and alcohol abuse, and as criminal acts of ethnic warfare and terrorism. The rediscovered power of forgiveness has great potential for healing society on a number of levels.

What are some of the psychological problems that the injured person group, or nation faces? On the individual level, psychologists have been able to substantiate that the injured person suffers from anxiety, depression and the general feeling that the world is unfriendly. The injured person feels a real battering to his or her self-esteem. Members of a group that have been attacked or injured generally feel that they were unjustly treated, that the injuring nation or group is evil, and that vengeance should be sought. This attitude can pose a serious problem, because there appears to be no alternative to injury other than retaliation and vengeance. What is needed is an empathic understanding.

Research was conducted with students to test under what conditions young individuals will forgive parents who deprived them of love and nurturing. Radhi H. Al-Mabuk and Robert D. Enright maintain that "Parental love deprivation is a condition where a child does not receive needed affection and nurturing, is not given assurance of value, respect, and acceptance by the parents" (Al-Mabuk and Enright 1995: 430). The authors designed an experiment in which a group of students who were deprived of parental love were given training that focused on such things as justice and forgiveness. As a result of such training, the students reported that they were able to forgive their parents.

Colin Tipping (2002) has criticized traditional forgiveness. He writes, "With traditional forgiveness the willingness to forgive is present, but so is the residual need to condemn. Therefore, victim consciousness is maintained and nothing changes" (Tipping 2002: 45). With "radical forgiveness, the willingness to forgive is present but not the need to condemn. Therefore, the *victim consciousness* is dropped and everything changes" (Tipping 2002:45). Tipping defines "victim consciousness" as "a conviction that someone else has done something bad to you, and as a direct result, they are responsible for the lack of peace and happiness in your life". He claims that radical forgiveness has a divine basis that comes directly from God and is a kind of divine truth. By the phrase "*divine truth*" he means it has no physical form and already carries the energy pattern of eternal life, mutability, infinite abundance, love, and oneness with God. Even though we cannot perceive this world with our senses, and we scarcely possess the mental capacities to comprehend its existence, we can get enough of a sense of it to know that it is real. Such activities as prayer, meditation, and radical forgiveness all raise our awareness of the world of divine truth and allow us earthly access to that world (Tipping 2002: 45).

Radical forgiveness is a purely spiritual path, and traditional forgiveness is more a means of living in this world. Radical forgiveness takes the view that there is no right or wrong or bad or good; only your thinking about it makes it so. Traditional forgiveness always begins with the assumption that something wrong took place, and that someone did something to someone else. In other words, the victim archetype remains operative. But radical forgiveness begins with the belief that nothing wrong happened, and there is no victim in any situation. Traditional forgiveness, Tipping says, is effective to the extent that it calls upon the highest human virtues-such as compassion, tolerance, kindness, mercy, and humility—the same virtues always present in radical forgiveness (Tipping 2002: 53).

Others also differentiate among levels or types of forgiveness. Richard Fitzgibbons (1998), coming from a clinical angle, defines forgiveness as the process of relinquishing one's feelings of resentment and thoughts of vengeance. A secondary part of the process is that of fostering compassion, generosity, and even love toward those who have inflicted pain. But abandoning one's angry feelings and thoughts is not an easy task. Fitzgibbons maintains that 40 percent of young Americans do not have biological fathers in their lives. Most of these young individuals have a hard time understanding this and therefore find it difficult to forgive their fathers for the pain of betrayal they struggle with daily. But Fitzgibbons argues that it is understanding that is necessary for true forgiveness to occur.

Fitzgibbons feels that the process of forgiveness can proceed on one of three levels: cognitive, emotional, or spiritual. The cognitive process of forgiveness implies the discussion, the evaluation, and the attempt to understand the victim's anger. By reasoning and reflection one may attempt to forgive, but Fitzgibbons feels that most forgiveness begins at the cognitive level. This is the level at which forgiveness seems like a good idea, when people *decide* to forgive. However, some individuals may feel that cognitive forgiveness is not really forgiveness at all, because they do not truly "feel like" forgiving.

The emotional level of forgiveness is when one comes to deeply understand the offender and his life struggles and is eventually able to develop empathy for the wounded boy or girl within the adult. As a result of this understanding, the offended party truly feels like forgiving. To the victim, being able to offer forgiveness is really a process of catharsis that yields emotional understanding and, ultimately, compassion for the offender. While such forgiveness does not imply an annulment of the wrongdoing itself, it does signify an attempt at an empathic understanding of *why* it happened. Healing may begin for both the injured party and the injurer.

The third level is the spiritual approach accessed when someone suffers from severe pain. Embracing a similar process to that of the Alcoholics Anonymous' 12-step program, victims conclude that forgiveness is not within their own power and instead look to a higher power to help them forgive. Statements such as "I am powerless over my anger and want to turn it over to God," or "Revenge or justice belongs to God," or "God forgive him, I cannot," or "God free me from my anger" are examples of this spiritual approach (Fitzgibbons 1998: 66).

Fitzgibbons sees the limitations of forgiveness. In his experience as a psychiatrist, he has seen forgiveness diminish the degree of sadness and lessen the severe pain of human betrayal. But he argues that forgiveness does not directly address the person's anger when it results from

> ... character weakness, such as narcissism, grandiosity, and patience, [or] the absence of moral values. While it is a very powerful tool, [forgiveness] alone cannot bring about a complete resolution of the excessive resentment, hostility, and hatred in our culture. (Fitzgibbons 1998: 67).

Everett Worthington (1997) proposes five steps for actualizing forgiveness: 1) Do not wait for an apology. Take the initiative to establish relations by giving the offending party the occasion to talk to you. 2) Allow yourself to empathize with the offender. He or she may well have acted out of ignorance and is the person who can heal your pain. 3) Perform a symbolic act. Make it public in some way to show you are willing to forgive. 4) Remember that forgiving is not forgetting. Hurt feelings can linger even after one has forgiven the offender. 5) Offended parties should include themselves in the forgiveness list.

Robert Enright, Elizabeth Gassin, and Ching-Ru Wu (1992) have constructed a similar list from their multiyear study of adults in the United States. They prescribe 18 "psychological variables engaged in a process intervention on forgiveness." Their expanded list shows a thorough appreciation of the steps involved in applying empathic understanding to forgiveness and benefits to the forgiver. All the major theories of forgiveness include processes aimed at reconciliation and restoration of a relationship emphasizing an applied empathic understanding.

Walter J. Dickey (1998) addresses the role of forgiveness in relationships that have been strained by a criminal offense. He considers the harm inflicted on the victim to the victim-offender relationship and to the community. Dickey raises the question of how this kind of harm can be repaired and views forgiveness as an integral part of the repair. In a criminal offense, the restoration of strained relationships must rest on two foundations; community, group, and individual healing must be the goal of any system that purports to administer justice. Apology, forgiveness, and restitution are important components of any restoration or healing, this process needs "undeserved qualities of compassion, generosity, and even love," to which Dickey attaches importance.

Joseph W. Elder (1998) delineates the characteristics and consequences of forgiveness and gives the example of Marietta Jaeger, who forgave the man who killed her daughter. Using the Hebrew and Christian scriptures, she reasoned that, "God is a God of mercy and compassion, who works unceasingly to help and heal." She concluded that her daughter's kidnapper and murderer "was a son of God, and, as such... he had dignity and worth." When the killer tracked down Jaeger in the middle of the night to taunt her, she showed mercy and compassion, asking him what she could do to help him. The killer was unable to reply and simply wept. He eventually confessed to the murder and went to prison. Drawing on the agony of her daughter's murder, as well as the closure brought by this experience, Jaeger concludes, "The only way we can be whole, healthy, happy persons is to learn to forgive" (Elder 1998: 150).

How can offenders ask for forgiveness, and how can victims forgive? Elder notes that the teachings of Judeo-Christian and Muslim faiths include divine forgiveness, and Buddhist/Hindu cosmology maintains that every virtuous act is rewarded, and every sinful act is punished in a manner similar to the law of physics.

> The punishments and rewards might happen in this life or in subsequent lives, but they will happen. There is no process of repentance or forgiveness that can affect the inevitability of the punishments and rewards. It would be both wrong and unnecessary to seek revenge. Punishment will happen on its own. Justice will be done through the dynamics of the law of karma... In the center of the Tibetan Buddhist 'Wheel of Life' are pictured a pig, a rooster, and a snake. These are identified, respectively, as the 'three poisons': ignorance, attachment, and hatred. Within the Buddhist cosmology, ignorance, attachment, and hatred are the central cause of suffering. They infect all sentient preachers everywhere and generate countless lives of misery. To overcome them, one must acquire wisdom and compassion (Elder 1998: 158).

Elder addresses the difficulties that arise when the injured party and the wrongdoer do not share the same moral community. Is forgiveness possible when one does not have moral values in common with the other? How does one deal with this? One answer to this question is to acknowledge that we do share fundamental moral values that are the same in virtually every religious tradition. No religious tradition condones murder, kidnapping, rape, or other violent crimes. Although this answer may not be completely satisfactory, we should realize that some things are universally considered wrong and unjust and simply cannot be tolerated. One example of transcending this problem of lacking a common moral community is the historic handshake between Israeli Prime Minister Yitzhak Rabin and PLO Chairman Yasir Arafat on September 13, 1993. After decades of hatred and violence, both men realized that their groups shared basic human values and had many common interests. Their handshake showed that even though each group considers itself to be the wronged party, forgiveness is still possible as a part of the reconciliation process. But the continuing violence and unrest in that area, and the ongoing hatred between the groups, shows forgiveness is no easy task; in some cases, it may take generations of work.

Charles Klein (1995) maintains that forgiveness is difficult because of a fear of being hurt again. It is only through love that this fear is conquered, and a crucial component of forgiveness is what he calls the "glory of love". Without love it is difficult to see that other human beings deserve a chance; besides finding the love within us, we must reframe our interpretations images of wrongdoers, and we must be willing to take a risk for reconciliation that involves reaching out and listening carefully to the person who was hurt or harmed. The person who was harmed must try to understand the reasons for the wrongdoer's hurtful actions. There are no endless tomorrows, and we should seriously consider the notion of reconciling with those we have harmed or who have harmed us. Forgiving another may reestablish harmony, which is especially important when one person involved is dying. To neglect reconciliation with a dying person is to ask for long-term pain for the survivor. From the Jewish perspective, it is vitally important to apologize and to forgive, especially during holy days. Klein cites a Jewish theologian, who is reported to have said, "One who has begged for forgiveness should not be so cruel as not to forgive".

African-American psychologist James M. Jones (2006) speaks about racial inequality and how to overcome it. He focuses on the Truth and Reconciliation Commission (TRC) in South Africa and the concept of *ubuntu*, which is a cultural concept of forgiveness. Ubuntu is the spirit of humanity characterized by the expression, "My humanity is inextricably bound to yours. I am human because I belong, [and] participate in humanity." Forgiveness is illustrated by African psychologist Dr. Pumla Gobodo Nadkizel, who interviewed a killer named DeKock, hired by the apartheid South African government as a professional murderer. Gobodo-Nadkizel was able to extract a sense of DeKock's humanity from him and was able to forgive. This example illustrates the universal concept of forgiveness as a healing and reconciliation process.

Italian psychologist Pierro Ferrucci's *Survival of the Kindest* (2005), presents an interesting contrast to the concept of survival of the fittest. Ferrucci argues that humanity has survived to a large extent because of its capacity for kindness, and that kindness reflects our true nature. He adds, "You can only be kind if your past no longer controls you" (Touber 2005: 44). Forgiveness is also important; someone who cannot forgive is like a city in which traffic has come to a standstill. To forgive, one must first recognize the suffering that one is experiencing. It is not good to hastily forgive just for the sake of forgiveness. Ferrucci discusses the virtue of attention and says that people who are suffering do not need advice, diagnosis, interpretation, or intervention so much as they need sincere empathy and attention. Once they have the feeling that other people are putting themselves in their shoes, they are able to let go of their suffering and begin healing. Ferrucci stresses this kind of attention as a vital factor in human relations and emphasizes that kindness is a very simple quality that may be able to save humanity.

It is saving humanity. Have you ever wondered why the world still has not fallen apart, despite all its complex structures? Mail carriers, train conductors, newspaper vendors, cleaners...of course they earn their livelihood with what they do, but it all happens largely thanks to their good will, to their kindness (Touber 2005: 47).

The most sensible way to look after our own self-interest, to find freedom and be happy, is not to directly pursue these things but to give priority to the interests of others. Help others to become free of their fear and pain. It's all really simple. You don't have to choose between being kind to yourself and others. It is one and the same (Touber 2005:47).

There are levels and aspects of the forgiveness process that elude categorization. Forgiveness presents a large and complex picture, some like the blind men feeling the elephant. At the same time, we can see some aspects that are universal.

Religion And Forgiveness

Muslim scholar M. Fethullah Gulen maintains that Islam, Christianity Judaism, Buddhism, and Hinduism teach love, compassion, tolerance and forgiveness as fundamental and universal religious values. These constructive social processes are vitally important, and without them society would simply fall apart. Theologians, thinkers, and social scientists—the Dalai Lama, Everett Worthington, Lewis B. Smedes, Bishop Tutu, Mother Teresa, Nelson Mandela, and others—agree with empirical data that shows altruism, empathy, spirituality, and forgiveness are very important in healing a violent world (Gulen 2003).

The idea of loving one's neighbor is vitally important in religion—and loving not only your neighbor, but loving even strangers unconditionally. The Jewish tradition prescribes loving the stranger because the Jews were strangers and slaves in Egypt. Jews must remember that and practice this great deed, known as mitzvah. In Buddhism, there is an important process called *bodhicitta*, referring to a selfless altruism that seeks to relieve the suffering of all. One example might be an effort to make a friend out of an enemy. In Christianity, the idea of love means unconditional love, the kind that entails a complete acceptance of the other, forgiveness, openness, being at one with all, and treating others as one would desire to be treated. The Jewish tradition also includes this concept of *unconditional love*. In the words of Rabbi Robert Kushner, "If you are hurting someone, and you are carrying around this unforgiveness longer than two days, you have failed to do your duty to humanity' (Lama Surya Das 1997).

Religious belief can play a powerful role in our actions. During flying combat in Vietnam in 1968, Richard Cunnare came across a number of bodies of American soldiers executed by the Vietcong. He experienced an oven whelming rage in his soul, as did his crewmembers. As he spotted Vietnamese farmers working in their rice paddies, he felt a tremendous pressure for revenge, but recalls, "I did not kill in rage when every part of my soul was telling me [it] was right. If I had shot the rice farmers, would I have been asked why? I do not think anyone would have even questioned the act" (Cunnare 2005). Cunnare felt that "Forgiveness is a powerful grace that the Lord offers us. I chose to take God's will for me and fought to live. I am sure the VC commander from February 1968 did not lose much sleep over executing American troops, or did he?" (Cunnare 2005).

While responsible for innumerable acts of kindness,

caring, and rescuing those in trouble, organized religion also plays a divisive role in human affairs. This is because organized religious groups, by their very nature, are groups that have clear "us" and "them" lines of demarcation. Religion almost always creates "saved" and "unsaved," "righteous" and "unclean," "godly" and "heretical," and so on. To a great extent it teaches us who we are and neglects or deemphasizes the histories and cultures, even the very essence, of others. In their edited collection titled Visions of Compassion (2002), Richard J. Davidson and Anne Harrington delve into the subject of who taught us to think this way:

> Certainly our religious traditions, the Jewish and Christian traditions, must take part in their responsibility for shaping our thinking here. The Christian tradition, for example, believes profoundly in compassion, but it also teaches that human beings are fundamentally flawed and can only be saved through the intervention of Christ, who alone possesses the compassion for our plight great enough to lift us out of our sinfulness. We have been granted eternal life as a gift we could never deserve on our own (2002: 12).

Of course, there is no mention here of Muhammad or of Buddha, leaving adherents to those traditions out in the cold when it comes to salvation. It is virtually impossible to have equal and empathetic relations when those kinds of distinctions underlie our relationships. At the same time, one can safely say that, in some contexts, many religions share similar themes and stress similar beliefs and behaviors.

All religions stress the importance of a foundation of love. The Dalai Lama, referring to love, writes:

> We express our quest for happiness through the language of love. Love not only allows us to access our

compassionate nature; it enables others to relate to us at the most human level. In contrast, suffering is closely linked to hostility and anger, for the full realization of hostility's goal is the destruction of the object of your wrath. By instinctually shunning suffering, we also express our dislike for destructive traits such as hostility, anger, and hatred. This is clearly a manifestation in our natural mind state: When we see death, destruction, or decay we feel uncomfortable; whereas we feel pleasant and assured when we see life, color, and growth (Dalai Lama 2002: 69).

This most "human" kind of love has been exemplified by a group of Jewish, Christian, and Muslim women who live in Jerusalem and recently participated in a conference. Their statement, which follows, has particular relevance:

Unless we understand that one life is lived in the other, our attachment to our identities, national and religious, is superficial, presumptuous, and meaningless" (Prince-Gibson 2004).

Precisely because of the potentially divisive nature of organized religion, ecumenism is a desirable attribute and may be strongly associated with forgiveness. Michael W. Foley (1999) reports on an ecumenical approach in his "Memory, Forgiveness, and Reconciliation: Confronting the Violence of History" from a conference on violence held in Northern Ireland. A number of participants in the conference had focused their discussion on ecumenical society. The participants—especially Adam Michnik, editor-in-chief of *Gazeta Wyborcza*, a major Polish newspaper—spoke of religious leaders having a great responsibility for fostering tolerance and acceptance of the traditions of others. Michnik pointed out that in the past, religious leaders had contributed greatly to war, violence, and hatred, but argued that now these leaders have a special responsibility to promote ecumenism and peace. Others addressed the notion of memory and noted that our grievance of historical hurt frequently comes to the forefront, which helps to ignite current conflict between groups. The interesting part of Foley's article deals with the question of forgiveness. Some discussants were somewhat skeptical about the role of forgiveness. Some argued that before forgiveness is possible, one must first overcome feelings of victimization, which may be the most important step toward healing—not only on a personal level, but also on a societal level.

Though there was skepticism among the presenters about the nuts and bolts of forgiveness, they concluded that forgiveness, which requires both acknowledgment and apology, may be a first step toward true reconciliation among groups. Some raised the question considered before by Simon Wiesenthal, of whether only victims can give forgiveness. A similar idea was expressed by Schimmel (2002). Auschwitz escapee Rudolf Vrba (1964) maintains that he cannot forgive for the crimes he has experienced. Others addressed the issue of the importance of understanding cultural backgrounds in considering how forgiveness and reconciliation can be accomplished. Forgiveness, however, cannot be dictated. Though some people believe there are unforgivable crimes, it is possible to have reconciliation *without* forgiveness. For example, in relations between Germany and Israel, Israel does not forgive the Nazi crimes of mass murder, but the two states and peoples are reconciled and have relations on all levels.

Spirituality

Ministers and priests, rabbis and imams, and religious workers are aware of divine forgiveness. Pastoral counselors try to help heal the pain of individuals by advocating forgiveness, in the image of the divine. Not only does God forgive those who trespass, but so must we as individuals. Forgiveness relieves the offender of shame and humiliation, and, according to John Patton (1985: 16), this is very much related to God's teaching:

> Human forgiveness is not doing something but discovering that I am more like those who have hurt me than different from them. I am able to forgive them when I discover that I am in no position not to forgive. Although the experience of God's forgiveness may involve confession of, and the sense of being forgiven for, specific sins, it is hard to recognize my reception to the community of sinners—those affirmed as God's children (Patton 1985:16).

Sheffield (2003) sees a strong relationship between forgiveness and religion that helps people cope psychologically in their lives. When we forgive others, we start to establish harmony in our personal lives; God forgives sinners because He is compassionate and wants to see love and harmony in the world.

Rabbi Harold M. Schulweis (2000), a religious scholar, looks at the Jewish Bible to see how religious teaching encourages people to be compassionate and forgiving towards each other and to avoid vengeance or holding grudges. He quotes from Leviticus 18:18 in decrying interpersonal unforgiveness: "You shall not take vengeance or bear a grudge against your fellow man." And similarly, against racism or other exclusionary practices he adds: "You shall not abhor an Edomite for he is thy brother, nor an Egyptian because you were a stranger in his land" (Deuteronomy 23:8).

There still seems to be a consensus among forgiveness scholars that there are methodological barriers to completely understanding the roles played by religion, culture, and the social-psychological facets of everyday life interaction. This must be addressed, or we will remain unable to comprehend theories of apology and forgiveness. We must include situational factors of culture, religion, personality, and socialization to shine proper light on the role of forgiveness in human relations.

There are many nuanced definitions of spirituality today. Facets of spirituality generally include some or all of the following overarching themes: a belief in a power operating in the universe that is greater than ourselves, a sense of interconnectedness with all living creatures, an awareness of the purpose and meaning of life, and the development of personal absolute values. Although spirituality is often associated with religious life, many believe that personal spirituality can be developed outside of religion. Acts of compassion, selflessness, altruism, and an experience of inner peace are all characteristics of spirituality. According to a 1997 survey of spiritual trends in the United States, "96 percent of Americans believe in God or in a universal spirit." Today, people in the U.S. look to their spirituality for practical applications—for example, "to promote healing, especially in cases where medications and other treatment cannot provide a cure." In a 1994 survey of people hospitalized in North Carolina and Pennsylvania, 77 percent felt that their doctors should consider their spiritual needs (*USA Today* 2004). This suggests that people in the U.S. appreciate the real benefits that can come through spirituality.

The National Institute for Healthcare Research has initiated a study looking into this important aspect of spirituality. It is believed that a person's most deeply held beliefs strongly influence health, and that a positive attitude towards a serious illness will help with recovery. Forgiveness, interestingly, is also vitally important. A 1997 Stanford study found that college students trained to forgive someone who had hurt them were significantly less angry, more hopeful, and better able to deal with strong emotions than those who were not trained to forgive. These studies found that love and social and emotional support were as important to people's spiritual health as prayer (*USA Today* 2004).

Others speak of spiritual wellness, a sense that life is meaningful, has purpose, and brings humanity together. Many people have spiritual needs, and as social beings, we feel a need to be connected to others. These feeling encourage actions such as prayer and meditation, seeking contentment (to seek the brighter side of life), forgiveness as an effort to reestablish relationships, religious attendance (sharing one's spirituality with a community), and altruistic behavior. So it is faith as well as hope that power most of us on this spiritual journey toward well-being (Hoeger. Turner and Hafen 2003).

Theologian Dr. Charles Stanley (1996) presents a Christian perspective on forgiveness. Using the letters of the various disciples of the New Testament—including John, Paul, and Matthew—he shows that if you forgive another person, it is the same as if God were forgiving them. Furthermore, God will look at the forgiver with great favor. Stanley passes along some lessons on how to forgive, as well as commenting on the consequences of forgiveness. He gives practical suggestions about how to face the individual who hurt you and how to go about forgiving him or her. He also speaks about self-forgiveness, because in doing so healing is possible. He says that it is psychological and spiritually unhealthy to continue being the victim and suffer as a result.

Addressing the issue of unforgiveness, Stanley has this to say:

Unforgiveness is actually a form of hatred. 'Oh, you may say, 'I don't hate anybody.' By such a statement, you probably mean that you wouldn't murder anybody or do anything intentionally to harm another person. But ask yourself these questions: Do I avoid encountering a certain person? Do I find it difficult to speak well of a certain person? Does the very thought of a particular person make me cringe or clench my fist? If your answer is yes, you are harboring hatred in the form of unforgiveness (Stanley 1996: 62)

Stanley maintains that hatred exists in various degrees and that an unforgiving spirit is marked by hatred. We know that when we have such a feeling we cannot shake the pain or memory of the hurt done to us. We cannot honestly wish the offending person well—on the contrary, we often want them to feel pain, to suffer and hurt to the degree we have hurt and suffered.

There are other consequences of unforgiving, according to Dr. Stanley. We may experience emotional bondage, and these memories may be tormenting, causing us to relive the pain we experienced. We may experience damaged relationships due to anger, quarreling, and other emotional eruptions. We can suffer spiritually because we feel that we cannot face unavoidable human suffering. Lastly, unforgiveness harbors anger, puts a heavy burden on our immune systems, and causes us stress and feelings of betrayal.

Biil Fields (2005) uses the Christian principle of reconciliation. He offers eight steps: confession by the offender to the offended; identifying the Biblical principles violated; determining how the offended person was offended; recalling similar offenses experienced by the offender; having the offender restate their offense while expressing Godly sorrow and wait for the offended's response; restating the response in their own words while expressing Godly sorrow; having offenders ask what they might do differently so as to not harm again; and, lastly, offering restitution.

Engaged Spirituality

By engaged spirituality we mean sustained moral action on behalf of others that is motivated by selfless love and kindness, rather than by selfish motives on the part of those helping. Jack Berry and colleagues (2005) state:

Warmth-based virtues (e.g., love, compassion, and generosity) contribute to cooperation and warm emotional bonds. Conscientiousness-based virtues (e.g., self-control, forbearance, and justice) inhibit selfish and antisocial behavior. We suggest that there are individual differences in the degree to which people value and practice the virtues in these two classes. Furthermore, differential preferences for the two classes of virtues should predict differential responses to transgressions (Berry et al 2005: 144).

Dr. Berry proceeds to present data concerning individual differences in preferences for the practice of moral virtues (Berry 2004).

There is a positive correlation between faith or religion and healing. For many, prayer, not only for loved ones but for those one does not know, helps in the healing process. Eighty-four percent of Americans think that praying for the sick improves their chance of recovery, and 28 percent think that religion and medicine should be separate. People who regularly attend church tend to live longer than people who are not churchgoers. Using brain scans, scholars found that meditation can change brain activity and improve immune response; other studies show it can lower heart rate and blood pressure, both of which reduce the body's stress responses. Forgiveness also has been found to have an impact on health and wellness. University of Michigan School of Public Health researcher Neil Kraus found that people who forgive easily tend to enjoy greater psychological well-being and suffer less depression than those who hold grudges (Kalb 2003).

While there are critics of this connection, two thirds of the studies find significant associations between religious belief and well-being: life satisfaction, hope, purpose, meaning, and lower rates of depression, anxiety, and suicide. Seventy of the 120 medical schools in the United States—from Harvard to Stanford—offer specific courses on spirituality or incorporate spiritual themes into their curricula (Kalb 2003).

Sir John Templeton donated millions annually to study the intersections of prayer, physical healing, love, forgiveness, reconciliation, and related studies. The National Institute of Health spent $3.5 million on "mind/body studies" (Kalb 2003). Many in the medical field, such as Duke University's Harold Koenig, Harvard's Herbert Benson, and Stanford's Robert Sapolsky, are finding that this kind of research is valuable.

Stanczak and Miller think of spirituality as "an integral part of everyday life among people who are dedicating themselves to social service. As an integral aspect of everyday life, spirituality is a feeling, an experience, a relationship, a connection of intimate practices that, much like other feelings or relationships in our lives, takes on the texture and color of what is going on around us. For some people, this means that spirituality must address the injustices that they perceive at work, the poverty that they see in their communities, or the global disparities that are so apparent in health services in developing nations" (Stanczak and Miller 2004: 5–6).

Inherited engagement is the connection between social and spiritual commitment that can be derived from family practice or long-term involvement within religious institutions. For example, Rabbi Leonard Beerman's lifelong commitment to justice was founded on his family's experience during the Great Depression. To individuals like Beerman, the combination of social commitment and spirituality is the only way to express faith that is deeply fused with one's sense of identity. The idea of *learned engagement* suggests that the pluralism and diversity of collegiate independence can open up many religious options, such as new ways of practice, discussions on histories of social engagement, or new philosophies about spiritual commitments to social change. Emile Durkheim describes the power of the social encounter as one of the universally fundamental building blocks of religious sentiment and meaning.

A *spiritual epiphany* in the form of visions, dreams, voices, or an overwhelming sense of clarity and direction constitutes the most transcendent and experiential connection between social action and spirituality. The basis of these transformations is perceived as undeniably otherworldly.

Serving as a *community volunteer* is a structured embodiment of the Good Neighbor. The volunteer works within his or her community, providing direct services or aid as part of an organized form of social service and, although spiritually motivated, may or may not publicly express this spiritual motivation. The conventional modern American image is the soup kitchen volunteer, which for many is their first introduction to service work. Similarly, the *moral advocate* focuses their spirituality on public education of particular issues or attempts to initiate changes in social policy or community development. Advocates are the instigators of policy change or community development; they are the educators, and the mouthpieces for particular platforms of social change and they can work either within or outside of institutional channels.

A *visionary prophet* sees the world not only as it is but also as it could be. Often the visionary acts in ways that disregard seemingly insurmountable odds. Spiritual practices are regimented parts of everyday life and often occur at scheduled times or in patterned ways. The five daily calls to prayer at the core of Islamic religious life, or the resurgence of the Daily Office among Christians, are notable examples of collective daily practice. These strictly scheduled practices connect each day with an otherworldly source.

Other individuals feel *empowerment* directly and literally as an embodied manifestation of a palpable physical force. This force might be articulated through a feeling of courage, strength, or energy but is typically experienced first physically. There is a common thread of *transcendence* or otherworldliness that infuses individuals with power. These individuals continually and solemnly refer to moments that could not be rationally explained.

Many people feel their spirituality in a sense of community, both real—in terms of one's friends, family, or religious congregation—and within imagined communities (for example, historical lineage of others who have engaged in similar endeavors for millennia), or in the greater communal body of the faithful around the globe. These individuals create connections to a tradition that provides cultural roots, affirmation, and validity for socially enacting one's spirituality. In doing so, they generate feelings of solidarity, love, trust, respect, unity, and belonging (Stanczak and Miller 2004).

We are seeing an increase in spirituality in our young people. Alexander Astin (2003) conducted a large survey—112,232 students, from 236 colleges and universities across the United States --- that focused on the spiritual development of college students and their involvement with society. One of the questions asked was, "How would you describe your current views on spirituality/religious matters?" Eighty percent of these college students responded that they are interested and tolerant in exploring their spirituality. Even though Elizabeth Svoboda (2005) documents that universities are often reluctant to offer courses that encourage the pursuit of such spiritual investigation, students can find their spirituality through many paths—for example, as community volunteers or moral advocates.

Epiphany

What epiphany promotes some scholars to look at the topic of engaged spirituality? How do scholars become interested in engagement? Recently I reviewed *Flourishing: Positive Psychology From a Life Well Lived* (2003), a collection of essays edited by Cory Keyes and Jonathan Heidt. Martin Seligman, a contributor to that volume, relays the following story: One day, Seligman was in the garden doing some weeding. His five-year-old daughter Nikki was present, but instead of helping with the weeding, she was throwing weeds in the air and dancing around. Seligman became irritated with her, because he had a goal in mind: to finish the weeding. He proceeded to yell at her and caused her to leave. After a while she returned and said to him, "Daddy I want to talk to you. You may not have noticed, but do you remember how I was before my fifth birthday? From the time I was three until I was five, I was a whiner, I whined every day, but when I turned five, I decided not to whine anymore. And that was the hardest thing I have ever done—but I did it, so if I can stop whining, Daddy, can you stop being grumpy?" This real-life episode had a profound effect on Seligman, who realized that he indeed was always grumpy and grouchy and that his daughter Nikki was correct. For 50 years he had walked around acting grumpy despite being surrounded by a wife and children who were all "rays of sunshine." In some sense, this single event made Seligman the father of "Positive Psychology," a field that has recently come into its own.

One dramatic example, previously mentioned, is the story of psychologist Everett Worthington and the murder of his mother. Stanford psychologist Frederic Luskin (2002) was motivated by an unpleasant and dramatic fall-out with a friend he valued greatly. Psychiatrist Aaron Lazare (2004) relates a similar experience, in which two friends betrayed his trust, causing anger and a need for understanding. Sociologist Nicholas Tavuchis (1991) had a similar experience of hurt. He says, "I trace my interest in apology to a bitter argument I had many years ago with someone close and dear to me. The precise details have faded from memory, but I can still recall feeling hurt, wronged, and angered by the accusation of misconduct and insensitivity' (1991: 1).

We can see that there are a variety of reasons why people get passionately involved with a subject. But is it possible, in the absence of dramatic epiphanies, to move more people from simply being bystanders to getting involved with others? How can we begin to inculcate and disseminate the behaviors of helping, getting spiritually engaged, and acting as moral exemplars so that more people will benefit their neighbors, their communities and the world?

Love, Empathy, And Forgiveness

One word frees us of all the weight and pain of life. That word is love.
-Sophocles

Closely connected with forgiveness is the power of love. "Without love what have we got? A world without a heart." This quote, from one of the more than 500 rescuers of Jews in Nazi-occupied Europe that we interviewed, had an important impact on our thinking. In considering the ways that we interact when we apologize and forgive, love must take a central role.

"Love is the language that can be heard by the deaf, seen by the blind, and felt by the loneliest of hearts. [It] is being happy for another person when they are happy, being sad for the other person when they are sad, being together in good times, and being together in bad times. Love is the source of strength...Love is the source of life," according to an Ohio-based Christian church (Agape Love Ministries 2004).

Stephen Post, in *Unlimited Love: Altruism, Compassion, and Service* (2002), and with others in *Research on Altruism and Love*

(2003), outlines an important process he calls *unlimited love.*
Citing Vladimir Solovyov (1853–1900), he says, "The meaning and worth of love, as a feeling, is that it really forces us,
with all of our being, to acknowledge for another the same
absolute central significance, which because of the power of
our egoism, we are conscious of only in our own selves. Love
is important not as one of our feelings but as the transfer of
all our interest in life from ourselves to another, as the shifting of the very center of our personal lives." Post believes
that those who have the virtue of meaningful spirituality
shape our love, and any spiritual transformation that is not a
migration toward love is suspect" (Post 2003: 42).27

David Augsburger (1981) informs us that love helps us
care enough to forgive. The following steps are part of this
process: 1) See the other as having worth and value; 2) See
the other as equally precious; 3) Recognize that changing the
past is impossible; 4) Work through anger and pain in order
to risk trusting again; 5) Drop demands for a perfect, risk-free
future. 6) Celebrate the forgiveness with love and compassion. Augsberger reports that letting go allows feelings, views,
and emotions to be fluid, and that accepting our humanity
and our powerlessness to force others into perfection relaxes
our grip on pain and allows ourselves to flow forward with
time and be present with us, our companions, and the universe. He argues that this is only possible when love is part of
one's cognitive and emotional being, which is strongly coupled with empathy and altruistic predisposition.

Menachem Eckstein (2001) argues that "Love, compassion, caring, [and] empathy are contagious and spread
from those who are fortunate to have these positive processes to others who do not have [them]." It comes about as a
matter of kindness and expression of caring. It is beautiful
and "endless," and we would like to see more of it diffused.
These ideas are "not just for the hassidically inclined, nor
even just for Jews." Rabbi Eckstein focuses on a "release

from self-centered consciousness, living the compassionate life, and the experience of oneness with the universe. These ideals are common to all traditions." (Eckstein 2001: 15)

My experience tells me that love is of the utmost importance, especially during childhood. At the age of 12, I found myself trying to survive in a dangerous world without parents, family, friends, or loved ones. The Holocaust had deprived me of all love and compassion. Until I was rescued, I felt lost, terrified, and alone. Then compassionate people took an interest in me and saved my life. After the war ended, other people showed me not only that they loved me, but also that they cared about me and respected me. It is easy for me to understand the ways in which love-deprived children suffer. The research on the topic of love shows that children who do not experience love early in their lives suffer the consequences for the rest of their lives.

At the "Works of Love" conference, held at Villanova University in 2003, attending scholars produced the following statement:

Unselfish love for all humanity is the most important point of convergence shared by the world's great spiritual traditions. We marvel at the... power of love, and find in it the best hope for a far better human future. People from all walks of life, often those disadvantaged themselves, excel in love and kindness, not just for the nearest and dearest, but also as volunteers and advocates on behalf of all the strangers (Works of Love: 2003).

Great numbers of scholars have dealt with this positive social process we call love. Psychologists, theologians, philosophers, social activists, marriage counselors, psychiatrists, and healing professionals of all stripes have made a convincing case that without love human beings cannot flourish. Harry Harlow's famous experiments with baby monkeys are instructive as to the importance and value of love to our successful development. Harlow separated infant monkeys from their mothers and raised them in separate cages with two substitute "mothers," one of cloth and one of metal wire. The wire "mother" had a bottle for the infant; the cloth "mother" did not. Although the infant monkeys were quick to determine that the wire mother had the bottle, and quickly learned to feed there, afterward they went to the cloth "mother" for comfort. Harvard Medical School professor Mary Carlson was influenced by the Harlow study and its relevance to human deprivation and lack of loving contact between mothers and their infants.28 When the infant monkeys were raised in a cage from which they could see, smell, and hear the mother monkeys but not touch them, the baby monkeys developed what Carlson called an "autistic like syndrome" with grooming, self-clasping, social withdrawal, and rocking.

Reporting on a study she did on orphanages in Romania, where conditions were shocking, the children were devoid of caring human contact, and their institutionalized care was not sufficient to maintain the social capacity for the human baby. The dictator Nicolae Ceausescu was a strong believer in technological progress and was highly skeptical of all things "touchy-feely." He clamped down on psychology and social work, preferring engineering and science. He greatly favored policies to raise the birth rate and established institutions for orphans and children whose parents could not care for them. Carlson's observations have many implications for our society, where she sees a consistent relationship between poor care and increases in cortisol levels, which are associated with stress. Her research raises questions about what happens to American children in poor day care centers.

Thomas Lewis, Fari Amin, and Richard Lannon address the importance of love in their major work, *A General Theory of Love* (2000). They seek to answer questions about the definition and meaning of love, why people are unable to find it, and about loneliness and why it hurts. The authors raise the question of the importance of attractors, which are patterns that are more or less imprinted in the limbic system from infant and childhood limbic connections. Lynn E. O'Connor notes that "Less than optimal limbic connecting, in whatever manner it fails to do the job, tends to get repeated throughout life in terms of choice of love partners and other close relationships" (O'Connor 2002). She agrees that people who have experienced dysfunctional and unloving parents tend to select and continue to select partners who essentially match the parents in some limbic way and that in the end are not good for them. Psychotherapy, when it works, helps to change the limbic patterns just enough to allow the person to begin to select more comfort-inducing partners and friends" (O'Connor 2002).

Faith-induced love is emphasized and embraced in Christianity, Judaism, Islam, Buddhism, Hinduism, Taoism, and Confucianism. For Christianity the notion of love is unconditional and emphasizes acceptance, forgiveness, openness, oneness with all, and treating others as you would wish to be treated. In Buddhism, especially Tibetan Buddhism, we have seen that the concept of *bodhicitta* means selfless or unselfish altruism, aspiration to relieve the sufferings of all, compassion, and service—also meaning love and forgiveness. There are a number of examples from real life in which unlimited love and loving kindness are exhibited, including in the hospice system and in L'Arche communities of people who have developmental disabilities.

There are different kinds of love, according to Anders Nygren in his book, *Agape and Eros* (1953). Nygren distinguishes romantic love (*eros*) from altruistic love (*agape*). Agape love is spontaneous and unmotivated, indifferent to values, creative, and initiates fellowship with God. Divine love is spontaneous, in that it does not look for reward. Divine love seeks those who do not deserve it and can lay no claim to it. Agape love is God's creative activity, and it initiates fellowship with God. It is deep, intimate, and selfless love, as portrayed in Christianity, Judaism, Islam, Buddhism, Hinduism, Taoism, and Confucianism. Judaism carries the message of agape in the passage from Leviticus that states, "You shall not hate your brother in your heart...you shall love your neighbor as yourself" (Leviticus 19:17). There is a similar statement in the New Testament: "You shall love your neighbor as yourself" (Mathew 22:39).

Stephen Post says, "In essence, unlimited love is abiding, regarding perspective and emotional attunement that affirms and serves all of humanity unselfishly and unconditionally, without any exception whatsoever" (Post 2002:5). Others, such as John Templeton (1999), maintain that unlimited love is a form of love that arises from every conceivable limit to embrace all of humanity in joy, creativity, compassion, care, and generativity; it lies at the heart at of all valid and worthwhile spiritual, religious, and derivative philosophical traditions. It is often associated with a divine presence that underlies the cosmos and makes life a meaningful gift. Indeed the life of unlimited love probably begins with the sense that every life is a gift. These explanations are the heart of agape.

In his book, *The Model of Love: A Study of Philosophical Theology* (1993), Vincent Brümmer maintains that *agape*, what he calls "gift-love," is the attitude of giving oneself in service to the other. He notes that two of the most important classical examples of the view that love is to be understood in terms of *eros* or "need-love," were Plato and St. Augustine. Brümmer discusses gift-love in some depth. "There is thus no way for man to come to God, but only a way for God to come to man: the way of divine forgiveness, divine love. *Agape* is God's way to man" (Brümmer 1993: 128). Brümmer continues that all love that has any right to be called *agape* is nothing else but an outflow from the divine love. It has its source in

God—God *is agape*" (Brümmer 1993: 131). Brümmer argues that the way in which God loves us is the perfect example upon which we should try to pattern our love for each other. Thus, God's love of human beings can be understood as a supreme appreciation of the individuality of each person. Discussing gift-love, Brümmer says that *agape* love is a kind of devotion for individuals to serve the good of others. A residual, though latent, effect of so doing is that we actually end up serving ourselves. In this sense, love is indeed unconditional love or gift-love, rather than a desire for fulfilling our own needs or interests.

In the Jewish tradition, it is stated that when we help others lovingly and unconditionally, we at the same time help ourselves in the eyes of God and humanity. Similarly, David J. Hassel (1985) states that love is other-centered and necessarily includes a discovery of God within this love. Understandably, Karol Wojtyla, the late Pope, said that "The desire for unlimited good for another person is really the desire that God has for that person" (Brümmer 1993: 139).

Rolf M. Johnson (2001) speaks about care love and union-love. Care love means concern for the good or welfare of someone or something. To love he says, in this case, is to care for or care about objects. The lover is concerned with the beloved and is supposed to act on its behalf. If the object of our care-love is endangered, our impulse is to protect it. Care-love is a form of agape love. Also he cautions that it should be clearly understood that care-love has a universally moral purpose only because one could also lovingly care for someone who is evil and destructive. Johnson cites Russian philosopher Solovyov in arguing that "we must join with others in order to join with God: we have no access to the divine as separate egos" (Johnson 2001: 95). Ilham Dilman speaks of "gift-love, which is always directed to objects [that] the lover finds in some way intrinsically lovable...divine gift-love in the man enables him to love what is naturally unlovable:

lepers, criminals, enemies, morons, the sulky, superior, sneering" (Dilman 1998: 162).

I became acquainted with the philosophy of Pitirim Sorokin in the late 1950s, when I was an undergraduate at Brooklyn College. One of my sociology professors told me that Sorokin might have lost his sociological direction and might instead have become a "philosopher of love." This implied that Sorokin was not worth reading, because he was not sociological or scientific-despite the fact that he had written 40 important books in sociology and had 400 articles published in professional journals. Sorokin's major works have been translated into at least 19 different languages and are read and discussed around the world. That single, somewhat offhand comment by my professor made me curious about this philosopher of love. In 1976, I became even more interested in his philosophy because of his creation of the Center of Creative Altruism at Harvard University. I wanted to know what he meant by "creative altruism," so I started investigating his writings. Besides reading his works, and the thoughts of those who critiqued him, I also wrote to some of his famous students who were by then full professors-scholars such as Neil Smeltzer, Robert Merton, and Edward Tiryakian because I wanted to find out what kind of a scholar Sorokin was. Each of them had something profoundly positive to say about Sorokin and his work. Some also commented on his conflict with the new upstart, Talcott Parsons, who later succeeded him as chair of the Department at Harvard.

Sorokin's monumental work, *Social and Cultural Dynamics*, and numerous other works, including the *Ways and Power of Love* (1954), have examined major social processes and how change occurs. Sorokin looked at 2,500 years of civilization to determine what causes social change. One of the positive social processes was love, which he felt was not well examined by social scientists. Sorokin felt love to be less well understood because social scientists tried to emulate the methods of physical scientists, involving themselves deeply in measuring and testing hypotheses. He was not very impressed with this direction. As a matter of fact, he accused social scientists, especially sociologists, of being involved in "quantomania" and *quantophenia"; testing little theories, subjecting them to rigorous statistical analysis, and coming up with results that are not earthshaking. Sorokin proposed another way of knowing: He introduced the notion of *integralism,* which is a system of thought that has the potential to fundamentally alter and redirect the social scientist in a positive and creative direction. The fundamental ideas of integralism are found in the writings of St. Thomas Aquinas, Pope John Paul II, and Sorokin himself. Integralism, which Sorokin formulated in the 1940s, offers a unique perspective in the social sciences, because it rests on the fundamental assumption that reality contains physical/empirical, rational/meaningful, and supersensory/super rational components. Therefore, the development of social scientists should include components that affect each part of this reality, and the epistemology should include methods of cognition that can be adapted to each of these aspects.

Sorokin's approach was a blending of Eastern and Western philosophical focus, fusing the truth found in human experience—truth of the mind, the senses, and the spirit. Sorokin maintained that integralism would free us from the pitfalls of one-dimensional thought and instrumental knowledge. He found it to be a necessary corrective to past domination by an instrumental but shortsighted and often destructive form of knowledge. Sorokin argued that sociologists spend too much time studying destructive social behavior, crime, violence, and war. If we wish to improve the human condition we should start emphasizing and understanding the positive aspects of humanity. With the help of a Lilly endowment, Sorokin established the Harvard Center of Creative Altruism, which sponsored many studies. Sorokin's research now positively impacts psychology and the topics of altruism, apology and forgiveness.

Biology And Forgiveness

There is little emotional activity that goes on in our brains that does not have a corresponding physical (bodily) reaction. For more than two decades, scientists have used various types of devices to scan brain activity while subjects are conducting certain tasks or thinking certain types of thoughts. Functional Magnetic Resonance Imaging (MRI) scanners are now used by researchers. Human activity "lights up" one or more parts of the brain on the MRI screen. A luminous spot represents intense electrical firing of nerve circuits or an unusually intense blood flow and oxygen consumption at a certain locale in the brain.

Science writer Keay Davidson (2004) reports that scientists have used fMRI evidence to find a link between empathy and physical pain: "When someone says, 'I feel your pain,' it isn't just an expression of empathy—it may literally be true." The pain-sensing part of our brains switches on when we're aware that someone else is in pain. And the more we feel empathy for someone else's pain, the greater the activity in the pain-sensing regions of our brain. Empathy, the ability to grasp the feelings of others, is one of humanity's most cherished traits. It is associated with great humanitarians, social activists, philanthropists, insightful novelists, and artists.

Recent research by Dr. Tania Singer of University College London points toward a neurological basis for empathy: "our brains' ability to mimic the 'internal bodily states' of others inside the neural jungle of our own noggins" (Davidson 2004: A2). The subjects were 16 male-female couples who were placed inside an fMRI scanner. The scientists applied painful stimulation-electric shocks or heat—to the women's right hands." Each woman faced a computer screen, and before each stimulation, she was informed by the computer when she was about to be hurt and by what intensity of pain. Later, the women's brains were scanned while they observed similar pains inflicted on their husbands. The fMRI scans showed that when women observed the suffering of their mates, the same parts of the women's brains illuminated as when they expected, thanks to the computer alert, to be hurt themselves.

Our ability to empathize may have evolved from a system for representing our own internal bodily states. Our capacity to tune into others when exposed to their feelings may explain why we do not always behave selfishly in human interactions but instead engage in altruistic, helping behavior. The journal *Neuron* reported fMRI evidence of how our brains distinguish between people who "play fair" and those who cheat (Davidson 2004: A2). The result of brain imaging experiments shows that human beings activate something within their brains when they see another person performing an action. That concept is currently understood as "mirror neurons," which implies that when people see joy or stress, they reflect the emotion they witness in sympathy. Singer and her colleagues had volunteers play the game "Prisoner's Dilemma," which tests how well two "prisoners" cooperate with each other. In the game, under certain circumstances, cooperation pays dividends; in other instances, cheating pays off. By fMRI-scanning the volunteers, Singer and her team discovered that the volunteers' brains illuminated in certain ways to players perceived as fair and differently to those regarded as cheaters. Such fMRI research is a new, high-tech contribution to long-standing debates over the possible biological roots of moral behavior.

For decades evolutionary biologists have argued over why humans and other animals risk their lives to help others. According to the "selfish gene" hypothesis, altruism make little sense—at first glance anyway—because it is only our own lives and genes that matter. But scientists have offered

Samuel P. Oliner

interesting arguments for why, under certain circumstances, altruism makes more sense. For example, it makes genetic sense for an elderly male to rescue a healthy young female relative who is genetically close to him, because her fertile years are still ahead of her.

Neuropsychological analysis of forgiveness may help us to understand mechanisms by which forgiveness contributes to improved psychological functioning. By utilizing autonomic and neurophysiological measures, in addition to more traditional psychological ones, some of the direct effects of forgiveness may be measured. Decrease in heart rate, respiratory rate, anxiety, depression, feelings of hostility and anger, and improved self esteem have been associated with practices such as meditation designed to augment parasympathetic activity. Changes may therefore occur in patients going through the forgiveness process. One might utilize brain-imaging techniques to measure aspects of cerebral functioning related to forgiveness. Forgiveness may improve a person's standing within the social group and enhance interpersonal relationships, and the forgiveness process may strengthen interpersonal bonds. Thus, encouraging forgiveness might be a powerful therapeutic intervention with transforming consequences.

Neuropsychological models suggest that forgiveness may ultimately have beneficial effects on the body, such as decreased levels of stress hormones and improvements in sleep patterns. Forgiveness and healing may go hand in hand. It is difficult to accomplish one without the other, and neuropsychological analysis of forgiveness may help to delineate why forgiveness is such an important phenomenon psychologically, physically, and spiritually.

Interpersonal And Intergroup Forgiveness

There are different types of forgiveness, from interpersonal to intergroup, and the factors and influences involved range from spirituality to love and empathy. Researchers have found neuropsychological correlations to forgiveness, and scholars see forgiveness as a critical distinction between restorative and retributive justice (see Chapter 6).

Apology can be an effective tool in reconciliation, but not if it is perceived as insincere. One example was found at the "Home Reading Room Message Board". Similarly, false forgiveness also obstructs reconciliation. Just as there are conditional false apologies, such as "I am sorry for what you made me do," there is false forgiveness, which does not really resolve the issue for the offender or for the offended. Some who are skeptical of forgiveness as a part of reconciliation are quick to point to these kinds of ineffectual instances of apology and forgiveness as the norm. But, as we know from our own experience, though some apologies and forgiveness exchanges may be attempts at a "quick fix," there are also many examples of sincere apology and forgiveness that form the basis of understanding and reconciliation.

There is evidence that people who are hurt and in pain are looking and longing for forgiveness. Recently, when conducting research on the Internet, we found numerous messages of apology asking for forgiveness.

Please forgive me for I know not what I do. All I wanted to do was make you happy. All I wanted to do was show you how nice and tender I can be. Please forgive me. I know sometimes I might have made mistakes. But I come to you, asking you, please forgive me. I just want you to know how I feel about you. So, I come to you asking, please forgive (Forgivenessweb.com 2001).

We don't know how effective such public notices are, but there are many of them, which seems to indicate that many people feel they have done wrong and are seeking reconciliation and hoping to reestablish harmony in their relationships.

Interpersonal Forgiveness

Mark Umbreit relates the following story as an example of a victim with a need to forgive in order to restore her own wellbeing:

> Sarah contacted me shortly after the parole hearing and expressed her strong inner sense of needing to meet the very man who killed her father so many years ago. Other than her husband, the rest of her family had no interest in following this path. From the very beginning it was clear that she was yearning to find peace within herself and her immediate family. Many months of separate preparation followed with both Sarah and Jeff. During our in-person separate meetings, I was able to understand the life context and needs of Sarah and her husband Rick, as well as Jeff, the offender. In addition to much deep compassionate listening to their stories, I explained how the process works and the fact that there are both benefits and risks in such a dialogue, particularly if people enter the process with unrealistic expectations. I also pointed out that even though many who have chosen a similar path of restorative dialogue have reported the encounter to be very therapeutic, the actual dialogue is not a form of psychotherapy. Jeff felt tremendous remorse for what he had done and was willing, though scared, to meet with Sarah. For all, this must be an entirely voluntary process. It became increasingly clear in Sarah's own words that she was on an intense spiritual journey to reclaim her soul, her sense of meaning, balance, and wholeness in life.
>
> The mediated dialogue was held in a maximum-security prison. Sarah's husband was present, as well as a support person that Jeff chose. Mediated dialogue refers to a humanistic approach that is very nondirective, honoring the healing power of silence and one's presence.

My comediator and I practiced mindfulness through centering and breath work both during the preparation and in the dialogue so that our egos and voices stayed out of the way, to allow Sarah and Jeff's strength and wisdom to emerge and flow as it needed to. After very brief opening comments by the mediators, we entered an extended period of silence as Sarah sobbed and tried to find her voice to tell her story. As mediators, we did not intervene to move the process along. Instead, we remained silent. We knew she had the strength, and our mindfulness practice allowed us to stay out of the way. Sarah and Jeff told us later that the energy of our presence, the nonverbal language of our spirit, was vital to the process being safe and respectful of their needs and abilities. After nearly four minutes, Sarah found her voice and her story of trauma, loss, and yearning for healing flowed out with strength and clarity. Jeff then offered his story of what happened, how it has affected his life, and the enormous shame he felt.

They continued to share deeper layers of their stories, interspersed with lingering questions both had. After five hours, and shortly before the session ended, following another moment of extended silence, perhaps a minute, Sarah looked directly at Jeff and told him she forgave him for killing her father. She made it clear that this forgiveness was about freeing herself from the pain she had carried with her for more than twenty years. She hoped this forgiveness might help him as well, but Sarah said she could not set her spirit free without forgiving him. Sarah had never indicated in our many months of preparation that forgiveness was an issue she was struggling with, nor did we raise the issue. When she and her husband came to the prison for the dialogue with Jeff, she had no plan whatsoever to offer forgiveness. Yet in the powerful moment of confronting her greatest fear, Sarah (spoke] of how she felt within her soul that this is the moment to free myself." In post-dialogue interviews with Sarah and Jeff, they both indicated the enormous effect this encounter had on their lives. Sarah spoke of how meeting Jeff was like going through a fire that burned away her pain and allowed the seeds of healing to take root in her life. She spoke of how before meeting Jeff she carried the pain of her father's death like an ever-present large backpack. After meeting Jeff, the pain [became] more like a small fanny-pack, still present but very manageable and in no way claiming her life energy and spirit, as before. Jeff reported a sense of release and cleansing, as if his spirit was set free as well (Umbreit 2005 with permission from the author).

There are many definitions of interpersonal forgiveness (Enright and North 1998). Interpersonal forgiveness, as distinguished from divine forgiveness, has as its major purpose to reduce the possibility of vengeance, revenge, or retaliation against those who have harmed us, thereby increasing reconciliation. This is pragmatic. Michael McCullough, Everett Worthington, and Kenneth Rachal (1997) define forgiveness as "a summary term representing efforts to reduce the motivation to avoid and to seek revenge and increase the motivation to reconcile or seek conciliation" (McCullough et al 1997: 229).

There are many situations that may call for forgiveness from people, including victims of crime, unethical work practices, workplace aggression, or discrimination, people who are unemployed; targets for racial, ethnic, gender, age, or religious discrimination, and members of ethnic groups that have a history of conflict and harm. Other groups that also may be included are separated or divorcing parents and their children, victims of child abuse, people involved in interfamily and intergenerational conflict, people dealing with unfaithful partners, and those who have been harmed or rejected by deceased parents. The list truly is endless. Forgiveness would help heal these wounds by decreasing the likelihood of vengeance and increasing reconciliation.

How can we sensitize, inform, and "prove" to people around the world that it is possible for mankind to live without hate, harm, war, and degradation of the environment (Dozier 2002)? There are two powerful human forces ultimately capable of reversing the trend of alienation and separation: The first is teaching, inculcating, and disseminating the positive consequences of altruistic behavior. We have seen that genuine altruistic behavior is helpful and regenerative, that it is strongly associated with enhanced general health, and that it leads to more harmonious relations. The second powerful force is apology and forgiveness. We know that hurt and alienation have been proven to have negative effects on mental and physical health, causing stress and physical and psychological pain. Professional healers are aware of this pain and the positive consequences of interpersonal forgiveness. They advocate apology, forgiveness, and reconciliation as a process of restoring loving and caring relations between individuals. A small percentage of people avail themselves of these healers. However, we do not see the results of the vast amount of research being done in these areas by schools and universities around the country.

It will take a focused vision on the part of educators to implement these ideas. In addition to the very important subjects of reading, writing, math, science, and computers, should we not also spend time learning about the consequences of harming? There is evidence that not only the victim is harmed, but the offender suffers for hurting or shaming another person, often feeling guilty for these actions but not knowing how to resolve them. Those who have been offended tend to carry anger and resentment, feeling that somehow they deserved the treatment. Their resentment often leads to a desire for vengeance. But positive, powerful social forces of altruism and apology/forgiveness can serve as an antidote to the spiraling need for vengeance. There are more than 80 million students in classrooms from elementary to college levels. Surely some way ought to be found with our present state of knowledge, to impress upon them how hurting or shaming others in their immediate environment has painful consequences and should be avoided.

The classic sociologist W. I. Thomas (1923) made a profound observation about how we treat each other as human beings. He is well known for his explanation that when a person defines a situation as real—whether it is real or not—it then becomes real in its consequences. This explains much about human behavior. For example, if an employer defines African Americans as "lazy," an unfair stereotype, that employer will be less likely to hire them. The employer has defined reality and makes real-life choices based on that interpretation. We tend to define people as good or bad, as one of "us" or one of "them," and then treat them accordingly.

There also is a psychological basis for forgiveness that consists of the need to overcome guilt, rage, and the desire for revenge, as well as a strong desire for reconciliation. There are several theories on the relationship between apology, forgiveness, reparations, and the restoration of harmony or reconciliation. Psychologist Seiji Takaku (2001) tested victims' abilities to take the perspective of the transgressor to facilitate the process of forgiveness as a result of dissonance/reduction motivation. He also investigates forgiveness as a model of dissonance reduction. Takaku challenges some of the explanations offered by authors such as Enright (1995, 1998) and others. He agrees with the notion that sympathy, compassion, and love increase the likelihood of positive behavior toward the offender. However, he feels that unless the offender takes the perspective of the other, and is thereby able to generate positive attributes toward the offender, forgiveness is less likely to be successful.

Takaku discusses other authors on perspective-taking. According to the correspondent inference theory (Jones and Davis 1965), if a transgressor apologizes for a transgression, the victim is less likely to infer a negative judgment of the transgressor's personality. The offense and the intention that produced it are less likely to be perceived as corresponding to some underlying trait of the offender. By breaking the link between the negative act and negative dispositional attributes, apology facilitates the process of interpersonal forgiveness. Forgiveness is more likely when others perceive the offender as having had good reasons for committing the offense, as in self-defense.

Holley Hodgins and Elizabeth Liebeskind (1999) analyzed two studies in which participants imagined themselves in "face-threatening" predicaments, examining the reproach and evaluation phases of predicament management. In the first study, participants gave accounts of their behavior after receiving hypothetical reproaches that were mild, moderate, or severe. Results showed that the severity of the reproach influenced the so-called perpetrators' accounts in opposite ways for females and males. Male perpetrators became more defensive under severe reproach, whereas females became less defensive. Expectations for a future relationship were more negative under severe reproach, and this was greater when the victim was an acquaintance rather than a friend. Individuals scoring high in self-determination were less defensive under mild-to-moderate reproach but not under severe reproach. In the second study, participants gave evaluations after receiving hypothetical accounts that varied in responsibility-taking. Results showed that greater responsibility-taking led to more positive victim evaluations and more positive expectations for future relationships. The advantage of responsibility-taking was especially pronounced when the perpetrator was a friend, suggesting that friends are more likely to be forgiven than acquaintances when they do take responsibility and apologize, but not if they fail to do so. Although claiming the results as useful in analyzing apology and forgiveness. The authors offer the caveat that the experiment scenarios may not fully and accurately reflect real life.

Another quandary occurs when someone does not ask for forgiveness such as Ali Agca, who attempted to assassinate the late Pope, John Paul II. The Pope personally forgave his potential murderer when he went to see him. Ali did not appear to be repentant. Many religious teachings maintain that a person has to repent first in order to be forgiven. We also must forgive ourselves and not blame ourselves for being the victim.

Lewis B. Smedes reminds us that forgiving a person does not require us to reunite with the person who broke our trust (1984). We do not forgive because we are supposed to, but rather when we are ready to be healed. Waiting for someone to repent before we forgive is to surrender our future to the person who wronged us. Forgiving is not a way to *avoid* pain but to *heal* pain. Forgiving is done best when it is done tolerantly.

Smedes maintains that forgiving is the only way to be fair to ourselves. Forgivers are not doormats; to forgive a person is not a signal that we are willing to put up with his behavior. We do not excuse the person we forgive, we blame the person we forgive. Forgiving is essential; talking about it is optional. When we forgive, we walk in stride with the forgiving God. When we forgive, we set a prisoner free and discover that the prisoner we set free is us.

Forgiving is a remedy for our pain but not for everybody else's pain. It is not our pain until we own it. An odd notion: How does one "own" pain? We appropriate and acknowledge that we have it and take responsibility for it. Smedes advises us of five steps in forgiveness: 1) Think; come to as much clarity as you can on what actually happened. 2) Evaluate; what is an accident? A misunderstanding? Lying? 3) Talk; consult with friends or counselors, and get the counsel that is needed after having been damaged. 4) Feel; take time to be alone with yourself to contemplate and clarify your feelings. 5) Pray; forgiving is a tough act to perform when bad things have been done to us. Give yourself a chance to be alone with yourself and your spirituality.

Smedes maintains that forgiveness should not be done in haste. It has to take time. He suggests ten stages: 1) take your time; 2) size up the risks; 3) wait for a signal; 4) do it sideways—talk about other things first; 5) begin at the end-forgiving hits its stride when the victim wishes good things for the victimizer; 6) don't claim holy motives; 7) improvise; 8) make it short; 9) keep it light-don't be too dramatic; and 10) give the other person time to respond.

The power of forgiveness is formidable, Smedes says. The most creative power given to the human spirit is the power to heal the wounds of a past it cannot change. We do our forgiving alone inside our hearts and minds; what happens to the people we forgive depends on them. The first person to benefit from forgiving is the one who does it. Forgiving happens in three stages: We rediscover the humanity of the person who wronged us, we surrender our right to get even, and we wish that person well. We forgive people only for what they do, never for what they are. We forgive people only for wounding and wronging us; we do not forgive people for things we do not blame them for. We cannot forgive a wrong unless we first blame the person who wronged us. Forgiving is a journey; the deeper the wound, the longer the journey.

In her book, Kathleen Griffin (2004) discusses steps for individual forgiveness. She maintains that forgiveness is liberating, and those who are unforgiving carry a burden with them that diminishes their joy in life. She realizes that for forgiveness to take place, one must forgive oneself for being a victim. Griffin gives us various examples of the positive effects of forgiveness, including Michael Lapsley, an Anglican priest in Africa involved in the antiapartheid struggle. In 1990, South African authorities sent him a letter bomb, causing him to lose both hands and one eye. He did not want to be stuck in his state of anger for the rest of his life. Despite his suffering, he used the power of forgiveness to transform himself from a victim into a victor. Griffin concludes that those who have already been hurt and have forgiven their offender, or who have experienced forgiveness themselves for hurts they have caused others, are more able to forgive. Our study shows that these people understand forgiveness better and are thus better able to forgive further hurts as they go on in life.

Kathleen Griffin had been sexually molested, as had Suzanne Simon, who also found release in writing about her own molestation. Those who have been hurt, like these two women, may be motivated to study and write about it in order to liberate themselves. Simon and her husband and co-author clearly take this approach. Their book (1990) offers explanations of forgiveness and discussions about its difficulties. Forgiveness can be a long process. There is self-blame involved; the victim may feel that they themselves actually caused the pain. Forgiveness consists of an internal process to seek liberation (Simon and Simon 1990). The Simons view it as a sign of healthy self-esteem to let go of intense emotions attached to past pain. They say that forgiveness involves accepting that nothing done to punish others will heal us. In order to heal, one must get rid of self-blame, victimhood, and indignation. Forgiving frees up all the energy consumed in holding the grudge and nursing wounds. An important first step in the forgiveness process is to refuse to deny the hurt or to downplay its impact. The victims will find themselves integrated when they are able to acknowledge that the people who have hurt them may have been doing the best they could, and they may come to the realization that if we are more than our wounds, then the ones who did harm must be more than their infliction of those wounds. It is possible that healing our wounds can result in being an acceptance of more loving relationships with people around us; it is possible to become closer, feel safer, experience more affection, experience more attention, as well as to feel more encouragement and validation of our self-respect. Suzanne Simon described her own victimhood:

> I reached the point where I no longer believed that being pretty or anything else about me drew my painful past experiences to me. Nothing I did made my father molest me. He did not have to do what he did—and because of him, my life was a mess. I was as powerless to change my life as I had been to prevent the abuse, I now thought. The situation was hopeless, I believed. I was not responsible for what he had done—or anything else. I had been victimized, and that was reason enough not to do anything more than just getting by (1990: 122).

This victimhood stage has many negative effects, from low self-esteem to the perceived need to victimize others. These effects occur until victims, as Simon said, "take off their blinders" and make room for a positive outlook, visualizing a different, brighter future. Smedes mentions the story of the German seeking forgiveness from Simon Wiesenthal, a Holocaust survivor, for having committed atrocities in the village of Dnepropetrovsk. The German had murdered many Jews by trapping them in a framed house, dowsing the house with gasoline, and setting fire to it. When people jumped out of the windows, he and other soldiers shot them. Wiesenthal could not forgive him, because he felt that only the victims could forgive.

Patterson and Roth (2004) address the important question, is forgiveness possible after Auschwitz? And if so, how can the victims who are dead forgive those perpetrators who are still alive? Thus, it raises a quandary: perhaps forgiveness is not possible. Haas (2004) addresses forgiveness from the Jewish perspective, citing the famous Jewish philosopher Maimonides, who maintained, "For one who sins against his fellow and his fellow dies before he asks forgiveness of him, he is to bring ten people and stand at the grave of the victim, and say in front of them, 'I have sinned against the LORD, God of Israel, and against so-and-so by doing such-and-such, [such as mass murder]. And if he owes him recompense, he returns it to his heirs, and if he does not know who the heirs are, he gives the recompense to the court and makes confession" (Haas 2004: 9). There are some victims of the Holocaust who have forgiven the Nazis their atrocities. For instance, Sidney Finkel, a Holocaust survivor who went through hell in various concentration camps, has since forgiven the Nazis for the trauma he experienced. "I began the unthinkable process of forgiving the German people, and it has released me."29 Another example of forgiveness is the recent Virginia Tech massacre. Christine Hauser—in her article published in 2007, titled "Virginia Tech Sets Out to Preserve Objects of Grief, Love, and Forgiveness"30—describes several students' reactions to the shooter, Seung Hui Cho, who murdered 32 people, including students and faculty at Virginia Tech in April of 2007—and then turned the gun on himself. The students are quoted in the article as saying, "Dear Cho, you are not excluded from our sorrow in death, although you thought you were excluded from our love in life." Another student wrote three words, "I forgive you" (Hauser 2007: A17).

Smedes believes if we concentrate on getting even, we will never see an end to cruelty and violence. There is no chance that Muslims will get even with the Serbs, or that the

Bloods will get even with the Crips. The more likely scenario is that in following the lure of vengeance and retribution, they will kill each other until all are dead, which does not resolve anything. We have to break the chain of retribution and start thinking about forgiveness.

Likewise, philosophers such as Emmanuel Levinas and Paul Ricoeur imply that forgiving does not mean forgetting; but if we refuse to forgive, we may block a brighter future and any relation between the offspring of the harmed and the harm-doer. As I have maintained, some acts are unforgivable, but perhaps we need to look at the offspring of victims and victimizer, who may have an obligation or moral authority to have an honest conversation about the tragedy affecting their families and subsequently themselves. This notion that only the victims can forgive gets us nowhere when the victims are dead. Pollefeyt (2004) speaks about *substitute forgiveness*, meaning that the descendants of the victims may have to get involved in forgiveness. He says, "I believe, however, that it is as illogical to refuse forgiveness in the name of the victims as it is to grant forgiveness in their name. Refusing to grant forgiveness is also a way of speaking in the name of the victims. Such acts are inappropriate attempts to 'manage' history" (Pollefeyt 2004: 65). Pollefeyt suggests that an intergenerational bond may be formed between victims and victimizers. One should not blanket the entire German population as those who were perpetrators and murderers of Jews. One reason offered is that offspring of both the perpetrators and the victims were born after the Holocaust; neither were involved in the event. Goodstein (2000) suggests that the document, Dabru Emet: *A Jewish Statement on Christians and Christianity*, which was signed in 2000 by Jewish leaders of all ranks, may be a hopeful step in the direction of reconciliation.31

To further emphasize the importance of offspring leading the way to forgiveness, authors Ervin Staub and Laurie

Anne Pearlman (2001) believe the incorporation of offspring in education is a step in the right direction. If the offspring of Jewish Holocaust survivors share the same schoolrooms as German descendants, through mutual learning and understanding they may be able to begin the process of reconciliation. The authors' emphasis upon this incorporation of offspring into mixed groups stems from their research in Rwanda, where they observed that the truth telling of victims of the Rwandan genocide seemed to aid the forgiveness and reconciliation process after decades of political unrest between the Hutu and Tutsi.

Truth telling as a path leading to forgiveness can be eminently practical, as in Nelson Mandela's implementation of the Truth and Reconciliation Commission in post-apartheid South Africa. There, the first step in forgiving is speaking honestly about what has happened and taking responsibility for doing wrong. Forgiveness is the price of reunion; it requires honesty about the person who wounded us and weighs future possibilities if one forgives or remains angry. Smedes says:

> The heart of my answer to the complaint against forgiving is that forgiving is the only way to get ourselves free from the trap of persistent and unfair pain. Far from being unfair, it is the only way for a victim to be fair to himself or herself. Far from being a dishonest denial of reality, forgiving is not even possible unless we own the painful truth of what has happened to us. Far from being alien to our human nature, forgiving dances to the melody of our own true humanity (Smedes 1996: 62-63).

Forgiving serves the forgiver and the forgiven as a reciprocal act. Forgiving must heal our pain before it helps the person we forgive. The act of forgiving is a wish for our perpetrator to heal as well. For those who are not repentant, forgiveness is a waste of time. It is important to understand that those who caused the pain and hurt are responsible. In this regard, Smedes mentions "the blame-share fallacy," which consists of blaming ourselves for having caused the victimizer to victimize us; for example, blaming the Allies for the Versailles Treaty of World War l, which crashed Germany's economy and sparked World War II.

Arie Nadler and Tamar Saguy (2004) discuss what it would take to end conflict between nations. They maintain that apology alone may not be enough. As in interpersonal forgiveness, it is necessary to first build trust between the groups, followed by social and emotional reconciliation. In some cases, a simple apology alone may not work. An example might be in the conflict between Israelis and Palestinians, in which much hatred and mistrust has developed over the years. What is required is slowly and surely building trust, beginning with face-to-face contacts between leaders, followed by other trust-building activities between people, organizations, and associations of both groups. Nadler and Saguy conclude that trust is a necessary condition to lead to the resolution of conflict.

Intergroup Forgiveness

In August 1995, the Prime Minister of Japan, Tomiichi Murayama, gave a "heartfelt apology" for the brutal crimes his country committed during World War II. The question naturally arises: Can a national leader ask for forgiveness for an entire nation? We conclude it is possible, because leaders represent groups that were perpetrators of the harm, even though not every member of the group agrees. Even if all the individuals who perpetrated the wrongs are dead, and none of the current group members are in any way responsible for these past wrongs, the leader can still take the moral high ground on behalf of the group. This can lead to the elimination of hatred and ultimately to reconciliation. Hatred is one of the most basic human emotions and is frequently justified, but it also proves to be a very persistent obstacle to forgiveness and reconciliation.

Forgiveness is not about reunion, nor does forgiving obligate us to go back to previous situations. Forgiveness does not necessarily mean restoring relationships. Smedes maintains that we must have an inner push to forgive, and that with some people or in some situations, it is not possible. He cites a story from Fyodor Dostoyevsky's book *The Brothers Karamazov*, about a young boy, the son of a poor peasant woman, who throws pebbles at a cruel landowner's dogs. The landowner, wanting to teach the boy a lesson, sets his vicious dogs on the child, and they tear him to pieces. How can a mother forgive someone for this?

Christina Montiel (2002) maintains that much of the discourse on public forgiveness actually addresses private forgiveness and calls for the development of ideas and practices for public forgiveness in the social arena. Social political forgiveness occurs when all members of the group of offended people engage in the forgiveness process in relation to another group that is perceived to have caused a social hurt or offense. Montiel writes that "Public forgiveness requires sensitivity to the historical, cultural, and political contexts of both conflicting groups" and "Collective forgiveness arises along with cultural transformations" (Montiel 2002: 271). When Germany apologized for the Holocaust, for example, it transformed its society as it introduced democratic institutions and changed its curriculum from dictatorial to democratic.

Intergroup forgiveness does not take place rapidly. It takes time, especially between unequal groups; the disadvantaged group must not be pressured into a quick accommodation. Healing has to take place slowly. Asking for forgiveness, in this social/political sense, must be performed by some prestigious authority, such as a president or another important leader. While the consequences of private and interpersonal apology are much better known, social/political forgiveness, or *collective forgiveness* is understudied.

Social thinkers, such as Vaclav Havel and Albert Einstein, maintain that we need to rid ourselves of the destructive and straight-jacketed views of human relations that guide us to confrontation rather than forgiveness and reconciliation. A global revolution in the sphere of human consciousness and forgiveness is needed to improve human relations. A number of solutions have been suggested to bring about a more caring world. The Buddhist monk Thich Nhat Hanh (1993) tells us that what is needed is revitalization of established religions, enabling them to be more relevant to the changes in our time. Religions seem to have become stagnated in practices and rituals and have become hostile toward other religions.

We are concerned with how nations or groups can forgive those who have committed unspeakable mass murders or genocide. How can Jews forgive those who participated in the Holocaust? How do Armenians overlook the genocide committed by the Turks? It is much easier to forgive lesser crimes and hurts; it is not so easy to forgive major crimes such as genocide. Leaders can make a profound difference. Chancellor Willi Brandt of West Germany knelt in silent atonement at the site of the Warsaw Ghetto. It may not have been therapeutic for the chancellor, but it raised global consciousness of a hurt perpetrated by the German nation. Forgiveness has the power of breaking the cycle of victimization and opens up space for political exploration that would otherwise be closed. Forgiveness is important toward reestablishing peace. The emergence of new sociopolitical institutions, nongovernmental organizations (NGOs), and citizen diplomats are opportunities for people to take part in improving international relations by facilitating helping, healing, and reconciliation. Also encouraging is the important push by some NGOs for economic, political, and restorative justice for all people on a global scale.

Henri Tajfels (1982; Tajfels and Turner 1986) developed a theory of group identity, which suggests that human beings divide the world into manageable categories to simplify matters. One of the ways in which we do this is to define and join groups. Our sense of identity depends upon our group memberships. This greatly eases the complexity of our daily interactions with others, because we are not constantly redefining ourselves. Instead, the underlying assumptions that go with our group memberships give us a ready-made and fairly solid framework for action. At the same time, unfortunately, discrimination, ethnocentrism, and hostility toward outgroups can be explained by this tendency to engage in categorization and identification. The notion of ingroup virtues and outgroup vices is implied.

There is a universal human tendency to form ingroups and outgroups: members of the "family and strangers. The ingroups have positive attributes—they are civilized, they are cultured, they are friendly, and they are "us." Negative characteristics are attributed to the outgroup. Statements such as "They are really evil," "They get what they deserve," and "They are not my people" are common; such beliefs make it more difficult to forgive those who are in the outgroup.

For thousands of years, philosophers, theologians, psychologists, and others have attempted to explain the nature of evil. In the recent past, sociologists, social psychologists, and therapists have tried to give evil a social or cultural explanation, such as being the absence of love, compassion, or caring and the presence of neglect or abuse. Those suffering would manifest destructive ideological beliefs—such as Nazism, racism, or homophobia—by relegating the other to a status of being less than human and not deserving to live among us.

In their article on the willingness to forgive among

adolescents, Genevieve Vinsonneau and Etienne Mullet (2001) report on their cross-cultural research on forgiveness between two young groups in France. They assessed willingness to forgive in a sample of 203 people, ages 15 and 16, adolescents from different cultures: French, Western Europeans, and a group from Maghreb of Islamic origin, residing in France. The aim of the study was to measure willingness to forgive under varying circumstances, and it noted the scarcity of cross-cultural studies on forgiveness. Some studies suggest stages of forgiveness, including revengeful forgiveness, restitutional forgiveness, expectational forgiveness, lawful expectational forgiveness. forgiveness as social harmony, and forgiveness as love (Al-Mabuk, Radhi Enright 1995; Enright, Santos, and Al-Mabuk 1989).

Vinsonneau and Mullet (2001) included samples of Druze, Shiite. and Sunni Islamic communities and Catholics, Maronites, and Orthodox Christians. These studies consider the effects of a number of circumstances on the willingness to forgive, such as intent to harm, cancellation of consequences, religious and social similarity to the offender, apologies from the offender, as well as variations of these effects as a function of age, gender, and educational level. The sample living in France was mainly Christian and Maghrebi. France, though a very multicultural society, experiences quarrels and unrest between the two groups on a frequent basis. One of the main findings of Vinsonneau and Mullet is that willingness to forgive is not substantially different between the groups. "The overall level of willingness to forgive was clearly different from zero, but not very high: among other lessons, forgiveness is far from being unconditional. The apology factor seems to be extremely important: when remorse and apologies are present, it is much easier to forgive. Willingness to forgive extends to the members of "the other" group. All these results hold true, irrespective of the respondent's origin (Vinsonneau and Mullet 2001: 267).

This ingroup/outgroup mentality, which is one ingredient of enemy making, regards the outgroup as having negative attributes; this is represented by the old adage, "We are the Greeks, they are the barbarians." Theoretician Fritz Heider's (1958) theory aims to explain how individuals attribute causes to events and how these cognitive perceptions affect motivation. In a nutshell, this theory divides the way people attribute causes to events into two types: One common way people explain causality of events is through external attribution, which assigns causality to an outside factor, such as the weather, or simply to the idea that "they" did it.

Internal attribution, on the other hand, assigns causality to factors within individuals, such as their level of intelligence or other variables that make the individual responsible for an event. Generally, people are more likely to make external attributions that are negative. Thus, those people who are "bad" are not only bad, but they "bring it upon themselves." Ulrike Niens and Ed Cairns (2002), who conducted research on intergroup forgiveness in Northern Ireland, have used Henri Tajfels's theory to demonstrate that much of human social behavior is determined by social group memberships. Human beings are more likely to forgive acts of violence perpetrated by ingroup members than to forgive similar acts by outgroup members. Understanding the insights gained from this type of research is important, because they explain basic aspects of human behavior. If we understand these behaviors better, we might be able to reconcile with the enemies that we make or perceive.

On an intergroup level, it is not easy to initiate the process of apology and forgiveness. If a leader apologizes, it will not be very productive if there has been no change in the perception of those who have been degraded and offended. Skillful and compassionate mediators may find a way for both sides to understand each other. From this foundation a relationship may be established, leading to apology, reconciliation, and ultimately to peace and cooperation. We know that humans are enemy-making animals with infinite ways to hurt one another. Hurts are frequently unintentional and are caused by unforeseen circumstances, misunderstandings, or misinterpretations. People are capable of carrying grudges for many years, making forgiveness a difficult process to initiate. How, then, do we motivate people to reconcile and release their heavy loads of resentment and revenge?

Researchers at the Conflict Research Consortium at the University of Colorado (2005) conclude that there are important steps in the process of easing pain between harm doers and victims. The first step is to establish or reestablish a relationship between the victim and the victimizer. A personal relationship offers the opportunity to progress beyond the problems that come with group memberships. This is usually not a simple task, and frequently a third party is necessary to get two conflicting groups together. Another goal of reaching out is to help deescalate the animosity felt by the harmed person. Some German chancellors apologized to other nations and groups that they hurt during the Nazi years. Reaching out at a grassroots level occurred when Jews and Arabs in the United States sought to create dialogue as a first step in fostering reconciliation. In attempting to reestablish contact between harm doers and the harmed, the first step is to build trust and respect between the groups. Once the parties sit at the same table, they can consider the problem. Harm must be acknowledged, anger admitted, and the offending side must genuinely promise to change its ways. At this point group members may perceive each other in a different light.

Summary

Benjamin Franklin once said, "Doing an injury puts you below your enemy; revenging one makes you but even with him; forgiving it sets you above him." While agreeing with the idea that forgiveness shows that one is a "big person," we feel that the whole point of forgiveness is to attempt to restore balance in relationships, and that using the imagery of someone being "above" or "below" another is not helpful.

Frederic Luskin of the Stanford Forgiveness Project shows that forgiveness is teachable and can reduce stress, blood pressure, and anger; it can also help lessen depression and hurt and increase optimism, hope, compassion, and physical vitality (Luskin 2003). Yehudith Auerbach (2004; 2005) maintains that an apology made by a nation's leader to a nation that was harmed is one of the major ingredients in conflict resolution and reconciliation. For Auerbach, forgiveness means the forswearing of resentment and the resolute overcoming of anger and hatred that are naturally directed toward a person who has done an unjustified and unexcused moral injury.

Beverly Engel (1990; 2001), Enright and Fitzgibbons (2000), and Kathleen Griffin (2004) document the benefits of forgiving those who have harmed us. Luskin, Ginzburg and Thoresen (2005) and Luskin (2004) have shown a positive relationship between forgiveness and physical health. The rage that a victimized person carries is debilitating, and it is in need of being released from the burden this individual carries. Not so long ago, the discussion of forgiveness and apology had been assigned as a weakness or deemed the domain of religious functionaries, whereas now the culture of apology is much more prevalent. When the world between the harm doer and forgiver is "right again," it may foster self-confidence and a sense of efficacy. In the medical arena, it may actually reduce disease, preventing pathologies that result in hostile feelings, depression, and hopelessness. Forgiveness also may provide a higher level of perceived social and emotional support, which may also include a greater sense of community. Lastly, forgiveness also may encourage self-healing, as well as help to refocus on the goodness and altruism that exist in the world. The forgiveness process helps us think in terms of higher values beyond the pain of the individual's ego.

There are literally hundreds of studies that show the power of forgiveness (Enright, Freedman, and Rique 1998). This proliferation of studies focusing on the positive effects of apology and forgiveness has begun to diminish some of the pessimistic views that have long held sway, such as with those who see only the "disuniting America," or the "fraying of America." Popular literature has taken notice of this trend. Jane Jacobs authored *The Death and Life of Great American Cities* in 1961. She said that the cities were being devastated by automobiles and showed a photograph of Manhattan, where thousands of cars occupied six lanes, bumper to bumper, hardly moving. Jacobs maintained, "This sort of culture and life will ultimately destroy us." Another pessimist is Samuel P. Huntington, who wrote *Who Are We: The Challenges to America's National Identity* (2004). He points out that massive Latinx immigration threatens the fabric of American culture, and says, "this will be disuniting America." Huntington is known for his earlier book, *Clash of Civilizations and the Remaking of World Order* (1996), in which he predicts the cultural battle for supremacy between Christendom and Islam. These writers predict that our proud American, or Western, culture and democracy will cease to exist. We will suffer from debilitations of bilingualism and multiculturalism. America will be negatively transformed, according to Huntington. Other pessimists, including evangelical Christians—such as Tim LaHaye and Jerry B. Jenkins, in their *Left Behind* novels (1995 and others)—warn us that we are on this earth for the last days, and that Armageddon is inevitably coming.

While some social critics offer valuable insights into our rampant individualism, acquisitiveness, waste, degradation of the environment, and perpetual engagement in wars,

Samuel P. Oliner

many promote their personal causes. But a profound question, one we are not sure is answerable, is this: What is the answer to the gloomy pictures that we regularly see? We are bombarded by media reports of how we harm and hurt, and yet we are still murdering each other on a mass scale. In the twentieth century, we killed approximately 100,000,000 people: innocent men, women, and children, as well as soldiers. What causes this massive universal separation, and what can we do about it? We are not so naïve as to think there is an immediate solution. For thousands of years, since the dawn of civilization, we have been murdering each other and making enemies of the "other." But perhaps we are now evolving as our world shrinks. Are we willing to listen to new evidence that we do not need to murder and harm each other, that there is enough space and food if we are simply willing to become true neighbors on both local and universal levels? Is this an impossible dream? Perhaps, perhaps not; however, many social scientists, philosophers, theologians, physical scientists, and others believe in this possibility. Perhaps not today or tomorrow, but there is an opportunity to change the minds, attitudes, perceptions, and hearts of humankind to see the "other" as a member of the human family. There is overwhelming evidence that almost all human beings are capable of feeling empathy, social responsibility, love, and compassion.

Reprinted From: *Altruism, Intergroup Apology, Forgiveness and Reconciliation*, Samuel P. Oliner, Assisted by Piotr Olaf Zylicz, (St. Paul, MN: Paragon House, 2008)

References

Agape Love Ministries. 2004. "Welcome and Be Blessed." Retrieved August 4, 2004 (http://www.ourchurch.com/member/r/ronlor777/).

Al-Mabuk, Radhi H., and Robert D. Enright. 1995. "Forgiveness Education With Parentally Love-Deprived Late Adolescents." *Journal of Moral Education* 24 (4): 427-445.

Astin, Alexander. 2003. "The Spiritual Life of College Students: A National Study of College Students for Meaning and Purpose." *Spirituality in Higher Education*. Los Angeles: Higher Education Research Institute, University of California.

Auerbach, Yehudith.2004. "The Role of Forgiveness in Reconciliation" in *From Conflict Resolution to Reconciliation*, edited by Yaacov Bar-Siman-Tov:pp.149-75.New York: Oxford University Press.

_____.2005. "Conflict Resolution, Forgiveness and Reconciliation in Material and Identity Conflicts." *Humboldt Journal of Social Relations* 29 (2): 40-81.

Augsburger, David. 1981. Caring Enough to Forgive: True Forgiveness. Ventura, CA: Regal Books.

Berry, Jack. "Forgiveness Among the Virtues." *A Campaign for Forgiveness Research*. Retrieved March 28, 2004 (http://www.forgiving.org/campaign/press/altruism_jackberry.asp).

Berry, Jack W., Everett L. Worthington, Jr., Nathaniel G. Wade, Charlotte van Oyen Witvliet, and Rebecca P. Kiefer. 2005. "Forgiveness, Moral Identity, and Perceived Justice in Crime Victims and Their Supporters." *Humboldt Journal of Social Relations* 29 (2): 136-62.

Brummer, Vincent. 1993. *The Model of Love: A Study of Philosophical Theology*. Cambridge, MA: Cambridge University Press.

Casarjian, Robin. 1992. *Forgiveness: A Bold Choice for a Peaceful Heart*. New York: Bantam Books (from Enright, Freedman, and Rique 1998:51).

Conflict Research Consortium.2005. *Beyond Intractability Project*. Retrieved September 29, 2005 (http://www.beyondintractability.org/essays.jsp?nid=2167).

Cunnare, Richard D. 2005. "Forgiveness." Retrieved October 17, 2000 (http:// www.deltadustoff.com/article. asp?ID=3).

Dalai Lama. 2002. "Understanding Our Fundamental Nature" in *Visions of Compassion: Western Scientists and Tibetan Buddhists Examine Human Nature*, edited by Richard J. Davidson and Anne Harrington: pp. 66-80. New York: Oxford University Press.

Davidson, Keay. 2004. "Empathy Found to Have Basis in Brain Chemistry: Neurological Link Seen." *San Francisco Chronicle*, Feb. 20:A-2. Retrieved May 24, 2006 (http://www.sfgate.com/cgi-bin/article.cgi?-file=/c/a/2004/02/20/MNGC65407H1.DTL&-type=printable).

Davidson, Richard J. and Anne Harrington, eds. 2002. *Visions of Compassion: Western Scientists and Tibetan Buddhists Examine Human Nature*. New York: Oxford University Press.

Dickey, Walter J.1998. "Forgiveness and Crime: The Possibilities of Restorative Justice" in *Exploring Forgiveness*, edited by Robert Enright and Joanna North: pp. 106-20. Madison, WI: University of Wisconsin Press.

Dilman, Ilham. 1998. *Love: Its Forms, Dimensions, and Paradoxes*. New York: St. Martin's Press, Inc.

Dozier, Rush W. 2002. *Why We Hate. Understanding, Curbing and Eliminating Hate in Ourselves and Our World*. Chicago, IL: Contemporary Books.

Eckstein, Menachem. 2001. *Visions of a Compassionate World: Guided Imagery for Spiritual Growth and Social Transformation*. New York and Jerusalem: Urim Publications.

Elder, Joseph W. 1998. "Expanding Our Options: The Challenge of Forgiveness" in *Exploring Forgiveness*, edited by Robert D. Enright and Joanna North. pp. 150-61. Madison, Wi: University of Wisconsin Press.

Engel, Beverly. 2001. *The Power of Apology: Healing Steps to Transform All Your Relationships*. New York: John Wiley & Sons, Inc.

Enright, Robert D., M. J . Santos and Radhi H. Al-Mabuk. 1989. "The Adolescent As Forgiver" *Journal of Adolescence* 12 (1) 95-110.

Enright, Robert D., Elizabeth A. Gassin and Ching-ru Wu.1992. "Forgiveness: A Developmental View." *Journal of Moral Education* 21 (2): 99-114.

Enright, Robert D., 1995. "The Psychology of Interpersonal Forgiveness." Paper presented at the National Conference on Forgiveness, Madison, WI, March 1995.

Enright, Robert D., Suzanne Freedman and Julio Rique. 1998. "The Psychology of Interpersonal Forgiveness" in *Exploring Forgiveness*, edited by Robert D. Enright and Joanna North: pp. 46-62. Madison, WI: University of Wisconsin Press.

Enright, Robert D. and Joanna North, eds.1998. *Exploring Forgiveness*. Madison, WI: University of Wisconsin Press.

Enright, Robert D. and Richard Fitzgibbons. 2000. Helping Clients Forgive: An Empirical Guide for Resolving Anger and Restoring Hope. Washington, DC: American Psychological Association.

Ferrucci, Pierro. 2005. El Poder de la Bondad (Survival of the Kindest). Barcelona, Espana: Ediciones Urano.

Fields, Bill. 2005. "Eight Steps to Biblical Forgiveness." Retrieved October 6, 2005 (http://www.peacemakers.net/peace/eight.htm).

Fitzgibbons, Richard. 1998. "Anger and the Healing Power of Forgiveness: A Psychiatrist's View" in *Exploring Forgiveness*, edited by Robert D. Enright and Joanna North: pp. 63-74. Madison, WI: University of Wisconsin Press.

Foley, Michael W.1999. "Memory, Forgiveness and Reconciliation: Confronting the Violence of History." Report on a Conference at the Institute on Conflict Resolution and Ethnic Conflict (INCORE) Derry/Londonderry, Northern Ireland, April 23-26, 1999.

Forgivenessweb.com. 2001. "Apology Room." Retrieved Mar. 21, 2006 (http://www.forgivenessweb.com/apologies.htm).

Goodstein, Laurie. 2000. "Leading Jewish Scholars Extend a Hand to Christians." *New York Times* Sept. 2000. Retrieved July 18 2007.

Griffin, Kathleen. 2004. *The Forgiveness Formula.* New York: Marlowe & Company.

Gulen, M. Fethullah. 2003. "Love, Compassion, Tolerance, and Forgiving: The Pillars of Dialogue." *Bloomington Muslim Dialog Group.* Retrieved Mar. 28, 2004 (http://en.fgulen.com/content/view/1339/13/).

Hanh, Thich Nhat. 1993. *For a Future to Be Possible: Commentaries on the Five Wonderful Precepts. Berkeley,* CA: Parallax Press.

Hartwell, Marcia Byrom. 1999. "The Role of Forgiveness in Reconstructing Society After Conflict." *The Journal of Humanitarian Assistance.* Posted May 3, 1999. Retrieved Oct. 11, 2005 (http://www.jha.ac/articles/a048.htm).

Hass, Peter J. 2004. "Forgiveness, Reconciliation, and Jewish Memory After Auschwitz" in *After-Words: Post-Holocaust Struggles with Forgiveness,* Reconciliation, Justice, edited by David Patterson and John K. Roth: 5-16. Seattle, WA: University of Washington Press.

Hassel, David J. 1985. *Searching the Limits of Love: An Approach to the Secular Transcendent God.* Chicago, IL: Loyola University Press.

Hauser, Christine. 2007. "Virginia Tech Sets Out to Preserve Objects of Grief, Love, and Forgiveness." *The New York Times* April 25:A17.

Heider, Fritz.1958. *The Psychology of Interpersonal Relations.* New York: John Wiley and Sons.

Hodgins, Holley S. and Elizabeth Liebeskind.1999. "Apology Versus Defense: Antecedents and Consequences." *Journal of Experimental Social Psychology* 39 (4): 297-316.

Hoeger, Werner H.K., Lori Turner and Brent Q .Hafen. 2003. "Spiritual Wellness." *Wellness: Guidelines for a Healthy Lifestyle*. Georgetown University. Retrieved March.28 2004 (http://data.georgegtown.edu/be/article.cfm?ObjectID=586).

Huntington, Samuel P.1996. *Clash of Civilizations and the Remaking of World Order*. New York: Touchstone.

_____. 2004. *Who Are We: The Challenges to America's National Identity*. New York: Simon and Schuster.

Johnson, Rolf, M. 2001. *Three Faces of Love*. DeKalb, IL: Northern Illinois University Press.

Jones, E.E. and K.E. Davis 1965. "From Acts to Dispositions: The Attribution Process in Person Perception" in *Advances in Experimental Social Psychology*, L. Berkowitz, ed.v.2:219-66. New York: Academic Press.

Jones, James, M. 2006. "From Racial Inequality to Social Justice: The Legacy of Brown vs. Board and Lessons From South Africa." *Journal of Social Issues* 62 (4): 885-909.

Kalb, Claudia. 2003. *"Faith and Healing."* Newsweek Nov. 10:44-56.

Keyes, Corey L. M. and Jonathan Haidt, eds. 2003. *Flourishing: Positive Psychology and the Life Well-Lived*. Washington D.C.: American Psychological Association.

Klein, Charles. 1995. *How to Forgive When You Can't Forget: Healing Our Personal Relationships*. New York: Berkeley Books.

LaHaye, Tim and Jerry B. Jenkins. 1995. *Left Behind*. Wheaton, IL: Tyndale House Publishers, Inc.

Lama Surya Das.1997. "Love and Forgiveness." A talk delivered in Cambridge, MA on January 27. *Dharma Talks*. Retrieved March 21, 2006 (http://www.dzogchen.org/teachings/talks/love.html).

Lazare, Aaron. 2004. *On Apology*. Oxford and New York: Oxford University Press.

Lewis, Thomas, M.D., Fari Amin M.D. and Richard Lannon M.D. 2000. *A General Theory of Love*. New York: Random House.

Luskin, Frederic, 2002. *Forgive For Good* (1st Edition). San Francisco, CA: Harper San Francisco.

_____2003. "An Experience of Peace." *Ions Noetic Sciences Review* 65:11-13.

_____.2004. "The Choice to Forgive." Greater Good 1 (2): 13-15.

Luskin, Frederick, Karni Ginzburg, and Carl E. Thoresen. 2005. "Efficacy of Forgiveness Intervention in College Age Adults: Randomized Controlled Study." *Humboldt Journal of Social Relations* 29 (2): 164-184.

McCullough, Michael E., Everett L Worthington, Jr., and Kenneth C. Rachal. 1997. "Interpersonal Forgiving in Close Relationships [Interpersonal Relations and Group Processes]." *Journal of Personality and Social Psychology* 73 (2):321-36.

McCullough, Michael E., Kenneth C. Rachal, Steven J. Sandage, Everett L. Worthington, Jr. Susan Wade Brown, and Terry L. Hight. 1998. "Interpersonal Forgiving in Close Relationships." *Journal of Personality and Social Psychology 75 (6):* 1586-1603.

Montiel, Cristina Jayme. 2002. "Sociopolitical Forgiveness." Peace Review 14 (3): 271-77.

Murayama, Tomichi. 1995. "On the Occasion of the 50th Anniversary of the War's End." Statement by Prime Minister Tomichi Murayama, Aug. 15, 1995. The Ministry of Foreign Affairs, Japan. Retrieved Sept. 6, 2005 (http://www.mofa.go.jp/announce/press/pm/murayama/9508.html).

Nadler, Arie and Tamar Saguy.2004. "Reconciliation Between Nations: Overcoming Emotional Deterrents to

Ending Conflicts Between Groups." The Psychology of Diplomacy, edited by Harvey Langholz and Chris E. Stout. New York, NY:Praeger.

Niens, Ulrike and Ed Cairns. 2002. "Identity Management Strategies in Northern Ireland." *Journal of Social Psychology* 142 (3): 371-80.

North, Joanna. 1998. "Ideal of Forgiveness: A Philosopher's Exploration" in *Exploring Forgiveness*, edited by Robert D. Enright and Joanna North: 15-34. Madison, WI: University of Wisconsin Press.

Nygren, Anders. 1953. *Agape and Eros*. Philadelphia, PA: Westminster Press.

O'Connor, Lynn E. 2002. *Review of A General Theory of Love*, by Thomas Lewis, Fari Amini, and Richard Lannon. *Human Nature Review* 2: 89-91. Retrieved Aug. 10, 2004 (http://human-nature.com/nibbs/02/leo.html).

Parachin, Victor M..2006. "How to Forgive: Ten Guidelines." *Unifier: European Unitarian Universalists*. March Newsletter: 3.

Patterson, David and John K. Roth, eds. 2004. *After-Words: Post-Holocaust Struggles with Forgiveness, Reconciliation, Justice*. Seattle, WA: University of Washington Press.

Patton, J. 1985. *Is Human Forgiveness Possible? A Pastoral Care Perspective*. Nashville, TN: Ebington Press.

Pollefeyt, Didier. 2004. *Incredible Forgiveness* "Emmanuel Levinas." Stanford Encyclopedia.

Post, Stephen G. 2002 *Unlimited Love: What It Is and Why It Matters*. Institute For Research and Unlimited Love. Retrieved Oct. 5, 2006 (http://www.unlimitedloveinstitute.org/publications/pdf/UL_What_and_Why.pdf).

_____.2003. *Unlimited Love: Altruism, Compassion, and Service*. Philadelphia, PA: The Templeton Foundation Press.

Post, Stephen G., Byron Johnson, Michael McCullough and Jeffrey Schloss. 2003. *Research on Altruism and Love*. Philadelphia, PA: The Templeton Foundation Press.

Prince-Gibson, Eetta. 2004. "Despite Our Differences…" *Na'amat Woman Magazine* Summer. Retrieved Nov. 3, 2005 (http://www.naamat.org/Mag_articles.html#).

Rye, Mark S., Kenneth I. Pargament, M. Amir Ali, Guy L. Beck, Elliot N. Dorff, Charles Hallisey, Vasudha Narayanan, and James G. Williams. 2000. "Religious Perspectives on Forgiveness" in *Forgiveness: Theory Research and Practice*, edited by Michael E. McCullough, Kenneth I. Pargament and Carl E. Thoresen: 17-39. New York and London: Guilford Press.

Schimmel, Solomon. 2002. *Wounds Not Healed* by Time. New York: Oxford University Press.

Schulweis, Harold M. 2000. "Forgiveness." Sermon delivered at Valley Beth Shalom. Retrieved Oct. 6, 2005 (http://www.vbs.org/rabbi/hshulw/forgive_bot.htm).

Sheffield, Jeffrey C. 2003. "An Investigation of the Relationships Between Forgiveness, Religiosity, Religious Coping, and Psychological Well-Being." Ph.D. Dissertation, Department of Counseling and Special Education, Brigham Young University.

Shriver, Donald W.,Jr..1995. *An Ethic for Enemies: Forgiveness in Politics*. New York: Oxford University Press.

Simon, Sidney B. and Suzanne Simon. 1990. *Forgiveness: How to Make Peace with Your Past and Get on With Your Life*. New York: Warner books.

Smedes, Lewis B. 1984. *Forgive: Healing the Hurts We don't Deserve*. New York: Harper and Row Publishers, Inc.

_____1996. *The Art of Forgiving: When You Need to Forgive and Don't Know How*. New York: Ballantine Books.

Sorokin, Pitirim A. 1954. *The Ways and Power of Love: Types, Factors, and Techniques of Moral Transformation*. Boston, MA: Beacon Press.

Stanczak, Gregory C. and Donald E. Miller. 2004. "Engaged Spirituality: Spirituality and Social Transformation in Mainstream American Religious Traditions." Los Angeles: Center for Religion and Civic Culture, University of Southern California.

Stanley, Charles. 1996. *Experiencing Forgiveness: Enjoy the Peace that Comes from Giving and Receiving It*. Nashville, TN: Thomas Nelson Publishers.

Staub, Ervin and Laurie Anne Pearlman. 2001. "Healing, Reconciliation, and Forgiving After Genocide and Other Collective Violence" in *Forgiveness and Reconciliation: Religion, Public Policy, and Conflict Transformation* edited by Raymond G. Helmick and Rodney L. Peterson: 205-27. Philadelphia, PA: Templeton Foundation Press.

Svoboda, Elizabeth. 2005. "School Spirit." *Science and Spirit*. Sept.-Oct.: 15-17.

Tajfels, Henri. 1982. "Social Psychology of Intergroup Relations." *Annual Review of Psychology* 33: 1-39.

Tajfels, Henri and John Turner. 1986. "The Social Identity Theory of Inter-Group Behavior" in *Psychology of Intergroup Relations*, edited by S. Worchel and L.W. Austin: 7-24.Chicago, IL:Nelson-Hall.

Takaku, Seiji. 2001. "The Effects of Apology in Perspective Taking On Interpersonal Forgiveness: A Dissonance-Attribution Model of Interpersonal Forgiveness." *Journal of Social Psychology* 141 (4): 494-509.

Tavuchis, Nicholas. 1991. *Mea Culpa: A Sociology of Apology and Reconciliation*. Stanford, CA: Stanford University Press.

Templeton, John Mark. 1999. *Agape Love: A Tradition Found in Eight World Religions*, PA: The Templeton Foundation Press.

Thomas, W.I.1923. The Unadjusted Girl: With Cases and Standpoint for Behavior Analysis. Boston: Little, Brown and Company.

Tipping, Collin C. 2002. *Radical Forgiveness: Making Room for the Miracle*. Marietta, GA: Global 13 Publications, Inc.

Touber, Tijn. 2005. "Survival of the Kindest." *Ode* 3 (3): 42-47.

Tutu, Desmond.1999. *No Future Without Forgiveness*. New York: First Image Books.

Umbreit, Mark. 2005. "Peacemaking and Spirituality: Touching the Soul Within the Energy of Conflict and Trauma." *Center for Restorative Justice and Peacemaking*. Retrieved June 26,2006 (http://www.rjp.umn.edu/img/assets/13522/Peacemaking_%20&_%20Spirituality_%20 Touching_%20the_%20Soul.pdf)

USA Today.2004."What is Spirituality?" Sunday, March 28. Retrieved June 30, 2007. (http://proquest.umi.com/pqdlink?PMID=7631&TS=1150734727&SrchMode=3&SrtM=O&PCID=15012901&VType=PQD&VInst=PROD&aid=1&clientID=17853&RQT=572&VName=PQD&firstIndex=60

Vinsonneau, Genevieve and Etienne Mullet. 2001. "Willingness to Forgive Among Young Adolescents: A Comparison Between Two Groups of Different Cultural Origins Living in France." *International Journal of Group Tensions* 30 (3): 267-82.

Vrba, Rudolf. 1964. *I Cannot Forgive*. Vancouver, BC: Regent College Publishing.

Works of Love. 2003. Scientific and Religious Perspectives on Altruism Conference, Villanova University, May 31-June 5. Retrieved Sept. 15, 2004 (www.metanexus.net/conference2003/).

Worthington, Everette L. Jr. 1997. "Interpersonal Forgiving in Close Relationships." *Journal of Personality and Social Psychology* 73 (2): 321-36.

_____2004. "The New Science of Forgiveness." Greater Good 1 (2): 6-9.

13

Elimination of Suffering

SAMUEL P. OLINER

Introduction

What is suffering? Anderson (2017) offers a taxonomy of four forms of suffering: physical suffering, or pain; mental suffering, including distressing thoughts and feelings; interpersonal suffering, trauma caused by interactional problems such as social rejection and isolation; and, finally, social suffering, a loss of a sense of worth and collective value due to social norms that stigmatize and lead to social discrimination of the victims (Anderson, 2015, p.4-5). These varying forms of human suffering are caused and perpetuated by many forces. However, as the primary focus of this volume is the alleviation of human suffering, this chapter explores the forces underlying extraordinary sacrifices made in order to rescue victims from extreme suffering. By examining the nature of suffering, we may envision some novel ways to alleviate human suffering in a variety of contexts.

The purpose of this chapter is threefold. First, after a brief account of the author's survival, suffering and rescue during the Holocaust, we characterize the nature of the Nazi's systematic mass murder of Jews and others, which is considered the most documented genocide in human history. Winston Churchill said of the Holocaust, "This is probably the greatest and most horrific crime ever committed in the whole history of the world" (Weber, 2000). Next, is an overview of some heroic rescuers (also called "righteous gentiles'), who reduced the suffering of thousands of victims by assisting or hiding them and saving their lives. These rescuers chose to act on their principles, risking all to help those in need during the Nazi occupation in Europe. Finally, we highlight several hero-producing projects and point out how altruistic individuals and robust social institutions may evolve to reduce suffering.

A Holocaust Survivor's Perspective

As a survivor of one of the most extensively documented genocides in human history, the Holocaust, I have been led by my experience to research the various aspects of human nature in order to understand how we may build a brighter future, in which another Shoah may never occur. Throughout my career, I have studied altruism, the nature of 'good' and 'evil,' apology and forgiveness, and the motivations of those who give selflessly, such as volunteers, heroes and others who devote themselves to the greater good. Dr. Pearl Oliner and I conducted a major study of rescuers of Jews and others during the Holocaust, The Altruistic Personality (1988). Our research team interviewed and tape recorded a number of gentile rescuers in their own language who acted in the interests of those persecuted by the Nazi regime, reducing their suffering and saving their lives. What we found was that although individuals' motives differed, there were consistent characteristics among our rescuers: they were raised by compassionate and nonviolent caregivers who encouraged them to think critically and to respect others who were different than themselves (culturally and ethnically); they were instilled with a sense of social responsibility and valued social justice, and they considered themselves responsible for the greater good of their communities, and were willing to act on that sense of responsibility, as opposed to 'bystanders'. Rescuers displayed behavior that can be defined as heroic altruism, an altruistic behavior that is voluntary, does not result in personal gain and involves risk of varying degrees to the helper (Oliner, 2003, p. 21). Similarly, we interviewed hospice volunteers whom we labeled as conventional altruists, those who perform compassionate acts that do not involve risking one's life. Much of the research we have conducted over the years has lent insight into how society may foster and encourage altruistic, caring behavior. While the trauma of my past has partly motivated this research, my focus on the nature of altruistic behavior may be traced in part to a Polish peasant woman named Balwina Piecuch.

I was born in a small village called Zyndranowa, located in southern Poland, on March 10, 1930. I lived with my father Aron, my brother and sister, Moishe and Feigele, and my mother, Jaffa. Sadly, my mother passed away from tuberculosis when I was seven years of age, but my family lived a relatively happy life on my grandparents' farm until the Nazi occupation of Poland began in 1939. As the occupation progressed, life became worse and worse for Jewish people. Homes and businesses were regularly looted by occupying forces and even some Poles. Food became ever scarcer. Jewish men were forced to shave their beards, and all Jews were forced to wear opaskas (stars of David) on the streets. By June of 1942, my family was forced into a hastily constructed ghetto in Bobowa, Southern Poland. Disease and hunger swept through the ghetto, and everywhere people were desperate. I would sneak out of the ghetto, at great risk, to find food for my family by trading thread, needles, and even watches for potatoes and other foods with surrounding Polish peasants. In August 1942, when I was twelve years of age, the fateful call rang through the ghetto *"Alle Juden-raus!"* (All Jews, out!), shrilly shouted by the *einsatzgruppen*, or mobile killing units. House by house, all occupants of the ghetto were forced to the Bobowa town square and made to sit on the concrete cobble stones. Loaded onto military trucks, everyone was driven to a pre-dug grave nearby forest of Garbacz, and the *einsatzgruppen* shot them all. I later discovered that my other grandfather and his family had been similarly massacred the day before. There was not enough time to properly bury the victims at the end of the day's massacre, and one victim that I knew crawled out of the grave. Driven insane and wandering aimlessly, he was later caught by the Gestapo and shot.

When the *einsatzgruppen* shouted for all Jews to come out of their homes, my stepmother Ester turned to me. I saw a dreadful look of fear and concern on her face—somehow she knew that our family would not survive this day. Clutching my stepsister Jaffa in her arms, my stepmother said to me, "*Antloif mein kind und do vest bleiben beim leben.*" (Run, my child, run away so that you will save yourself). I asked my stepmother where I should go, and she told me to hide, anywhere. As I contemplated what this warning entailed, what I should do next, I turned to the door and heard my stepmother's last words "Shmulek, I love you. I know God will protect you."

I hid on the roof, and both heard and saw the horrors taking place below. Eventually I was able to leave the roof, and with great fear and despair made my way out of the ghetto to a nearby village and to the house of Balwina. She was a Catholic peasant woman who had known my family and had even traded with them before the war. It was from Balwina that I learned the fate of my family and the others who had been taken from Bobowa. At great risk to herself and her family, Balwina advised me to pose as a Catholic boy. She taught me the catechism, and gave me the name of Jusek Polewski. Balwina's son Staszek posed as my brother, and helped me authenticate my false identity. I was able to get a job as a pastuch, or cowhand, on a farm (whose Jewish owners had been killed) that was now rented by a childless Polish couple, the Padworskis. Mr. and Mrs. Padworski hired me to assist on the farm, and in this way, I was able to keep up the deception (with the help of Staszek and Balwina) and survive the war.

Why did Balwina help me to reduce my fears and suffering? She was a mother, certainly, and felt great pity for the fate of my family and for all the Jewish people condemned in Nazi occupied Poland. It was with tears in her eyes and a broken voice that she told me of the liquidation of the Bobowa ghetto. What made Balwina different? The cost of her heroic altruism, had it been discovered, would almost certainly have cost her life, perhaps even the lives of her entire family. One way that the Nazis ensured that no help would be offered to Jewish persons during this time was the principle of *collective responsibility*: if anyone was caught giving aid then there would be consequences, not only for the person providing help but also their family, and potentially everyone in the community where they lived (Tec, 1986, p. 32, 64).

In the Holocaust, as in other genocides, people suffered tremendously. However, the Holocaust is unique in the sense that the Nazis systematically devoted efforts and treasure to murder every Jewish man, woman, and child. The murder took various forms, including mass execution by bullets, gas chambers, starvation, and experimentation. The Holocaust is undoubtedly the most documented genocide; there are miles of documentary footage, and eyewitnesses, victims and victimizers, many survivors and a number of scholars who have done research on this tragedy. Organizations devoted to Holocaust research include the International Institute for Holocaust Research at Yad Vashem, located in Jerusalem; the Polish Center for Holocaust Research, based in the Polish Academy of Sciences in Warsaw; the Center for Advanced Holocaust Studies, operating from the Holocaust Memorial Museum in Washington, D.C.; the Vienna Weisenthal Institute for Holocaust Studies, and many other academic groups and individuals (Berger, 1991; Berger & Berger, 2001; United States Holocaust Memorial Museum, 2016).

How Was The Holocaust Possible?

It was perpetrated by a "civilized" nation, in collaboration with other nations. In a time marked by the loss of the First World War and the German empire, the punitive Versailles treaty, severe economic depression, a psychological need to blame the 'other', and general social unrest, a charismatic leader named Adolf Hitler was able to come to power. Fascist dictatorship became the political model, resulting in arrest of opposing parties, the establishment of concentration camps such as Dachau, the spread of anti-Semitism, and ultimately *Kristallnacht*—the Night of Broken Glass, during which citizens openly destroyed and looted Jewish homes and businesses, their former occupants dragged away. Nationalist propaganda such as the popularized German phrase "the Jews are our Misfortune" *("Die Juden sind unser Ungluck")*, hate literature like Hitler's *Mein Kampf, The Protocols of the Elders of Zion* (manufactured by the tsarist secret police), and famous Protestant theologian Martin Luther's book *The Jews and Their Lies* were circulated (Luther, 1971; Weber, 2000). In a divided nation socially conditioned to punish the "other,' the tragedy of the Holocaust was possible.

Heroic Rescuers Of The Holocaust

After interviewing a number of gentile rescuers, Carnegie Heroes, and Hospice volunteers, we have found common motivating factors of altruistic behavior (Oliner and Oliner, 1998). One is normocentric motivation; others are empathic reasoning and principled motivation, all associated with Professor Janusz Reykowski of the Polish Academy of Sciences (Reykowski, 1987).

The normocentrically-oriented respond to an external event that arouses or heightens their empathy. The impact of a direct encounter with a distressed Jewish person was sometimes overpowering. Consider, for example, the following encounter related by a Polish woman, then approximately thirty-five years of age. In 1942, I was on my way home from town and was almost near home when M. came out of the bushes. I looked at him, in striped cap clothing, his head bare, shod in clogs. He might have been about thirty or thirty-two years old. And he begged me, his hands joined like for a prayer; he had escaped from Majdanek and could I help him? He joined his hands in this way, knelt down in front of me, and said: "You are like the Virgin Mary." It still makes me cry. "If I get through and reach Warsaw, I will never forget you." (Oliner, 1988, p.189).

Another rescuer we interviewed, Stanislaus, demonstrated altruism based in normocentric principles as a Holocaust rescuer. During one of our interviews with him, he explained that his reasoning for giving aid to twenty Jewish individuals could be traced back to his mother and grandmother. He stated, "I learned to respect the world from my mother," and learned how to care for others by watching her extend a helping hand to relatives who needed a place to stay until they found work (Oliner, 2003, p. 198-199). An interesting factor that contributed to his dedication to helping others were the sacrifices that his maternal grandmother made before he was born. Stanislaus's grandmother was raised Jewish but decided to leave that part of her life to be with his Polish Catholic grandfather (Oliner 2003, p. 199). Stanislaus's inclination to help stemmed from his mother's teachings and his grandmother's sacrifices, along with the fact that he was raised in a region that had many Jewish people, so he had Jewish friends. In Stanislaus's case, these relationships had a great impact on his appreciation of diversity, which motivated him to provide care for the Jewish people in a time of persecution.

In an interview recounted in *Do Unto Others* (Oliner, 2003), Ilsa, another rescuer, initially favored the Nazi view of Jewish people for political reasons. However, she came to disagree with their beliefs because it was affecting her husband negatively. She also believed that the Nazi party was not aligning with the values of her church. Ilsa's actions changed in response to how her most treasured values, such as those of her faith, and her concern for her husband were being affected by the Nazis. Although some people may have initially benefitted from the persecution of the Jewish people, they came to realize that the systematic oppression and the atmosphere of hate and suspicion would affect everyone.

The Post Holocaust Future

Some see the world as having a brighter future. Stephen Pinker, in his book "The Better Angels of Our Nature," argued that violence has been declining and will continue to do so. He wrote: "For all the tribulations in our lives, for all the troubles that remain in the world, the decline of violence is an accomplishment that we can savor—and an impetus to cherish the forces of civilization and enlightenment that made it possible" (Pinker, 2011).

Jeremy Rifkin, in his work *The Empathic Civilization* (2009), describes a social world that is evolving to be more altruistic, caring, empathic, and compassionate. I concur with Rifkin, who sees this current century as entering the "Third Revolution," which consists of raising consciousness about the destruction of the biosphere and the need for economic sustainability. This 'Third Revolution' is associated with what global consciousness, as well as the effects of intergroup apology, forgiveness, and reconciliation.

The Global Consciousness

The emergence of global consciousness, which relates to the digital communication revolution, instantly informs people about events occurring around the world, whether good or ill (Oliner 2003). Remote communication of the hurtful experiences of others arouses an empathic response by many fellow human beings, which we have witnessed time and again during catastrophic events or natural disasters affecting people worldwide.

People's inclinations to help can also be explained *by dual inheritance theory*, which claims that an individual's altruistic and empathic tendencies stem simultaneously from both genetic evolution and cultural evolution. Social groups in which altruism and empathy are exercised tend to live longer and reproduce (Pinker, 2011; Rifkin, 2009). Neuroscientists and have found convergences between the human brain and social situations (Franks 2015). The human brain contains *mirror neurons*, a neurological response to others' actions or emotional displays, allowing people to empathize and experience others' emotions (Winerman, 2005).

Our research on rescuers during Nazi occupied Europe, 9/11 first responders, Carnegie heroes, and unpaid volunteers around the world provide examples that many people are innately good. This is due to the influences of important others in an individual's life and the values they internalize. In *Do Unto Others: Extraordinary Acts of Ordinary People* (2003) I found that one of the most common characteristics of empathic people was that they had internalized ethical responsibility for diverse others. The global consciousness now allows people around the world to become aware of the circumstances of others, and thus have more opportunities than ever to take action to alleviate suffering in one's own region or on the other side of the globe.

Intergroup Apology, Forgiveness And Reconcilatiion

One way of demonstrating social responsibility is to offer apology for wrongdoing and forgiveness to those who seek it. We found positive results from our study on apology, forgiveness, and reconciliation in a number of countries (Oliner & Zylicz 2008). For instance, there are Truth and Reconciliation Commissions around the globe, and many nations, such as Rwanda and South Africa, who have apologized to those that they have harmed in an attempt to heal the hurt and open the path to reconciliation. Another example of apology and reconciliation took place between Poland and Ukraine. Both nations committed tragic massacres of each other's people during World War II, known as the Volhynian Massacres (taking place from approximately 1943 to 1945). Hoping that after the defeat of Hitler these nations would be free and independent, Ukrainian partisan groups targeted "undesirable" ethnic groups, systematically killing many Polish people. Many Ukrainian citizens heroically aided Polish people, warning them of impending attacks and sometimes hiding them (Zajaczkowski, 2013). After World War II, this resulted in the closure of borders and the breaking of economic, cultural, and educational ties, tourism, and other social and political interactions. In 2002, after a historical 2001 visit from Pope John Paul II (the first time a Pope had ever visited Ukraine), the two Presidents, with the approval of their respective Parliaments, met on the grounds of the massacre and apologized on the behalf of their people for this tragedy (Zawada, 2005). This was a massive step forward in healing for both nations, and resulted in the opening of borders, trade, cultural exchanges, and political cooperation.

Another example of apology is practiced by a group of nuns in Kentucky who desired to make amends for the exploitation of African Americans. The nuns inherited a group of convents, which were built by slaves in 1800s. In 2001, the Sisters of Charity, Sisters of Loretto, and the Dominicans of Saint Catherine decided to confront the "enduring sin of racism." The nuns publicly apologized to the African American community in Bardstown for historically mistreating them and for not doing more to oppose slavery. As a result of the apology, the three orders helped establish scholarships for African American students in high schools and colleges, and they helped improve diversity in their school boards. While racism has not disappeared, many African American people interviewed in the Kentucky area have reported that race relations have improved in their communities.

There are tangible positive results from both individual and intergroup apology. Forgiveness is a gift and an act of reconciliation that has tangible consequences. Forgiving helps both body and mind to heal. Offering apology and seeking forgiveness has spiritual consequences, and under the right conditions, it is able to reestablish a relationship between groups or individuals. "I am sorry" is a difficult phrase in any language. It is particularly crucial that a perpetrator of wrongdoing acknowledges the truth and is willing to apologize when a relationship has been damaged (Oliner and Zylicz, 2008). For global harmony, we stress the importance of intergroup apology, forgiveness and reconciliation—a practice that has rendered some of the most positive results in social and political reparation throughout the 21st century.

Humanitarian Projects Facilitating Heroic Rescue

Suffering occurs when people hurt because they are deprived of their basic needs, both physiological and social. Social connections and physical safety are endangered by violence, conflict and instability in the social environment. Suffering, then, can be reduced through efforts to provide safety and stability for all people. What follows are examples of organizations and projects where aid workers and others function as heroic rescuers and thus reduce suffering. We begin with an overview of the exemplary non-government organization Doctors Without Borders.

During the time of the Holocaust, where hate, racial discrimination and genocide abounded, many compassionate individuals risked their lives to help and protect. On a macro level, it can be observed that different organizations have grown in order to address economic and social inequalities that have contributed to human suffering. One global humanitarian effort that was born from the tremendous need of medical care in war-torn countries is called *Doctors Without Borders*, also known as *Medecins Sans Frontieres* (MSF), the title chosen by the French doctors who founded the organization. A quote from the Doctors Without Borders website (http://www.msf.org) sums up its purpose: "MSF was created on the belief that all people have the right to medical care regardless of gender, race, religion, creed, or political affiliation and that the needs of these people outweigh respect for national boundaries."

According to psychologist Maslow's "hierarchy of needs," in order for a person to achieve higher levels of well-being (love, self-esteem, and self-actualization), their basic needs must be met, and for most people, having basic safety and security means having access to shelter or housing (McLeod, 2014). *Habitat for Humanity*, a non-profit organization created in 1976 addresses poverty and lack of housing (Habitat for Humanity, 2016). This organization has been able to gather resources in order to build homes with families under certain requirements, and has successfully been able to address these issues not only in the United States of American but also in over 70 countries worldwide. Every year the Habitat for Humanity attracts over 1 million volunteers, who make it possible to place 310,000 families per year into housing units. In their 40 years of operation, they placed 3 million people into safe housing solutions worldwide.

The Danish Refugee Council (DRC) is a humanitarian, non-profit, nongovernmental organization (NGO) that works in more than 30 countries throughout the world. Its mandate is to develop durable solutions among conflict-ridden populations, particularly those with refugees and displaced persons. Denmark itself has integrated many of these refugees. Established in 1956, they have aided over one million people in their history. In recent years it has ranked among the top ten of the Global Journal's ranking of the top 100 NGOs.

Mercy Corps is a small NGO with a budget well under a half million dollars. Yet they have a major presence in several countries, achieving demonstrable impact. Mercy Corps started out as an organization to help the Cambodian refugee crisis, but evolved into a much broader role of a combination of disaster relief and development. From their beginning, their primary mission was to "alleviate suffering." That is still their primary goal, but their focus is to eliminate oppression and to help build productive and just communities. Unlike most NGOs, they explicitly define their stakeholders as the people and communities they serve; their explicit value premises are the dignity of human life; the stewardship of the earth's health; and their stakeholders participate in all decisions. Mercy Corps was ranked in the top 10 NGOs in 2013.

Bringing in the Bystander is an unusually robust violence prevention program, of which there are hundreds of programs. Rather than focusing strictly on the roles of perpetrator and victim, this highly interactive, researched and evaluated program offers a curriculum and evaluation tools, using a community of responsibility approach. It teaches bystanders how to safely intervene in instances where an incident may be occurring or where there may be risk of violence. The program, which was developed and evaluated by University researchers and program practitioners, is customizable to reflect the locations, colloquialisms and cultures of diverse campuses. The program was developed and currently managed at the Prevention Innovations Research Center (http://cola.unh.edu/prevention-innovations-research-center) at the University of New Hampshire (UNH), Durham NH USA. The Center designed several Bystander Program Evaluation Tools. The program is working in colleges and other organizations all over the world. Research such as that of Moynihan, Banyard, Cares, Potter, Williams, & Stapleton (2015) demonstrates significant impact in training young adults in intervening or rescuing victims of sexual violence.

An organization called Humanitarian Outcomes maintains the international Aid Worker Security Database available at (https://aidworkersecurity.org/about). In their 2015 report, there were an estimated 450,000 aid workers worldwide and over the past decade, an estimated 3,000 workers encountered extreme violence. About a third of these workers were killed, a third wounded, and a third kidnapped. These estimates do not include the local or national aid workers. Often these violent victimizations of international aid workers are widely publicized in the media. Therefore, the aid workers are truly heroic rescuers, knowing that they are risking their lives by the decisions they make in the field.

This risk applies to workers for all of the organizations above except the *Bystander project*. In Bystander projects, ordinary students and adults are trained to take risks in order to reduce the likelihood of violent relationship, usually sexual violence. Undoubtedly, on occasions the bystander person engaged in intervention encounters physical harm; however, these project organizations do not report statistics on such instances. Those engaged in (or considering) intervention are called *bystanders* because this label has emerged from the enormous number of academic research projects, which have examined the factors that predict whether or not an individual will intervene if s/he observes a violent or morally reprehensible action taking place. The most persistent finding is that the larger the group of observers of a situation or crisis, the less likely someone is to help, which is called the *bystander effect*. The Bystander projects are designed to counteract the bystander effect.

Conclusions

The pursuit of education and the process of personal and social growth are deeply connected. From research on the nature of people's moral and altruistic motivations, we can conclude that building upon the altruistic impulse from early life into the adult years is crucial to cultivating a caring society (Oliner and Oliner, 1995). In the classroom environment, where young people spend so much of their formative years, there is unlimited opportunity to teach and reward compassionate, socially responsible behavior. One model, called the "jigsaw classroom," places students in ethnically diverse groups and requires them to work together to complete a task. Students who experience diversity and learn cooperation in the classroom tend to be less prejudiced, more cooperative and more empathic than students who are not required to work with others of different cultural backgrounds and cognitive abilities. The students are intrinsically rewarded for working together and tend to internalize and retain the values of cooperation and empathy (Clay 2006).

Reduction of suffering is possible by encouraging and empowering the altruistic potential within each individual. Any contribution to others, whether volunteer work, donation or random acts of kindness offers the potential, if not the reality, of the reduction of suffering. The key to promoting this type of behavior is to teach children and youth the importance of caring and social responsibility. It is encouraging to see that education in caring and empathy in the classroom can be effective (Clay 2006). Empathy in classrooms builds positive classroom culture, strengthens community and reduces suffering. Empathy training prepares students to be responsible leaders in the community. Teaching tolerance can build a positive classroom culture and results in reduced bullying. By instilling the values of caring and social responsibility in our young people, and rewarding those behaviors and practices that empower and assist, the future of our world can look much brighter.

Because of the risk involved in aid work or bystander intervention, ordinary persons are not likely to take on these challenging roles unless they are altruistic and have a moral sense of social responsibility. Such an inclination may be inculcated within the family, the school, communities, or other social institutions where training is offered. Fortunately, there seems to be a growing trend in North America to incorporate empathy and social responsibility in elementary and secondary schools.

The Holocaust has become a metaphor in Western societies for both the evil and good hidden in the human spirit. It is comforting that contemporary societies continue the heroic rescuing that emerged from the righteous gentiles of the Holocaust; select altruistic individuals and specific social institutions that maintain the recruitment and training of professionals and ordinary people, continue to engage in heroic rescuing when violence comes to our attention.

Reprinted by permission from: Ronald E. Anderson, Ed., Alleviating World Suffering, Samuel P. Oliner, *Suffering During the Holocaust and Heroic Rescuers*, Springer International Publishing, Minneapolis, MN, 2017.

References

Anderson, R. (2013). Human suffering and quality of life. Dordrecht: Springer.

Anderson, R. (Ed.) (2015). World suffering and quality of life. Dordrecht: Springer Science+Business Media Berger, A. (ed.) (1991). Bearing witness to the Holocaust, 1939-1989. Lewiston, N.Y., USA: E. *Mellen Press.*

Anderson, R. Ed. (2017). Alleviating World Suffering, Springer International Publishing, Minneapolis, MN, 2017.

Berger, A. and Berger, N. eds. *(2001). Second generation voices: Reflections by children of* Holocaust survivors and perpetrators. Syracuse, NY, USA: Syracuse University Press.

Clay, R. (2006). "Helping kids care." Monitor On Psychology, Vol. 37 No. 11., p. 42. American Psychological Association. Retrieved from http://www.apa.org/monitor/dec06/kids.aspx

Luther, M. (1971). "The Jews and Their Lies." In The Christian Society. Vol. 4, of Luther's Works. Ed. F. Sherman, Philadelphia: Fortress Press. McLeod, S. (2014). "Maslow's Hierarchy of Needs." Simply Psychology. Retrieved from http://www.simplypsychology.org/maslow.html

Moynihan. M. M., Banyard, V. L., Cares, A. C., Potter, S. J., Williams, L. M. & Stapleton, J. G. (2015). Encouraging Responses in Sexual and Relationship Violence Prevention: What Program Effects Remain One Year Later? Journal of Interpersonal Violence, 30, 110 132.

Oliner, S. P. (1979). Restless memories: Recollections of the Holocaust years. St. Paul, MN: Paragon House. Oliner, S. P. (1982) "The Heroes of the Nazi-Era: A Plea for Recognition." Reconstructionist 48:7-14.

Oliner, P. (1983). "Putting Compassion and Caring into Social Studies Classroom." Social *Education 47, no. 4: 273-277.*

Oliner, S. *P. (2003). Do Unto Others: Extraordinary acts of ordinary people. Boulder, CO, USA: Westview Press. Oliner, S. P. & Oliner, P. (1988). The Altruistic Personality: Rescuers of Jews in Nazi Europe.* New York, NY, USA: The Free Press.

Oliner, S.P, & Oliner, P. (1992). Embracing the Other: Philosophical, Psychological, and *Historical Perspectives on Altruism. New York University Press: New York,*

Oliner, S. P. & Oliner, P. *(1995). Toward a caring society: Ideas into action. Westport, CT,* USA: Praeger. Oliner, S. P., & Zylicz, P. (2008). Altruism, Intergroup Apology, Forgiveness and Reconciliation. St. Paul, MN, USA: Paragon House. Pinker, S. (2011). The Better Angels of Our Nature: Why Violence Has Declined. Penguin Books.

Reykowski, J. (1987). "Activation of Helping Motivation: The Role of Extensivity." Unpublished paper.

Reykowski, J. (1987). "Dimensions of Development in Moral Value: Two Approaches to the Development of Morality." In Social and Moral Values: Individual and Societal Perspectives. Ed. N. Eisenberg, J. Reykowski, and E. Staub. Hillsdale, N. J.: Lawrence *Erlbaum*.

Rifkin, J. *(2009)*. *The Empathic Civilization: The Race to Global Consciousness in a World in* Crisis. Penguin Books.

Tec, N. (1986). When light pierced the darkness. New York: Oxford University Press.

United States Holocaust Memorial Museum. (2016). Research in collections. Retrieved from https://www.ushmm.org/research/research-in-collections

Weber, L. (2000). "Winston Churchill." The Holocaust Chronicle. Lincolnwood, IL: Publications International.

Wiesel, E. (2006) Night, Revised Edition. NYC: Hill and Wang Publishers. Winerman, L. (2005). The mind's mirror. Monitor on Psychology, October 2005. American Psychological Association.

Zawada, Z. (2005). "Ukraine mourns Pope John Paul II, recalls 2001 visit." Ukrainian Weekly, April 10, 2005, No. 15 Vol. LXXIII. Retrieved from http://www.ukrweekly.com/old/archive/2005/150504.shtml

Zajaczkowski, M. (2013). "Polish-Ukrainian historical disputes over the Volhynian massacres." Institute of National Remembrance. Retrieved from http://www.volhyniamassacre.eu/spory-o-wolyn/polish-ukrainian-historical-disputesover-the-volhynian-massacres.

14

Conclusion

SAMUEL P. OLINER

This book sought to describe the two sides to the future our children stand to inherit: the glass half full and the glass half empty of what has been the trajectory of the world, it seems, since the beginning of human history. The arc of human progress has at times taken major leaps forward; at other times it appears to have lain dormant, only to burst forth with a new energy at a later time. In this collection of writings, we have attempted to show both sides of the picture because to do otherwise would leave this endeavor incomplete. Depicting only the negative would lead one to think that there is nothing positive moving us forward; depicting only the positive would suggest that we have no further work to do.

As raised in the introduction to this collection, Stephen Pinker informs us that, despite public perception, the incidence of violence has diminished worldwide since World War II. Since that time, despite military conflicts in various parts of the world, the loss of life has been a small percentage of what was seen in the two world wars combined. According to Pinker, our species is finding other ways of resolving conflict. Positive trends, such as the spread of democracy and the rise of women's movements along with human rights and animal rights movements, all bode well for a more peaceful world—for the glass of tomorrow to be half full.

Notably, there has been a rise of xenophobia, nativism, bigotry, and racism, as well as a political move to the right in America and Europe. Nevertheless, based on current data, Evan Oliner gives us a vision of the glass being half full instead of half empty. He argues that a different kind of world exists—one where we are economically interconnected; where ethnic diversity, open-mindedness, and charitable giving are also qualities that manifest in society.

Likewise, Pat Devine, in writing about the nature of genocide and the Holocaust, portrays a positive future where people work together to prevent future holocausts and genocides. She outlines for us how academic scholarship is flourishing in these two areas and how we know more than ever before about the crime of genocide. She emphasizes that, for the very first time, there is a decentralized group of international organizations committed to proactively preventing genocide. Bypassing the United Nations and governmental agencies, they have established their own early-response warning systems and early-intervention action teams that they hope will decrease incidences of, if not eliminate, the crime of genocide.

Nichole Wagner vividly describes how the glass is half empty for thousands of women worldwide; at the same time, she brings to our attention the sources of hope that are beginning to surface globally. One such source is the Me Too movement that arose in the United States in 2007, bringing women's long-standing experiences of sexual violence and harassment to national awareness. Via social media, the Me Too movement has spread to many parts of the world, planting seeds for positive social change surrounding sexual violence and harassment towards women. In this case, the future glass is becoming half full.

Many in the present day have sounded the death knell for the human family. Pat Devine paints the glass as being half full, however, when she describes how the family of tomorrow will benefit from the tide of economic growth fueled by continuous technological innovation and globalization. As accelerated change continues at an unparalleled pace in the history of the world, the family will reinvent itself to meet the needs of the future by assuming a variety of forms, such as the traditional nuclear family sharing space with the extended family, cohabitation, and other old and new forms.

Sitaram Sandin, Ronnie Swartz, and Bryan Kraus graphically and extensively describe for us the present-day issues connected with climate change and the role that humans play in exacerbating it. The picture they paint, however, shows a glass that is neither half full nor half empty. It is somewhere in between. As they warn, looking at only the bright side of the picture prevents humanity from solving the problems connected with the dark side. They depict for us how there is growing awareness and action taking place on many different levels across the planet. Examples include clean energy solutions, taxing carbon, the Green New Deal (GND), phasing out gas refrigerants from air conditioners, and new forms of energy such as wind and solar, to name a few. They stress the importance government support in bringing about a sustainable future and the need for involved citizen groups that support individuals to become active in politics, vote, run for office, and adopt sustainable lifestyles. These are all hopeful endeavors we can participate in today to contribute to the glass of the future being half full.

The chapter "Heroic Acts of Extraordinary People" asks this question: "Why did they do it?" What differentiates the person who commits heroic acts from the bystander? In every time and every place, there are those individuals who step out of the norm and perform acts of heroism. Such acts are associated with human compassion and social responsibility. The prevalence of such individuals in human societies gives hope for a future where the glass is half full.

Pitirim Sorokin informs us that altruistic love is important to the future of society. We know that this quality has historically existed. For example, heroic rescuers of Jews in Nazi Germany risked their lives for a higher moral value of saving Jewish friends, neighbors, or strangers who were in peril. In order for the glass to be half full for the society of tomorrow, we need such altruistic heroes as role models for our young people, by teaching and telling their stories. In other words, the health of our society will depend on the extent to which we promote the value of altruistic love.

In the chapter "Altruism in Different Religions," we learn how many world religions teach altruism and how it may be taught in various forms. This has been the positive contribution of the world's religions to societies throughout the ages. Notwithstanding the shadow side of religion, there remains this positive side that continues to inform the modern day, contributing to the glass being half full.

Pat Devine demonstrates that the walls between various faith traditions are beginning to break down, and that they are moving towards a model of mutual respect and understanding. As a result, an interfaith movement is flourishing in many communities across the country and around the world. The more that religions can overcome their differences and come together in the sharing of core values, the more that the glass of the future will be filled, increasing the chances that our children will inherit a more peaceful world.

In the chapter "Apology and Forgiveness," we learned of the positive correlation between apology and forgiveness (on both the personal and group level) and the importance of the process to maintaining a peaceful society. Interpersonal and intergroup apology are essential ingredients for all societies. The more a given society can develop these qualities in its population, the more it moves towards a society where the glass is half full rather than half empty. We have modern-day examples of apology and forgiveness that can serve as templates for the future.

We know that suffering is a universal phenomenon. All beings suffer. There are many types of suffering in the world, including personal, economic, political, physiological, and psychological. At the same time, there is a desire to eliminate suffering in the world, not only for humans, but in the animal kingdom as well. Advances continue to be made to reduce human suffering in the medical, psychological, and physiological realms. There are also growing numbers of animal rights activists and animal rescue operations and a growing emphasis on human stewardship of other species. Such trends to end the suffering of humans and other species render the glass half full.

This is the future our children will inherit. It is a future like all futures—it contains both an evolution of our species towards a higher level of consciousness and a resistance to such change. This has been the balancing act throughout human history. It will be incumbent upon our children to make sure that the glass of the future is half full.

Made in the USA
Las Vegas, NV
22 October 2021